D1029957

Community
Media
Handbook

Second Edition

A.C. Lynn Zelmer

The Scarecrow Press, Inc.
Metuchen, N.J., & London   1979

Library of Congress Cataloging in Publication Data

Zelmer, A   C   Lynn, 1943-
  Community media handbook.

  Bibliography: p.
  Includes index.
  1. Audio-visual equipment--Handbooks, manuals,
etc. 2. Mass media--Handbooks, manuals, etc.
I. Title.
TS2301.A7Z44   1979   621.38   79-12989
ISBN 0-8108-1223-1

To Jennifer,
my six-year-old daughter,
who makes better posters than I do,
and is fascinated by media and computers.

She knows when something
doesn't meet her needs,
and is willing to say so.

TABLE OF CONTENTS

TABLES AND CHARTS

ACKNOWLEDGMENTS

The Community Media Handbook was prepared out of a need for training and reference materials for workshops with community groups. Individual sections were prepared for specific workshop sessions and distributed to the participants. Testing and revision came from actually using the materials with these sessions and by the workshop participants using them in their own programs. The materials have evolved over the last fifteen years and it would be impossible to give recognition to every person or organization who assisted in this work. Likewise it would be impossible to individually credit the source of ideas, illustrations and even the content of many of the articles. I would however like to thank all the individuals who served as "guinea pigs" for my writing. Whether they knew it or not they were responsible for much of what I have done. Equally I would like to thank all of my colleagues who have contributed to the technical aspects of this Handbook. I sincerely apologize for any accidental omission or unwitting misidentification of any credits. As with most technicians and educators I can't claim to have many original ideas. I have picked up useful tips from many sources and hope that they will find a wider audience through my work.

In particular, I would like to thank those persons who have contributed specific articles or who have given me particular help for major sections:

Learning Environments in the Community, by Amy Elliott Zelmer;

Comparisons of Media, assistance from Dave Sands and Jack Smith, the University of Alberta;

Production Planning, assistance from Dave Sands of the University of Alberta and Allan Stein of Filmwest Associates Ltd. ;

Interviewing Techniques, assistance from Darrell C. Hockett, international management consultant;

Editing: The Unique Skill, by Harry Paney, St. Charles, Ill.; reprinted courtesy of Behrend's, Inc., Chicago, from their catalog of motion picture equipment;

Community Development and Film-Making, by Amy
   Elliott Zelmer;
Street Theatre: A Tool for Action, assistance from
   the International Development Street Theatre Troupe,
   Calgary;
Gaming in the Community, by Irene McRae and Amy
   Elliott Zelmer;
The Publicity Chairman, by June Sheppard; reprinted
   courtesy of the Edmonton Journal;
Broadcast Community Television, by I. Switzer, Toron-
   to; and
Citizen's Media: Some Cases, interviews with Don
   Kimerly, QCFM; Station Staff and Volunteers,
   CFRO-FM; Cathy Clavier, QCTV; and Ernie
   Poscente, Capital Cable.

INTRODUCTION TO THE
FIRST EDITION

Even the most casual observer of the media scene today is aware of vast changes. Members of the public are becoming aware that mere amateurs are capable of producing quite acceptable mediated messages, and the professional is preparing for an assault upon his previously sacred media center. "Community Media" has become a new term in our vocabulary and a surprisingly strong force among the potential users and producers of media.

- minority groups are operating their own radio and television stations, as well as organizing "resource centers" or "media centers."

- regulatory agencies are requiring locally produced community channels on cable systems.

- citizen participation is reaching into every facet of government and education.

- community schools provide access to media facilities.

- libraries are promoting community programs.

- underground publishing ventures provide a viable voice for the youth.

- elementary school students learn about photography, film-making and VTRs as part of "visual-literacy."

- educational institutions are gearing up to train community facilitators.

Unfortunately, through all the list of achievements of the new wave of media utilization we continually hear pleas for simple, non-technical instructional and reference materials that can be read and understood by the enthusiastic community media neophyte. The professional was trained through several years of sacred rites using primarily a textbook ap-

proach. When designing a training program or when asked
for information, he usually responds with technical data which
does not allow the learner to participate in the planning and
execution of his own education.

This handbook is an attempt to partially meet this need
by providing basic data on most of the media commonly en-
countered by community groups. It is primarily designed to
be a handy reference and training tool for community organizations and volunteer groups who do not have the resources
or the desire to employ "professional" media "experts. "

Each section of the handbook covers a separate topic;
however, many of the sections are related in that they cover
different aspects of an overall topic or because a basic procedure is common to several media. As far as possible the
articles have been written to include practical tips and basic
operating procedures. For more detailed theory or technical
information you should consult your local public library or obtain the reference materials noted in the bibliography section.

Because of the changes occurring in the media field
this handbook will never be completed. It is hoped that users
will add their own chapters as they develop materials to solve
their own particular problems. Community media will only
be a reality when community groups undertake the development of their own materials.

P. S. Readers who send along revisions or additional material on community media will be helping us to prepare
the next edition of the handbook. The source of any
material used in the handbook will always be acknowl-
edged.

How the Handbook Was Prepared

The development of this handbook sprung out of a
series of workshops that I organized for media users. These
workshops ranged from the use of television to the design of
simulations to the production of simple motion pictures.
Throughout the workshops I was asked repeatedly for simply
written instructions and operating tips that the students could
take home for future use. I found, in fact, that many of the
students (both youth and adults) participated in a workshop

and then went back home and didn't use the techniques they had discovered.

The utilization usually depended upon whether or not the workshop had broken through the "mystique" about how difficult and expensive media was to use, and whether the participants had received (or developed) written and visual materials that they could use at a later date. Conventional training methods and "handouts" were not satisfactory. The students had to participate and get involved in the design, production or use of media. The usual type of handout materials had to be revised to exclude jargon and highly technical references. The writing had to be very readable and contain enough visuals to be interesting and explanatory.

Thus was the Handbook born..........

Over a period of about a year I worked to assemble and write the required materials. Initially I had hoped that much of the content could come from articles which had been written for magazines and the like. In actual fact, I found that there really was a lack of usable articles and set out to write my own. All articles included here are by me, except those specifically credited to other authors.

As part of the process I worked with a group of individuals and institutions scattered all across Canada and part of the United States, testing the effectiveness of each article. These people were all involved as media users or trainers at the community or college level, and they became my community. Surprisingly, to me at least, very few major changes were requested; most comments were for minor revisions and for additional areas to be covered. Thus the Handbook expanded as my media community required materials for the work they were doing. It seemed, of course, that every new article spawned several more, but gradually a form emerged that was agreeable both to myself and to the major users of the draft edition. As with any community media project, we had our disagreements and conflicts over what was best; but the ultimate control rested with me and I trust that I have made the best decisions possible about what to include or how to approach an area.

I would like to thank sincerely all the participants in this community media project and to acknowledge in particular the assistance of the following who were contributors to parts of the Handbook:

Dave Sands: Motion Picture Services, the University of Alberta.

Jack Smith: Printing Services, the University of Alberta.

Allan Stein: FilmWest Associates Ltd., Edmonton.

Darrell C. Hockett: Management Consultant, Edmonton.

Harry Paney: Behrend's Inc., Chicago.

E. Burke Nagle: Public Affairs Communications, The Government of Alberta.

Ken McKersie: Rogers Cable TV Ltd., and Canadian Electronics Engineering magazine, Toronto.

Irene McRae: Edmonton.

International Development Street Theatre Troupe: Calgary.

Judy Brown: Northern Medical Services, Department of National Health and Welfare, Canada.

I. Switzer: Maclean-Hunter Cable TV Ltd., Toronto.

June Sheppard: The Edmonton Journal.

And last but not least:

Amy Elliott Zelmer: a media user and continual critic of my pompous prose.

Another segment of the professional media community was indirectly involved in the design and production of the Handbook: the publishing industry. To those of us most closely involved, it was especially frustrating to be working on something that we felt was useful, which the wider community of users was indicating was needed, and yet which the publishing industry declared to be "too technical" or, alternatively, "not academic enough." We accordingly worked out a budget which would have allowed us to publish the Handbook ourselves, and we were appalled at the costs involved. Sheila McFadzean of the Canadian International Development Agency (CIDA) in Ottawa worked unsuccessfully to obtain a subsidy. In the face of the costs involved, we faced a dilemma--the answer to which was to go outside of Canada for publication. The Scarecrow Press agreed to be the publisher, relieving us of printing and distribution problems. Ultimately, I suspect the Handbook will obtain wider circulation through the United States and the resulting royalties will enable us to subsidize a second volume dealing further with the administration and management of a community media or resource center. The dilemma we faced is a very real problem for many media projects: at what point do you turn to outside professionals to assist your production?

A. C. L. Zelmer

International Communications Institute
P. O. Box 8268, Station F,
Edmonton, Alberta, Canada, T6H 4P1

INTRODUCTION TO THE
SECOND EDITION

Chinese fortune cookie: "Lessons Learned in
Past Can Now Be Utilized."

I am constantly reminded that the more things change,
the more they remain the same. I have spent much of the
last four years working in South East Asia as a consultant
to community groups, government agencies and various non-
government health service units. Upon returning to Canada
I felt that it was likely that enough had changed in the community media field to justify working up a revision for the
now five-year old Handbook. After all, many of the small
cooperative media groups that I had known have disappeared;
community cable television has become big business "competing" with CBS, NBC and the CBC; audio-visual equipment
sales have seemingly soared (as also their prices); and the
local community college is graduating Audio-Visual Technicians that the school boards cannot afford to hire. There
must be many changes to report and I had learned some new
things too.

My dream world of community operated radio stations,
village health workers preparing posters, and high school students making their own animated films was bumped back to
reality in one short conversation. Nothing seems to have
changed! It began like this:

Joan: Hello, Lynn, this is Don Researchus, he works for
        the East Overshoe Begal Aid Society and he wants
        to buy some television equipment. Can you help
        him out?

Don: Hi--I really want you to look at this quotation that
        I got from the TONY salesman. It is a lot more
        expensive than I figured it would be. I know that
        the school just got a new television at about one-
        half the price.

Me: O. K., Don, back to basics first; is the Begal Aid
        Society a non-profit educational institution?

Don: No!

Me: How are you planning to use the equipment?

Don: I don't know, the executive-director just said that
        the board had authorized us to get some audio-
        visuals. He wants a color television system.

Me: Does he have any idea how much that will cost?

Don: No.

Me: What kind of a budget does your organization have?

Don: Well, not much. We are actually trying to cut
        back, but we have some money left over from last
        year's equipment budget.

Me: O. K., let's look at your quotation.... It all seems
        proper, the prices are about right since you don't
        get the educational discount. You have a 3/4 color
        recorder, one monitor/receiver and an office style
        storage cupboard. What about tapes? Do you
        need a camera? Where will your programs be
        coming from? What do you need color for?

Don: I don't know, we've never had TV before.

Joan: We have a couple of programs that we could loan
        them. And some are available from some of the
        Begal departments at the universities.

Don: Oh, I've never seen them. Are they in color?
        The director said that color was the only thing to
        get these days....

    And so it went. Another voluntary agency which might
quite likely spend a lot of its scarce bucks on a "television
system"--lots of gold stars and bangles for the executive
director's ego trip, and salesmen are so hard up they won't
ask too many questions. Anybody want to watch the football
game in color down at the Begal Aid office? (I'm sad to
report that this story actually happened. I've changed the
names involved but have reported the conversation almost

verbatim. We talked for about 40 minutes and "Don" went away to buy his director a color television system.)

Perhaps I am naive, but I had hoped that as equipment became more expensive the potential buyers would think more about WHY they needed something. I had hoped that the "demystification" of the hardware would lead to some sense and a critical examination of software (or content) before making an equipment purchase decision. Perhaps a friend of mine at the local community cable station is right: "We have made it seem too simple, everybody thinks that he can and should be a television producer. Nobody wants to learn how anymore. " If so, I am sorry, but I offer this revised Handbook to those people who are still trying.

I've made a number of changes in content and organization of the Handbook. First, many things in the media field have changed in the last five years. Secondly, my own ideas and skills have changed. The first edition was prepared from my work within an adult education institution, primarily teaching workshop type courses, preparing media productions and consulting on media use. Since the Handbook was published I have primarily been working as a free-lance media and education consultant. I still don't have a darkroom of my own, we have moved too many times. Our own "media center" is a basement room with shelves of equipment, supplies, and references. We can however, find almost anything that we want fairly quickly and we use our "clients'" facilities for most of our work. This means, that we cannot do everything ourselves and must depend on community resources. I no longer want to have my own television/film studio. It really is more interesting out in the community.

A. C. L. Zelmer
June, 1978

xviii

1 COMMUNITY MEDIA CENTER

INTRODUCTION

Eventually any discussion of community access to media services will become a discussion of access to some kind of equipment and production center: the establishment of a Community Media Center. Such discussions have been carried on by people both inside and out of various community organizations, local government communication services and educational authorities. Usually, the employees of these institutions will argue either that their facility is already open to the public (such as through the provision of a film projector to the local youth club for their monthly meetings) or else that the institution's resources are already so taxed by internal demands that it would be impossible to open up their resources to the public ("we don't have enough space for our own students, how can you expect us to allow an additional 450,000 people in ... "); members of the outside community will point up the lack of use of the institution's facility and their own need for such facilities.

This section on the Community Media Center is intended to look at the style of operation necessary to enable members of the community to use such a center, and at some of the requirements for specific facilities. While each of the specific facilities (film and TV studio, darkroom, etc.) is described as a separate entity, there will often be occasions when the media center will house several facilities under one roof. Obviously, this may result in savings of space and money, plus the added advantages of the cross-fertilization of ideas between various interests. Equally important, none of these facilities is essential, as media services can operate almost anywhere.

Planning the Center

One of the most difficult tasks of an aspiring community group will be to participate in the planning and design of the community media center. Where a school or other established group is opening up its facilities to the community it will often be almost impossible to obtain more

2

than token representation on the planning body. The average
community member does not have a very good grasp of the
technical aspects of such a center, and the institution will
usually decide to use their own expertise or hired consultants
in the planning process. In some cases the institution will
go so far as to hold a community meeting or to appoint a
representative to the planning committee; but rarely, if ever,
is the community allowed to do its own planning for its own
perceived needs, making its own mistakes if necessary. I
feel quite strongly that the community itself can and will do
a competent job of planning and operating such a center if it
is allowed to, and if the "experts" can be kept from inter-
fering. (It is very difficult for the media professional to
stand aside and allow a group to make a decision that he
knows is wrong; many times, however, the experience is useful for the group and, often, the decision is not wrong in the
context of a non-professional service.) Some points to remember:

- involve as broad a spectrum as possible of the community
  in the planning of any facility, and plan around demonstrated community needs.

- use professionals and experts as consultants only; do not
  allow them to make decisions or to control the group.

- obtain a broad funding base (remember that volunteer labor
  and donated materials count as matching funds for many

grants), since this will lessen the probability of control by
one organization or institution.

- establish a reputation for honesty and integrity, take good
care of borrowed facilities and equipment, and follow through
on promises.

- keep the formal organizational structure as flexible as possible. Some kind of structure and delegation of responsibility will be necessary for ad hoc projects but far too
many organizations get bogged down in formal committee
structures that dilute energies and merely serve as a base
for power struggles (meanwhile, the dedicated and creative
workers who originally proposed the ideas have become
disgusted and left, and the political shell remaining will
never be effective).

- be realistic and start small. One individual can build up
a very effective motion picture production and editing outfit over a period of two or three years by careful saving
and wise selection of equipment. Trying to do it all at
once will leave him broke and frustrated (imagine a great
pile of equipment but no money for film or processing).
Small successes will give the group confidence and, equally as important, show prospective sponsors and donors
that the group can carry through with its ideas.

Locating the Center

The most effective community media facility will probably be located in the heart of the community. This has
been demonstrated in recent years by some of the very effective minority radio stations operating out of the U.S.
ghettos; often the studio is a disused office or store, or perhaps the basement of the existing community center. In this
manner residents of the area can participate without traveling great distances (it is just as far to walk up the stairs to
the fancy studio in a marble fronted office block or school
as it is to travel several miles by bus or subway to a cen-
tralized facility across town). While new buildings and expensive decor give "status" and "prestige" they do not add to
the operation of the center. In fact, such facilities seem
actively to discourage volunteer participation, and definitely
deter workers from using low-cost or homemade solutions
to operating problems.

A potential community media center.

- old warehouses, ground level stores (particularly those
  with basements), disused office blocks, or converted ga-
  rages will be adequate for most aspects of a community
  media center. Conversion costs can be reasonably inexpensive (using volunteer labor and donated materials?) and
  continuing costs for rental or lease should also be low.

Operating the Center

Community media implies community involvement, and
at the risk of repeating myself, I feel that the community
media center should be staffed and directed by volunteer or
paid members of the community using the center. Professional media experts should only be involved as consultants
(or as individual members of the community group) and
should not dominate the operation. While schools and libraries have operated what they would class as community
media centers for many years, it is the exception rather
than the rule that the operators of the center actually involve the community they supposedly serve. Most librarians
and media personnel are trained according to a school of administration that puts expert opinion and the convenience of
the institution ahead of the community or the customer.
Hopefully, if the community being served actually operates
the media center, this attitude will not develop.

- carry adequate insurance against theft and damage of equipment, plus liability insurance against accidents.

- educational services must have first priority. Teaching materials (instruction sheets, practice materials and equipment) must be readily available, simple and open to all who are interested. Instructional sessions must be workshops or similar activities where everyone is encouraged to participate without censure or embarrassment.

- keep good records of equipment borrowings and issue of supplies but refrain from developing the red tape common to many professionally run centers (a $5.00 or $10.00 deposit along with the borrower's name and address will probably insure against misuse).

- do whatever you can yourself, using local resources, but send out for major repairs of equipment that you can't handle yourselves. This will often save the necessity of hiring expert staff (how many ham radio clubs do you know that have to hire technicians?). Maintain an up-to-date directory of the skills of the group's membership, and a list of competent repair services and sources of materials and assistance.

- budget carefully to avoid duplication or waste of resources. Many professional centers are full of "white elephant" equipment that is seldom if ever used. Even with the best of planning some equipment is seldom used; with several cameras, tape recorders, etc., around our house we all seem to end up wanting the same equipment, usually the simplest to operate and other equipment sits on the shelf unused.

Human Dynamics

There is a very thin line between having an institution similar to many university media centers, with their restrictions and red tape, and having a "media freaksville." The first type of operation generally commands the respect of the community at large but seldom allows an individual the freedom to be creative. The latter system has freedom bordering on anarchy but can seldom get the cooperation of its own members, let alone that of other organizations.

- incorporation as a company or society is seldom necessary

to carry on business, but it has advantages, as well as
placing some very formal restrictions on your organization. Whatever structure you decide to operate under,
you should endeavor to keep rules and by-laws to a minimum. In my experience, a group which does not have a
well-defined goal or task will soon dissolve into jurisdic-
tional disputes among members or various committees.
Keeping the formal structure simple will lessen the possibilities of disputes.

- "control" is an important issue with many people, and becomes particularly crucial if you decide to collect a center
full of "things" (hardware, software or people) or have a
large budget. In any group of people there will be several
who will be most interested in the politics of the group
and will attempt to manipulate it. The best safeguard is
a simple constitution which provides for the orderly change
of executive officers and defines responsibility for funds.

- keep a record of meetings (minutes) and other occasions
where decisions are made, and make these available to
all members of the group. Evaluate decisions in terms
of whether they advance the goals of your group.

- secrecy breeds distrust! Keep all operations open and
honest so that all members of the group are well informed.
Sharing in communications, so that everyone knows the
rationale for a decision, is as important as actually being
involved in the decision.

- build a good reputation through your dealings with outside
organizations and they will be willing to cooperate when
you need them in the future.

A Continuing Introduction

    This Community Media Center provides a framework
for members of the community to train themselves in the
operation of the media that are needed to solve their own
particular problems. If the center is designed with the community's needs in mind and operated by interested members
of the community, then it will probably be an effective resource. The center may contain a community newspaper,
or a studio for the local origination of programs for a community cable system or community-oriented radio station,
or it may merely be a place where individuals or groups

can get together to experiment with media. It can be a very
expensive waste of money or it can be the heart of a very
viable community....

What do you need?

ON THE STREET

One of the reasons for the existence of any community media group or of a media center will be to involve
people in media use. One organization will set up to publish
an underground newspaper, another will want to provide programming for the local community-access channel on the
cable system, and still another will have the objective of
facilitating citizen access to all media; but all will have the
objective of involving people with media. Unfortunately, all
too often, the structures that we use to operate within do
not allow optimum human contact and involvement.

A studio is a very frustrating place for most begin-
ners:

- studios are usually the property of media professionals
  whose expertise tends to put down non-professionals.

- studios are full of expensive, complicated equipment that
  often intimidates the learner (things that we don't understand scare us).

- studio productions lend themselves to "talking face" types
  of programs; often, a studio program is nothing more than
  one person in the studio talking to another at home (this
  situation exists in both radio and TV).

- studios are usually cold environments with hard floors;
  this makes it easy for camera operators to move their
  dollies around but makes it very difficult for people to
  interact.

- because studios are alien environments, most people are
  conditioned to "pose" and to be unreal.

- people who live in studios (technicians and experts),

however, soon find the studio is more comfortable than
the street and begin to lose contact with the community.

A place to
work and meet is
very important to
the functioning of
a community media
group but this need
is often translated
into a game of one-
up-manship with the
other media services.
I doubt that it is ever
possible for a com-
munity group to de-
velop facilities (stu-
dios, etc.) as fancy
or as costly as those
used by the commer-
cial broadcasters.
Luckily, there is no
need for such facili-
ties--the community
does not function in
a studio (but the com-
mercial media people
have never realized this, therefore their programs have
never reflected the true life of the community).   To develop
a media-conscious community requires community involvement.   Community involvement requires going to the people!

Street Workshop

Imagine that a local media group is interested in
holding a short (3-5 days) conference on citizen access to
cable TV.   Not having any facilities of their own, they decide that they have several alternatives:

a) Hold the conference in a local hotel with the financial help of a government grant.   Participants would be the
members of the media group (actually only the few whose
work enables them to attend during the day will get maximum
benefit), plus invited representatives of other media organizations across the country (probably members of their execu-
tives since these persons are best known and most likely to
be invited).   Evening sessions would be open to the public.

b) Hold the conference at the local university or community college to take advantage of that institution's studios. Other plans would be similar to the "hotel" situation.

c) Hold the conference in a shopping center mall or similar location (outdoors perhaps, if the weather is good). Equipment would be borrowed from local educational institutions and continuous workshops would be run to allow passing individuals to learn to operate the equipment and to help overcome people's fear (if any) of being on TV. Recording equipment would allow them to make short televised statements or to react to the previous speaker's statements. Resource people would be available to assist persons who had questions or wanted to interact. Coffee and donuts would be provided.

Which alternative would you select? Is it possible to get people "on-the-street" involved in such a program? Are community media people forming a new media elite?

Media Is Mobility

One of the major problems in using most community media is the need for bulky or heavy equipment. Street television and film require battery-operated cameras and recorders which are reasonably heavy and require frequent recharging (this is still better than being tied to a 110v power line). Most groups therefore improvise and develop equipment that can be quickly disassembled and easily transported.

- some cars are too small for carrying anything but the bare minimum of equipment (although we have used a VW Karmann Ghia to carry two people, a full 16mm equipment package, plus food and clothing--it was a tight squeeze). Any van (VW Microbus, Econoline, delivery van) or bus will make an excellent portable media center or can be used just for carrying equipment. Wherever possible, shelves or other storage racks should be installed.

- outfit suitcases or trunks with foam padding around equipment. I have carried VTRs, monitors, cameras, etc. by air in this manner, and have shipped them by truck and bus. Just make sure that fragile objects are firmly held in position and can't rattle. Use at least two inches of foam (soft kind or styrofoam) around any heavy object.

- battery units can be built into "belts" to make carrying

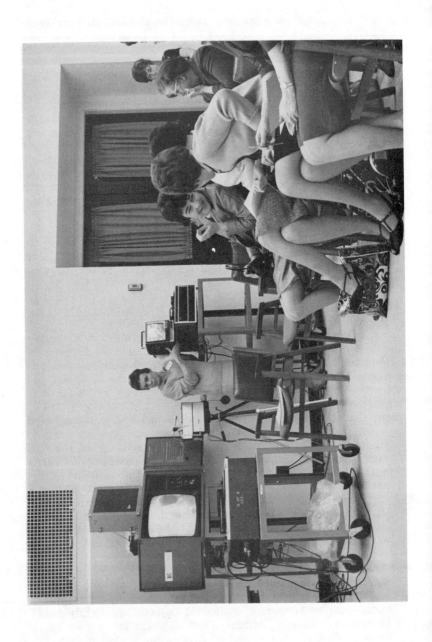

easier. A portable VTR can be fastened to a pack-board for back-packing rather than being carried over one's shoulder.

- lights and other accessories are now being sold complete in their own suitcases. (Often they need added foam packing materials to prevent breakage.)

- television and 16mm equipment is heavy--try using Super 8mm film or still photography on the streets. There are ways that these can both be converted to film or TV use if desired. These lighter-weight media also have the advantage of being less conspicuous and less complicated.

There are ways of making almost any media equipment portable, but in the interest of economy, try and select equipment and media that can easily be packaged and carried, is safe to move (not easily broken), and is necessary! The professionals have developed all kings of ways of faking outdoors in a studio; it's up to us to do competent media productions on the streets.

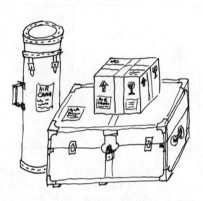

USE LIGHTWEIGHT EQUIPMENT.

DEVELOP CARRYING CASES AND TRUNKS.

FORGET THE EQUIPMENT AND GET INVOLVED WITH PEOPLE!

LEARNING ENVIRONMENTS IN THE COMMUNITY

It has been said that fish will be the last living creatures to discover water. Sometimes those of us who work

in communities also become so used to our environment that
we fail to see what is around us.   We may be so accustomed
to "making do" with what is available that we overlook some
very simple things which we might do to make learning or
working more effective for community groups.

We communicate very powerful messages to co-
workers and the community without saying anything, simply
by the way in which we organize our work-spaces.   For
example, if you were arranging chairs in a room for a
small group meeting, which of the plans shown below would
you use? (The o designates the group leader's chair; the
x's, chairs for the group members.)

Which of these schemes would you prefer if you were
coming into the meeting late?   How else might you arrange
this circle ... and with what effect?   (Try out some different ideas in the blank above.)

Where Will People Sit?

Shifting furniture around is one well-known way to
change the way in which people will interact with each other.
Probably the most efficient way of seating a large number
of people in a small space is by arranging seats in the formal "lecture" fashion.   This can be quite useful if, in fact,
that is the kind of presentation to be given, but what if you
want to promote discussion or work in small groups?   Then
the most logical thing is either to use moveable chairs which
people can shift into small groups or to set up a series of
small circles to begin with.

Will they need tables?   A good general rule is to
omit tables whenever possible--they tend to separate people

and often make it harder to hear. But, if you expect the
groups to do some work which will involve writing or manip-
ulating materials, then you had better provide some facility
for groups to handle this--perhaps they can work on the
floor!

Adults generally (in North America) are becoming
more comfortable sitting on the floor for work and discussion groups, but before you decide on this strategy as a way
of promoting informality you had better check out the group
expectations (perhaps related to average age and the formal-
ity of the situation), how people are dressed (people in tight
clothes, "good" suits or dresses, will generally resist working in floor-sitting groups), and you should also check the
condition of the floors. Carpeted floors (which are becoming
more plentiful in public buildings) lend themselves well to
this type of activity; dirty, splintered or cold floors do not.

One final word about chairs; most people who come
into a strange room will sit at the back. To keep your
audience closer to you and to promote more interaction
among the members of the group, don't set up too many
chairs. If you have an overflow crowd it won't take long to
set up extras and it starts the proceedings off with an aura
of success. If you're working in a large room with a small
group, try turning off the lights at the back of the room (if
you can). Most people will sit in the lighted portion and it
will help to keep the group from feeling lost in all that
space.

What About the Noise Level?

Some of the factors here may be
beyond your control but ... if it's a
lecture situation can everyone hear? Or
do you need a P.A. system? (Plan
ahead!) If you want to encourage questions from the floor have you made it
possible for people to be heard from the
floor? (There is nothing so frustrating,
or so quick to kill a promising discussion, as the inability to hear the questions which are being raised.) Many
speakers are reluctant to use mikes;
but what does the lack of a mike say about where we place
most importance--on the speaker's hang-ups or the group's
functioning?

My own pet peeve is the hotel P.A. system which isn't switched off, so that the meeting is continuously interrupted by paging calls and music. Again, what does this say about the hotel's (or our) priorities?

If you're working in an informal discussion situation the noise level can get pretty high and can interfere with the flow of ideas within a group. Have you made plans for the groups to spread out so that there is sufficient separation between them? Can you use additional rooms for some groups? (If you do use separate rooms, does everyone know where and when they are supposed to get together again?) Have you kept the size of the groups down so that everyone can hear what is being said within their own group without straining? What will you do if everyone wants to go off to the same small group?

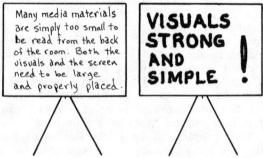

Many media materials are simply too small to be read from the back of the room. Both the visuals and the screen need to be large and properly placed.

VISUALS STRONG AND SIMPLE !

And what about translation? Most of us can't afford or don't need elaborate simultaneous translation services, but what about providing a "way in" for those who may not be comfortable about speaking in public in a language with which they are not familiar? Having someone ready to act as a translator for a few sentences--and making this known to all the participants--can "say" a good deal about the willingness of this group to have everyone participate.

Can Everyone See What's Going On?

How you handle this will depend on the importance of visual material to the group's work. Perhaps everyone should have a copy of the materials being discussed (though this makes it hard to know if they're looking at the diagram that you're talking about); perhaps you should be using some larger visual aids. If you are using a blackboard or flip chart, is your writing and drawing large enough? With some poorly lit halls, the glare from bare light bulbs may in itself make people uncomfortable. If you're going to use that hall very often it might be worthwhile to do something about inexpensive shades.

Do People Feel Comfortable?

Do they feel comfortable psychologically as well as physically? This is a harder one to answer and will depend a good deal upon the previous experience and expectations of the group. For example, if the usual practice is for the men to sit on one side of the hall and the women on the other, you may meet considerable resistance to trying to mix up the groups for discussion, no matter how beneficial you think an exchange of different viewpoints would be. (This same situation applies to mixtures of status.) Perhaps setting up an arbitrary system for formation into groups (by numbering, for example) will make more people comfortable than a vague request to form into groups.

Coffee, tea, milk, juice ?
Fruit, biscuits ?

In most meetings provision of coffee is almost a ritual, but it does help to make people feel more at ease, particularly if they're meeting with a new or strange group. (So does the provision of alcohol for some people, but I'm confining this discussion to low budget, basic solutions.) While it's almost traditional to provide a coffee break at the end of a meeting or in the middle of a work session, perhaps providing coffee at the beginning (or making a coffee pot available throughout the meeting) might make for better rapport. (Some participants might prefer tea or juice; can these be made available?)

For all-day meetings you'll need to think about meals. If the group has to break up to go to a restaurant this may become more of a social function; more work-time will likely result if food is brought in, and a certain camaraderie

may result.   If participants have to pay extra for meals,
what will the average cost "say" about your expectations of
their pocketbooks?

Babysitting services can be costly and difficult to
provide, but will certainly indicate your desire to have active participation from people who often are left out of community decision-making.

Pros and Cons to Smoking

Many adults will not appreciate a "no smoking" sign in a room
where they are expected to meet and
work; others will not appreciate the
blue air which sometimes results.
Neither group will appreciate a lack
of ashtrays and the resulting butts
on the floor.

Ventilation and temperature control can be a real
problem, especially in older buildings, but fresh air can be
a real help in keeping individuals and groups awake and pro-
ductive.

Equipment

If people are
expected to work, do
they have the tools?
If you've ever watched
someone frantically
trying to borrow a
pencil to complete a
questionnaire, you'll
know how uncomfor-
table it can be to be
"caught" without
"proper" equipment.

At least until a group norm becomes established, you should
be prepared to provide materials to those who come without.
If the activity is going to be messy, is there some provision
for cleaning up?   Most adults have had this need well ground
into them and will be uncomfortable if they have to sit
around with sticky or dirty hands, if there is not a way for

them to clean up at the end of the activity. (Even dry paper towels and some water will do if conditions are pretty primitive.) Work tables may also be required.

Print Materials

One of the facilities which is frequently overlooked for informal groups is the provision of a browsing area if there are print resources. Putting several books or pamphlets out on a table at the back of the room is definitely not adequate if you want people to do more than glance at the titles. Providing a couple of comfortable chairs, making provision for borrowing the materials and/or providing a list of sources where people can get their own copies will help to make print materials more useful to your groups and indicate that you do think they are important. (If they're not, why use them?)

Permanent Work Spaces

All of the foregoing suggestions have been based on the premise that you will be using temporary facilities for a meeting or work session and that you won't have the authority or resources to make any permanent changes in the environment. If, however, your group has its own work space, then you can do a good deal more to make the environment work for you. It's often a temptation to keep putting off fixing the place up because there are "more important" things to do, but working in dingy or ill-planned surroundings can exact quite a toll in efficiency and group morale too. One day's effort with a paint brush or some posters may give the place quite a different atmosphere.

A little time spent in organizing the physical resources of
the group so that they are in
some kind of order may save
a good deal of time, money
and effort for those involved.
Time spent rearranging tables
and chairs may make for
quite different interaction
within your group.

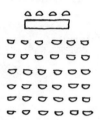

　　　One final suggestion:
when you finally get a work
space arranged to the group's
satisfaction there will be a
temptation to spend too much
time in it! Nothing could be
more stifling for a community
organization than to lose
touch with its community.
Try to move out to new
places, to meet new people
and to learn new things for
yourselves. Shopping centers,
public parks, laundromats,
art galleries and other spots
where people gather should
all be considered.

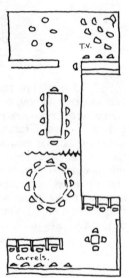

Individual Study
Small groups.
Large groups.
Media facilities
Book stacks.
Magazines.

　　　For those of you who
would like to find out more
about the effect which the
environment has on individuals
and groups, and on the way
in which we work, I'd recommend the following books:

　　Personal Space by Robert
　　Sommer, published by
　　Prentice-Hall, Inc.;

　　The Hidden Dimension and
　　The Silent Language, both
　　by Edward T. Hall, pub-
　　lished by Anchor Books.

FACILITIES

Every situation is different, and no two media centers will need exactly the same physical facilities. Determining a real need before the purchase of equipment or the building of a physical plant will keep your center more flexible and less burdened with an expensive overhead.

1. Many technical services will be available in your own community. Do you really need a TV studio when there are already studios at all four of the stations, seven educational institutions and two commercial producers? Surely it is possible to work out a usage/rental agreement with one of these studios, even if it means use only from one to six A. M.

2. Often facilities are not required. I have prepared very acceptable tape recordings out in the community, sometimes with a blanket strung from wall to wall to soften outside noises. Editing and splicing was done on the kitchen table. Most freelance radio journalists work this way.

3. Seldom used equipment should be rented, not purchased. Ask almost any photography buff if he really uses all those lenses and gadgets that he carries around and his answer would have to be "no." Acquire the basic tools that you will need regularly and either rent or "make-do" without the expensive frills.

FILM OR TV STUDIO

Film or TV studios can cost hundreds of thousands of dollars; however, quite adequate facilities for a community group can be constructed for a couple of hundred dollars (less if labor and materials are donated).

Basically, a studio is a room or rooms which have been sound-deadened and well enough lighted for use in film or television production. In fact, a single room of about 150 sq. ft. can be used.

CONVERTING A GARAGE (14' x 20' or larger)

(This is the size of a standard single car garage!) Lumber yard specials would build the building for $3,000.00 plus labor.   Allow another $2,000.00 for converting and insulating, plus, of course, the cost of all equipment, etc.

Control Room:
for TV or as
editing room
for film
studio

Studio (14'x14'):

Sound proofed, insulated and heated.
Curtain and/or backdrop on 2-4
   sides.
Double or triple paned windows
   to control room for TV studio if
   desired
Lighting system is hung from
   rafter truss units.   Provide lots
   of power.

Reception:
Library,
Coat racks,
Coffee,
Telephone,
   etc.

Emergency
Exit: if
garage
style doors
replace or
insulate!

A government media unit here in Edmonton had a studio that was approximately this size and design in a regular office building.   The offices for the staff and director occupied an additional space about twice as large.   Small cable TV studios locally (rural systems) have studios no larger than this.   Again staff offices occupy additional space.

22

A Basic Studio

One of the reasons why studios are so expensive is that they contain facilities which are not part of the actual production requirements. Thus the studio area will often contain offices, darkrooms, control rooms, storage rooms, a set construction workshop, preview and editing rooms. The intermittent necessity for a quiet studio may actually allow some of the other functions to use the same space. Thus the "studio" may double as screening room, workshop, and meeting room. In a TV studio the control room will also be used for tape editing; a film studio really needs a separate editing room (easier to keep clean). In either case a basement, garage or disused store will be more than adequate. (The same space may be used for both film and television work too.)

- floors can be covered with indoor/outdoor Non-Static carpet if required. Wood, concrete, or tile floors are adequate (as long as there are no squeaks).

- walls insulated with fiber glass insulation batts and covered with burlap.

- doors covered likewise and weather stripped for additional sound protection.

- ceiling as high as possible, open beam or joist preferred for hanging lights etc.

- quiet heating and/or air conditioning.

- entry and Control/Editing room finished inside with painted plywood, masonite, or plaster board.

Sound Deadening

The studio itself should be finished so that it will keep out outside noises and prevent internal noises (such as camera operators working, machine noises) being bounced around the room. Whenever possible the deadening materials should be aesthetically pleasing and inexpensive. Fiber glass insulation batts covered with burlap will be adequate for most purposes. On concrete or other hard surfaced walls, 2" x 2" framing at 16" spacing will be needed to support the wall coverings; otherwise, the 2" x 4" studs (or

Maintenance

Washroom

Storage and Workroom:
    Set building, props, etc.

Often older stores will have
high ceilings and a second
story at the back over the
storage area — useful as a
planning and workroom.

Building Approximately 24'x40'
Studio approx: 20'x25'
All walls painted flat (matte)
    colours to use as backdrop as
    required. Sound proofing
    materials can be covered with
    burlap or cotton (fireproofed).
Two walls set up with curtains
    for changable backdrop.
One corner can have a raised
    platform for a permanent
    announcers "set." Another
    corner can have lights and
    a stand for graphics, also
    a stand for projectors — use
    the wall as a screen and
    film directly with a
    regular studio camera.
Use wall space in halls for
displays, books, etc.

Hallway.

Control or
editing room.
Also reception?
(Cover this window
w. plywood or pegboard

Basement Use?
Business office? Files?
Window for noticeboard?

Suggestions for a CONVERTED STORE or office space

Washroom converted to DARK ROOM

WASHROOM

Furnace Room

Office of Service Station - use as library, meeting and work room. - cover windows as necessary for security, warmth and added wall space. - coffee pot - silk screen press. RECEPTION cum WORK-Room

Storeroom, Can be used as FILM EDITING

Storeroom, can be used as T.V. Control Room, equipment repair, materials storage.

Two stall repair shop, with high ceiling. Cover floor and use as STUDIO cum WORKSHOP.

~ soundproof walls (Burlap?)
~ level floor
~ hang lights from ceiling.
~ build storage cupboards along one wall.
~ hang backdrop curtains
~ old garage doors allow access for mobile van, equipment, etc.

Ex- SERVICE STATION ~
Why not convert to
Community Media Centre?

metal curtain wall framing in an office building) will work.
The burlap should be stretched smooth and straight, and can
then be stapled. Burlap curtains weighted at the bottom (to
hang straight) and hung from a 1" pipe "curtain rod" will be
adequate to hide the wall in a quiet location (they can also
be rolled-up out of the way; very useful when the room is
used for other functions). Unbleached cotton dyed in various
colors will also make inexpensive curtains.

Lighting

Ceiling-mounted lights are more useful than similar
lights on floor stands (floor stands take up space). Lights
can either be mounted on brackets fastened to the ceiling
(mounting brackets and sockets for PAR bulbs work very
well) or a pipe grid may be built and lamp sockets mounted
with special pipe clamps. To build your own lighting grid,
hang 1" O.D. pipe (new or used) about 6" down from the
ceiling. Two or three rows of pipe will be adequate for a
small studio. Always run the pipe across the normal direction of your studio (a studio will generally have one end
which is the front where sets are normally placed). Being
able to move the lights anywhere along the pipe makes your
lighting much more versatile. Locate several electrical
outlets on the ceiling to plug the lamps into. Each outlet
should have an on-off switch in a central, convenient location.
Plan ahead and provide sufficient separate circuits so that
fuses or breakers will not blow (three 500-watt bulbs are
maximum on a 15-amp circuit, a 2000-watt bulb will need
20 amps).

A second set of lights should be permanently mounted
in the room to serve as "work" lights (normal incandescent
or fluorescent bulbs are much cheaper to operate than the
more powerful studio lamps).

NOTE: Many schools and industrial training departments
       use only the normal room or work lights and do not
       have any supplementary lighting. This may be ade-
       quate for some simple television work but is gener-
       ally not adequate for creative television or film pro-
       ductions.

Television Control Room

The main purpose of a control room for low-cost

productions is to eliminate the noise of the video tape recorder. Thus some kind of sound-absorbing screen in one corner of the room will work just as well as a more elaborate "room."

If a separate room is used, it should have a large window to enable the operator to see into the studio (otherwise an intercom system is required). To make this window soundproof, at least two and preferably three panes of glass are required (the dead air space between deadens the sound, so make sure there are no air gaps around the edges of the window).

All cable holes must also be sealed against sound transmission.

Film Editing Room

Film editing requires extreme cleanliness so a separate room is preferable. (Even so, equipment and film should be covered with dust covers at the end of each work session.) This room doesn't need to be very large unless it will be used by more than one individual at a time. A film editor needs a large editing bench (equipped with rewinds, editor/viewer, etc.), some storage space (for materials, film, etc.) and either a film bin or a wall where film clips can be hung during editing. Pegboard covered walls facilitate storing spare reels and other materials when not in use. The professional editor will have a quite expensive horizontal type editing table occupying a room of its own. For the occasional film or the low budget film you will not have the same level of equipment or space needs.

DARKROOM

Black and white or color photography is one of the most versatile of the simple media. While the average amateur photographer may not be able consistently to equal the quality of the professional, his fresh ideas and enthusiasm will often more than compensate. Thus, for a very reasonable investment you can obtain photographs for displays and exhibitions (many shopping centers welcome exhibits which portray activities in the community); to illustrate

reports (or your own newsletter); to expose pollution or similar problems (photographs can be used as evidence in court
cases); to show your organization's activities (for recruiting
new members or soliciting money); or to promote your activities through the media (the mass media will all use
original and interesting photographs when submitted with a
minor press release or as part of a major promotional campaign). A photographic record is also useful as a history
of the organization and special series of photographs are
easily prepared to illustrate your training manuals.

As the center becomes more active the darkroom may
include some or all of the following:

- negative and slide storage files
- slide sorting racks
- film developing darkroom(s)
- contact printing and enlarging darkroom(s) (black and
    white)
- chemical mixing room
- color printing darkroom
- washing, drying and mounting area
- combination studio/projection/training room
- equipment and materials storage
- display area.

Small Darkroom

A darkroom suitable for developing film and making
prints can be installed in a large closet or unused bathroom
if necessary. From one to six photographers will be able
to use this facility (individually, not all at the same time)
provided it is kept neat and clean. Access to a large sink
for washing negatives and prints is essential but the sink
does not have to be in the darkroom. A regular white light
and a photographic safelight should be mounted on the ceiling
(controlled by separate switches); at least one double convenience outlet is also required. The door should have strip-
ping installed around all four edges to make it "light tight."
Painting the room a light color will make it seem larger and
brighter under safelight conditions. Space under the work
counters should have shelves or be enclosed for storage,
and shelves or cupboards similar to those in a kitchen can
be used for storage above the counter. Clocks, timers,
spare reels and other small equipment can be mounted on
hooks on the wall behind the work area. Even the back of

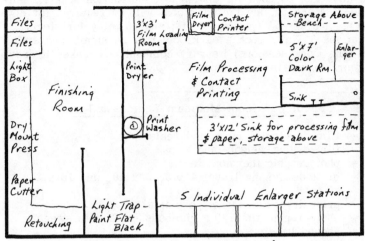

<u>16' x 26' DARKROOM</u>: Suitable for use by
6-30 people; black & white, color, processing & finishing.

3' x 4'6" DARKROOM:
Converted from closet, no
water, suitable for one
person or apartment use.

Work bench for
developing trays.

2'x2'
Enlarging
Bench   3'x 4'6"

5'x 6' DARKROOM:
Converted from bathroom
with fixtures removed
or covered.

Fibre glas sink 2'x5',
developing trays sit in sink
(use a wooden rack).
Storage above & below.

2'x3'
Enlarging
Bench   5'x6'

1'x5' Work bench

Note: Drawings not to
consistent scale.

the door can be used for charts and instruction sheets. Additional space outside the darkroom will be required for drying, mounting and spotting prints; and possibly for storing negatives. While such a darkroom will be small (and stuffy for long work sessions) its very compactness makes it easy to work in and to keep clean.

Small Darkroom Minimum Equipment List

- film developing tanks and reels
- film drying weights and clips
- photographic thermometer
- print developing trays (4 x 5, 8 x 10, and 16 x 20 sizes)
- print dryer (or ferrotype plates)
- photographic timer (or luminous clock with sweep second hand)
- contact printing frame (proof printer)
- scissors
- enlarger, lens, easel
- negative cleaning brush
- chemical storage bottles
- chemical stir rods
- darkroom graduates
- rubber squeegee
- safelight
- 35mm film cartridge opener
- exhaust fan

Large Darkroom

To accommodate more photographers it is possible simply to provide additional small darkrooms, but it will probably be more economical to design a darkroom which has been divided into usage areas. Thus a person wishing to process film need not disturb someone else who is using an enlarger, yet both can use the same sink area. It is important however to separate wet and dry work areas. As well as being more economical (and probably more convenient) a properly equipped large darkroom can be used for instructional purposes (two people can't even get into some darkrooms and it is impossible for two or more people to work together in most small darkrooms).

As in the smaller darkroom, space under the work

Large Darkroom Equipment List

- film developing tanks and reels
- film washer (hurricane style)
- film dryer
- photographic thermometers
- print developing trays (8 x 10, 16 x 20, 20 x 24 sizes)
- print dryer
- scissors
- large photographic clock
- contact printer (11 x 14 size)
- enlargers and lenses (at least one enlarger should be 4 x 5, rest should be common camera sizes, probably 35mm)
- easels for printing (one 8 x 10 for each enlarger, plus an assortment of larger sizes)
- enlarger timer for each enlarger
- negative cleaning brushes
- polycontrast printing filters and holders
- chemical storage bottles and tanks
- chemical stir rods
- chemical mixing pail
- darkroom graduates
- photographic funnels
- rubber squeegees and ferrotype plates
- several safelights
- 35mm film cartridge opener
- color enlarger and developing equipment as required (probably with automatic water temperature and heat control)
- electric tacking iron
- electric dry mount press
- large paper trimmer
- ventilation system or exhaust fan
- refrigerator for storing film and paper
- light box for inspecting negatives
- photographic paper cutter
- optional: stabilization print processor
- water temperature controls
- chemical recovery equipment on drains

areas should be used for storage, and careful layout of equipment will make work easier. Splash guards and light baffles (low walls between sinks and enlargers) can be used to keep chemicals out of the dry areas and to keep light from one enlarger from shining on another enlarger's work

area.   Finishing activities (drying, mounting and spotting
prints) and negative filing require space in an adjacent area.

Darkroom Lighting

It seems strange to say that a darkroom must be
well lighted but poor illumination will produce severe eye-
strain.   First, there should be an adequate system of normal white light to use when cleaning the darkroom.   Secondly, one or more safelights should be provided and equipped
with the proper filters for the type of work being done.
No safelight should be closer than 4 feet to a work surface.
A light-colored wall (matte finish preferred) will help utilize
all of the available light.   The two lighting systems should
be separately controlled and properly wired to prevent electrical shocks.   Grounded double-convenience outlets should
also be provided for all equipment (keep the outlets high
enough to prevent splashing from sink or chemicals).

All cracks where light can enter the room from
other areas must be plugged; watch particularly around the
door casing and in corners.   The entry must be light-proof,
either using a light trap or a carefully fitted door.

Ventilation

Working in a darkroom is damp and stuffy if an exhaust fan has not been provided.   Try to filter the air entering the darkroom to prevent dust being sucked through by
the fan.   Photographic chemicals may cause problems when
they are being mixed if they are allowed to escape into the
air, as they will contaminate everything they land upon (mix
chemicals in another room if possible).

Cleanliness and Water

A dirty darkroom is worse than no darkroom at all.
Chemical spills may contaminate later work; thus, arborite
or similarly covered counters are essential (use arborite
part way up the walls too, if possible) and the darkroom
furniture should be designed to prevent liquids from dripping
into storage areas.   Every piece of equipment should be provided with a storage space where it can dry if necessary and
also be kept clean.

Darkroom sinks are always too small, I think, so equip your darkroom with the biggest one you can build. Plywood and a 2 x 4 framework on 4 x 4 legs can be covered with fiber glass to make a sink at a reasonable cost. Get a plumber to hook it up and install chemical filters for anti-pollution control if you can afford them (now required in many localities, and always a sensible idea). Special connections and pipes should be used to prevent the chemicals corroding the remainder of your plumbing system. A temperature-controlled water supply is fairly expensive but there are several inexpensive devices which will fit on a tap to monitor the water temperature (you adjust the taps manually). Water supply filters are also available where tap water is not pure enough to use. Since good water is becoming a scarce resource, every effort should be made to use equipment that will not waste water (e.g., stabilization processors for prints do not require any water for their use) and to ensure that you do not pollute unnecessarily.

Finishing and Storage

Well lighted, clean work areas must be available for the finishing touches on a photograph. This will include drying and mounting the print as well as the retouching necessary to remove dust marks, etc. When the darkroom is part of a media center these operations can be carried on in adjacent multi-purpose work rooms.

Since you will undoubtedly have several hundred dollars' worth of chemicals, film, paper and other supplies on hand at all times, a lockable storage cupboard or room is advisable. A refrigerator is useful for storing unused film for long periods of time. A common practice is to store all supplies and small equipment (such as enlarger lenses) in a central office where individuals can check out the materials they need (this discourages petty theft as well as facilitating inventory control).

You will not want to save every negative shot but a simple filing system should be developed to save important negatives for future use.

Check First

Finally, before you start building a major darkroom,

check to find out the alternative facilities available in your
community; if you decide to proceed, visit as many darkrooms as possible to get ideas for design and layout.   The
following Kodak publications will also be useful.   They are
available at most camera stores or direct from Eastman
Kodak, Rochester, N.Y., 14650 or Canadian Kodak Sales,
Toronto, Ontario, M6M 1V3.

  AK-3   Darkroom Design for Amateur Photographers.

  AK-13   Photolab Design.   A manual for planning layout
          and work flow in photographic facilities.

                          LIBRARY

        The one facility that is often lacking in even the best
equipped media center is a decent library, both of reference
materials and of production samples.   Often it is impossible
to find a complete set of the organization's annual reports,
minutes of meetings, and newsletters.   Invariably, it seems,
the center does not even have a file copy of their other publications (training manuals, special reports, briefs, mono-
graphs, etc.).

        Personally, I feel that any media center must have
a basic set of reference materials relating to the agency services.   For example, a community radio station needs copies
of all the relevant regulatory publications, basic technical
books (operation and repair), service manuals for all equipment, basic textbooks on radio production, training manuals
from other similar stations, files on program ideas, files
on "contacts" (names, addresses, etc., of friends, consultants, persons to be contacted for opinions on various topics,
service and repair personnel, salesmen, etc.), and a library
of music.   In addition the station needs to keep tapes of
their programmes.   The station budget will likely determine
whether to keep tapes of everything produced or just special
programs (in addition to those "log" tapes kept for regulatory
purposes).   Subscriptions to a few relevant journals are also
required.

        Style books, dictionaries and similar references are

FIGURE SKATING   B2019   15 min   col $2.50

    Canada's top skaters demonstrate their world champion form and children enjoy their very first attempts at simple figures. For the youngsters, a turn on the ice develops poise and timing and is an ideal way to meet new friends. For adults, the fun can range from apparently effortless grace of dancing on skates to a rousing demonstration of the speed and skill required for the most rugged figures.

FINAL GAME, THE   E3198   55 min   col $2.50

    This film covers a championship basketball game between the Boston Celtics and Cincinnati Royals. Playbacks and stops throughout the film provide for a commentary on the various plays, techniques, and patterns used.

FISHING IN NEWFOUNDLAND   B1070   20 min   col $3.30

    Fishing amidst the grandeur of Newfoundland, where sport fishing is finest and trout only serve to whet the angler's appetite for still bigger trophies.

FISHING VAGABONDS   A1284   9 min   bw $2.50

    Shows four fishing vagabonds engaged in some carefree hours of sun and fun.

FLIGHT IN WHITE   B3596   15 min   col $2.50

    An amused look at skiing in the Alberta Rockies. Music and sound effects provide all the narration required.

FOOTBALL ASSOCIATION CUP FINAL, I   A1231   9 min   bw $2.50

    The Football Association Challenge Cup Final, 1954, between Preston North End and West Bromwich Albion, played at the Empire Stadium, Wembley, showing the huge crowds, the highlights of the game, and the presentation of the cup by H.M. Queen Elizabeth, the Queen Mother.

FOOTBALL ASSOCIATION CUP FINAL, III   PA72   10 min   col $2.50

    An account of the match between two leading London football clubs. Tottenham Hotspurs and Chelsea, in which Spurs beat Chelsea two goals to one thus winning the F.A. Cup for the fifth time.

A sample film catalogue page

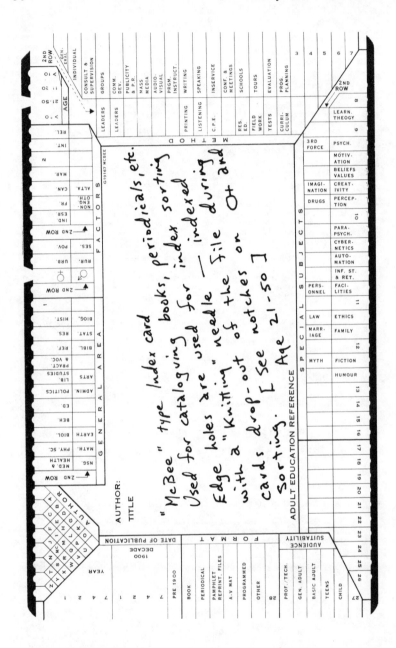

"McBee" type Index card - books, periodicals, etc.
Used for cataloguing for index sorting
Edge holes are used — indexed
with a "knitting" needle — the file during
cards drop-out of the notches on and
sorting. [See Age 21-50]

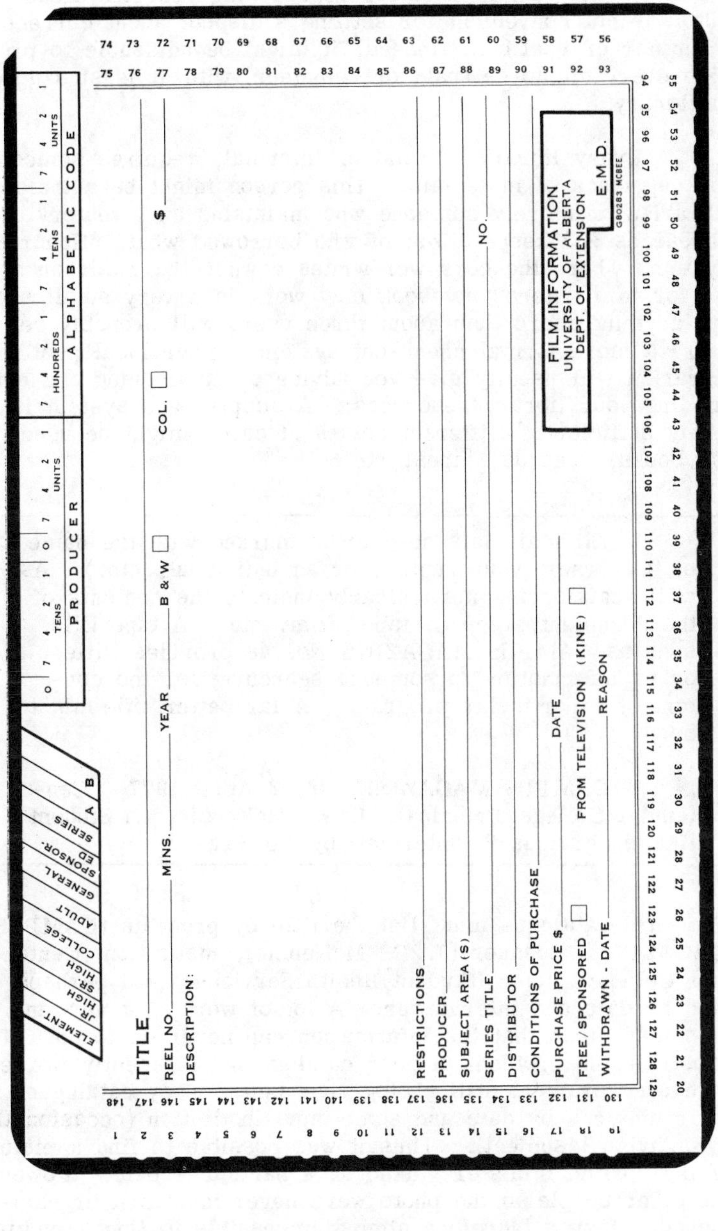

Film Information Card for library card catalogue

essential for any center, regardless of its function. The
public library can be used for researching program ideas
but it is not convenient for settling a dispute about correct
grammar or spelling. Indeed, it might be advisable to provide every employee (paid or volunteer) with at least a good
dictionary.

Every library, formal or informal, requires someone
to keep track of materials. This person might be a trained
librarian or merely someone who maintains an inventory of
resources and keeps a list of who borrowed what. Honor
systems where the borrower writes down withdrawals on a
list or in a "steno" notebook may work in a very small shop
but anything more than about three users will probably require a more formal check-out system. Your local public
librarian will usually give you advice on cataloguing and con-
trolling your library resources. A simple card system is
likely sufficient. Different colors of cards might be used
for books, records, tapes, etc.

All materials need to be marked with the name
of the owner (your center, or an individual, etc.). As
well, cataloguing must clearly indicate the contents of
the document, record, tape, film, etc. A tape title
such as CAMPUS MAGAZINE No. 48 provides little
or no information to someone searching for the content of a particular program. A far better title might
be:

CAMPUS MAGAZINE, 48, 3 April 1977, "Centennial College Principal, J. R. McKenzie, on Student
Health Services." Interview by Fil Fraser.

The card catalogue must list the title by program (CAMPUS
MAGAZINE), speaker (J. R. McKenzie), institution (Centennial College), topic (Student Health Services), and perhaps
also by date and interviewer. A lot of work, but anything
less may mean that the information can never be found. To
illustrate the problem of poor cataloguing, I recently worked
with a government still photography unit. They catalogued
their pictures by date and sometimes institution (occasionally
by individual subject). Thus it was possible to find a picture
of the "prime minister" taken on a particular date. However
the other people in the photo were never identified or catalogued. It was therefore almost impossible to find a picture

of a visiting dignitary or a local institution unless you could
remember exactly the date when the person met the prime
minister, or when some particular minister opened the institution.   Needless to say, the negative files were seldom used
by anyone who wanted a particular photograph in a hurry.

COMPUTERS AND MEDIA CENTERS

Macro, micro, or mini?   Magnetic storage on disk,
computer tape or a home cassette recorder?   With the ad-
vent of mass-produced, very low-cost central processing
units and other computer parts it is now possible to look at
owning your own home computer.   The conventional image
of an air-conditioned building full of very expensive equipment is slowly dissolving into very useful computer systems,
portable and extremely versatile in the $10,000 price range.
For the home market it is possible to purchase systems in
the $500 to $2,000 price range that will perform many useful functions--but how useful are they?

We have been renting computer time on a large system to produce our printed materials for the last several
months.   Rough drafts of written work are typed into the
computer memory, corrections are made very simply, and
special notations are used to produce underlining, titles,
pages, paragraphs, etc.   Multiple copies of the document
can be computer generated, or a single original can be reproduced by any photomechanical printing process.   Expensive?
No, it costs less than a commercial typist who would have to
prepare at least one rough draft and a final copy.   I wish I
could have afforded the cost of revising this Handbook on the
formatting system but I had started the revisions before we
began the computer service and I couldn't afford to have a
professional operator type all the original materials onto the
computer (for our other work my wife and I have been typing
our own drafts on the computer terminal).   There are a number of programs available for the $10,000 and up range of
computers which will do this kind of work; however, the programs for home computers are still too limited for our work.

It isn't even necessary to go to the main computer
with a commercial system--on our present use we have a
choice of several locations where we can rent "terminal"

S/G IN NURSING EDUCATION   3

world situation we have a universe of component items, some of
which are crucial to the operation of the system. The first
task in designing a simulation will be to look at the 'universe'
in question and extract its essential characteristics (see   *line 50*
illustration). / Having obtained a list of the essential   */JP*
components of the system it is now necessary to design a
simulation or gaming model which will all___ __ to manipulate
these elements in a w__ __   _ designing, as
we[ll]   system or
p[ic]   aching nurses
to   stethoscope ear
pi[e]   t, etc., of
the   nting her to
rec[o]   ver, we
want[e]   diaphragm and
the d[we would
need [r a complex
switch[__ by pressure on
differe[nt]   __ ine model. Perhaps a real patient would
be preferable in the last example.

CONTENTS   *** U[

LINE #	PAGE	PFX	KEYP
1			NO CAP
1.1			SPAC 2
1.2			SEPA 2
1.3			NO JUST
1.4			SENTENCE SEPARATION = 2
1.5			INDENT (5,0) (5,5)
1.6			TAB 6
1.7			UNDERSCORE BLANKS
1.8			REPEAT TITLE ON EVERY PAGE
1.9			TITLE
2			S/G IN NURSING EDUCATION
2.1			)E
2.2			GO
2.3			
44.2	2		GO
44.5	2		

FIGURE 2 0

    Many people have an aversion to mouth-to-mouth contact and
to teach artificial respiration we might build a doll which fits   */e*
W28J28

inside a suitcase, yet can be unfolded and inflated to human
size with all of the necessary body parts for effective
practice. Once a would-be first aider has practiced on the
dummy he will have sufficient skill and confidence to go on to

time (the typewriter type unit for entering data) and we could
connect to the computer from anywhere (almost) in North
America that is on the telephone system. One of our options
therefore would be to purchase or rent a terminal for use in
our office and connect to the main computer by telephone
when we need the central processor functions. We would
then only pay for the time when we are actually connected.

There are a number of large library systems which
have formed special computer access to their information
files. On a much smaller scale a media center could prepare a complete "card catalogue" listing on a home style
computer. Reasonably quick access can be provided to the
data for searching for titles, etc., and given sufficient time
for operation the system could provide booking services for
films and could even prepare simple catalogues, bibliog-
raphies, inventories, etc.

- LOOK BEFORE YOU LEAP. Subscribe to one or more
  of the computer hobby magazines and get an idea of what
  various systems offer. Talk to users of a particular home
  computer system before you purchase.

- Clearly define your needs and select a hardware and software system that will fit your needs.

- There isn't very much software available for home systems.
  This means that many home computers have programs
  available to play computer games such as "Star Trek" but
  haven't anything available to operate a simple billing system, or to keep track of materials bookings. Unless you
  want to prepare your own programs you should stick to
  rental on a commercial system or a home system which
  does have the necessary software.

- Be prepared to do much of your own equipment maintenance
  (and construction) if you purchase a home computer system.
  IBM and Amdahl provide systems engineers and repair services but most home computers are produced by small
  companies who do not have large distribution networks,
  and definitely do not have local service facilities.

Talk to the members of your local computer hobby club
for advice and assistance. Likewise get to know the
local equipment and/or software suppliers--their assistance and integrity will save you many problems and
perhaps lots of money.

For many years we have advised community groups to stay away from computers to solve their problems, whether it is operating simulation games or keeping track of finances. Today however, it looks as if commercial rates are low enough that a community group can afford proper services for many routine tasks and the inexpensive computers will soon have enough scope for the more esoteric tasks. Only you can decide whether the computer is an appropriate solution to your organizational needs. I would hope that just as with any other media you look at your needs first and choose a system to fit your needs rather than the other way around. (Incidentally, if you think that audio-visual professionals often try to snow you with jargon, you should listen to the computer bugs, they have refined the jargon game to a fine art!)

BASIC REPAIR KITS

One of the soundest investments anyone working with media can make is to buy tools for maintenance and minor repairs. Ordinarily it is not possible for the user to perform major repair work but regular maintenance and cleaning will add years of service to most equipment. To accomplish this you need a selection of good quality tools (not $.49 specials or half broken cast-offs from the local garage) and you must save all of the repair or operating manuals that come with the media equipment (almost all instruction manuals show how user adjustments can be made and indicate cleaning techniques).

> NOTE: Never attempt to disassemble delicate equipment such as cameras, lenses or electronic equipment. Clean them regularly but leave repairs for an authorized repairman.

General Operation and Cleaning

- flashlight
- pocket knife
- spare bulbs: projection, exciter and indicator (for various machines)
- adapters for 3-prong grounded cords to 2-prong

Equipment repair facilities need not be elaborate.

- extension cords
- 110V octopus plugs
- Q-tips (keep them away from video heads)
- cleaning solvent (get a nonflammable type)
- cheese cloth or "J-cloths"
- glass cleaner
- soft paint brushes for dusting
- vacuum cleaner (for inside tape recorders, projectors, etc.)
- light string and heavy twine ⎫
- brown wrapping paper   ⎬ wrapping and shipping
- butcher's brown tape   ⎪
- nylon filament tape   ⎭
- small first aid kit
- hand cleaner
- stapler (heavy duty model which will open to staple to wall)
- staple remover
- carpet layer's tape (for taping cables to floor) or Gaffer's tape
- masking tape
- felt tip marking pens
- lens cleaner and lens cleaning tissues (for camera lens)
- metal engraving tool (hand held, for identifying tools, etc.).

Wood and Metal

(Set construction; equipment and general repairs; building a work bench, storage cupboards, etc.)

- regular pliers (make sure the jaws meet squarely)
- screwdrivers: slot, phillips, robertson
- allen wrenches
- crescent wrench
- wrenches: open/box end (buy only sizes needed)
- screwdriver type socket wrenches
- work bench and bench vice
- hack saw
- crosscut saw (choose a general purpose size)
- keyhole saw
- wood plane
- hammer
- wrecking bar (goose neck bar)
- Yankee drill, 3/8" power hand drill and high speed bits
- brace and bits

- sandpaper and emery cloth
- combination 12" square
- many miscellaneous clamps
- tape measure.

Electrical and Electronics

(Cleaning VTR's, fabricating cords, etc.)

- spare batteries
- film cleaning solution (works for cleaning VTR too)
- video head cleaner and cleaning swabs
- plastic electrician's tape
- friction tape
- soldering gun, solder and paste
- wire cutters
- needle nose pliers
- set of needle point files
- tweezers
- 110 volt circuit test lamp
- inexpensive multimeter (amps, volts, ohms)
- methyl-hydrate
- test (inspection) light on long cord.

Tape Recording

(Splicing tape and cleaning)

- single-edge razor blades
- splicing block for audio tapes
- splicing tape for audio tapes
- head de-magnetizer
- bulk tape eraser.

Disc Recordings

(Cleaning)

- magnifying glass
- record cleaning cloth or tube
- anti-static spray/solution

Film and Slides

   (Cleaning, repair and mounting)

   - 16mm/Super 8mm splicer
   - splicing cement
   - white cotton gloves
   - dry mount tacking iron
   - scissors
   - film rewinds
   - film cleaning solution and cleaning pads
   - razor blade knife
   - liquid opaquing solution (to blank out unwanted areas
     of slides)
   - film leader and tail material
   - film sprocket repair unit.

Miscellaneous Supplies

   - wire, various sizes and types (speaker, microphone,
     power)
   - fuses (for various machines)
   - fuses 15 amp and 20 amp, 100 volt
   - electronic plugs and sockets
   - coaxial video cable
   - coaxial audio cable
   - speaker wire
   - washers, metal and fiber
   - assorted screws and nails
   - 110V plugs and sockets
   - contact cement, epoxy cement
   - white wood glue
   - charging unit for rechargeable batteries.

Organization

       A small tool box or fishing tackle box works very
well for transporting a flashlight, spare bulbs, extension
cords, tape and various tools when going out on a projection
or recording job. A solidly built work bench with storage
cupboard underneath and a peg board tool rack above will
make the repair job much simpler and keep one's tools in
neat readiness. Adequate lighting and power supplies will
also be required (remember to have a couple of 110-volt
outlets for testing equipment).

Equipment and materials storage is essential.

The tools and materials listed above can be obtained over a period of several years as they are needed (or preferably before). Expensive oscilloscopes, tube testers, power tools, etc. are not needed for routine repairs.

Again, save all instruction manuals and keep them in a central location where they will be available when needed. From very practical experience I would strongly recommend the idea of a work bench, storage and repair area. When tools and equipment are stored away in "corners" or cupboards they tend not to be used. If you want to keep your equipment and materials operating well your tool kit and repair center must be close at hand (this is especially important with the high use facilities such as for film inspection/cleaning).

A PERSONAL TOOLKIT

Every person who uses a media tool--whether it is
as simple as a marking pen or as fancy as a video tape re-
corder--needs to be accountable for maintaining that tool.
I am personally quite displeased with a number of people
who have worked for or with me over the last several years--
almost invariably when people borrow tools they fail to keep
them clean--in my case these individuals have failed to clean
my lettering pens! It seems like an insignificant matter,
however; if it takes me half an hour to clean a set of pens
every time I want to do a simple lettering job then I just
can't loan them out. My solution has been to develop a "kit"
of basic tools which I will assign to anyone who works for
me. These tools will be their personal responsibility, and
if the individual fails to keep things clean then no one else
will suffer.

Perhaps if your organization has a number of people
working on newsletter layout, or photo copying, or tape-
slide preparation then you might also buy a number of "fishing tackle" boxes and equip each person with their "own"
tools--let them keep their messes to themselves. This system won't work with large or expensive pieces of equipment
but for small tools....

Photographer's Toolkit

- camera (with lenses)
- light meter
- grey scale card
- tape measure
- flash unit
- cleaning kit
- tripod and/or copy stand
- carrying case
- marking pen.

Recording Kit

- tape recorder
- microphone (with wind screen)
- cleaning kit
- battery charger

- extension cord
- editing block
- editing tape
- single-edged razor blades
- grease pencil
- take-up reel.

Graphics Toolkit

- one 24" T-Square
- one 12" 45° Triangle
- one 12" 30-60° Triangle
- one straight pen holder
- several lettering pen nibs (assorted)
- one mapping pen (very fine nib straight pen)
- roll masking tape (1/2")
- roll transparent mending tape
- set pencils, HB, 4H, 7H
- one eraser, pink pearl
- one eraser, art gum
- bottle India ink
- one 12" steel ruler, cork back
- bottle typist's white correction fluid
- pkg. single-edged razor blades
- sandpaper, fine (sharpening pencils)
- piece emery cloth (cleaning pen nibs)
- pads, rough tracing paper
- pads, 100% rag ink quality tracing paper
- pads, newsprint paper.

Each of these "kits" is very minimal, obviously a
person preparing a lot of graphics materials would need lettering supplies, ruling pens, drawing tools, etc. However,
a quite credible job can be done with minimum investment
in tools--$30 each for the graphics kits for example.

For very low budget work in rural areas I have developed a variation of this idea as a complete kit for village
workers. With the kit of materials illustrated the village
worker should be able to:

- construct and use a chalkboard,

- make hand-lettered posters, charts, etc.,

- prepare cut-out stencils for spray or silk-screen application,

- prepare flannelgraph display materials,

- prepare multiple copies of simple posters and hand-out leaflets,

- enlarge or reduce sketches, illustrations, etc.,

- trace photographs or drawings to produce illustrations,

- sew and use puppets,

- make dioramas, models, and sectional models.

Basic Kit for Village Workers

As the budget increases we can substitute commercial materials for locally produced items. In the Canadian Arctic, for example, we issued scissors, press-on lettering, etc., rather than asking the village health workers to make their own. These workers did however prepare their own cut-out lettering guides (similar to the cardboard guides used by school children).

MANAGEMENT OF THE MEDIA CENTER

In planning the revision of this Handbook I had anticipated a neat orderly arrangement of several topics for

this discussion of operating a media center. As my ideas
began to take shape, however, I realized that many of
the operational guidelines were interrelated and would need
a more unified consideration. One cannot talk about "public"
access to files for example without also looking at the
philosophy of staff-client relationships. In the end I opted
to record a number of the directions and guidelines that I
felt important in the orientation of a new staff member to
a community resource center. The comments which follow
therefore relate to one very specific center, materials
oriented, rather than production oriented. Your center may
well need quite different guidelines and indeed I would approach a number of issues quite differently if I was orienting
a staff member to a fee-for-service institution, etc. It
might be useful to remember here that these comments come
from myself (as Chairperson of the Board) to a hired employee. The center is publicly funded (mainly government
type grants) as well as from limited service charges (film
rentals, etc.); it is controlled by a Board of Directors
(volunteers who have limited time to devote to the operation
or management of the center) and is staffed by one resource
librarian (who also ships films, etc., cleans the toilet, and
sweeps the floor) and a community animateur (working with
one specific community). The center is, in effect, a
special library with an out-reach program. Resources
include films, tape-slide sets, audio-tapes, books, magazines, vertical files and equipment. Some print materials
are stocked for resale, mainly as a means of "laundering"
grant monies (buy the resources from the regular budget,
and apply the revenue to non-funded outreach activities).
Cataloguing, etc., is very weak although this is being
rectified.

Volunteer and Client Relations

        The center is in the process of moving at the time
of writing, all contacts with volunteers and "clients" (film
users, etc.) should be used as a means of encouraging continuing contacts through the period of disruption.

- Phone everyone on the mailing list to obtain postal codes,
  explain the move for the center (overt reason for calling)
  and solicit help in the moving process as well as participation in regular activities (covert reason). Personal
  contact is very crucial, letters and visits to agencies,
  schools, etc., should be basis of our relationships. Staff

should contact all our major customers at least once per
year, and others as possible.

- A list should be kept (file cards, organized alphabetically)
  with the name, address, phone number, organizational af-
  filiation and interests of EVERY contact with the center.
  We have neglected potential volunteers, partly because no
  record has been kept indicating their interests and/or willingness to help.

- Every query to the center should be followed up.   Too
  many situations have occurred in the past where someone
  has called for information and simply been told "I don't
  know," or "We don't have that."   Record in the daily "log"
  all questions, whether by phone or in person, as well as
  relevant data about the person inquiring.   Direct queries
  to other agencies where appropriate or take the name, etc.,
  find out the information yourself, and call back promptly
  with the required information.

- The file cards on people should be up to date.   Names,
  phone numbers, etc., need to be confirmed at least once
  per year and preferably twice.   Ensure that when you direct someone to another agency that you provide a current
  contact name as well as agency phone number.

- Follow up on all queries to ensure that the inquirer did in
  fact find a useful answer to his/her question.

- Every contact is a potential source of funds and/or volunteer labor.   Be polite, admit your ignorance when appropriate and generally cultivate a positive image for the center.   Follow up on everything that you have promised--keep
  a record in the "log" of your response to queries and cross-
  check regularly to ensure that you haven't missed anyone.

Calendar

- Maintain a personal date calendar to remind you of important engagements.   Be on time for engagements, do not
  commit yourself to more than one activity for any particular time period.

- Maintain a "booking" calendar to indicate when the center's
  "meeting room" has been booked by an organization or
  group.   Do not doublebook.

Film Title				
B & W/Color Quality:	Silent/Sound Quality:	Length/Time	Previewer Date	Rating
Producer		Series		
Supplier		Cost	Production Date	
Type of Production			Audience Category	
Subject				
Synopsis			Comments	

Ratings: 1-Purchase immediately, 2-Consider for purchase, 3-Acceptable/no immed. need, 4-Not recommended, 5-Unacceptable.

Film Evaluation Card for assisting in ordering films

- Booking cards exist for every film, tape-slide presentation and other major resource item. Write bookings on the cards. Confirm bookings by phone and/or mail. Leave enough time between bookings for maintenance (films, etc., need regular inspection and cleaning). Notify customers immediately and personally (by phone, etc.) if unforseen delays or other circumstances will cause a cancellation or delay in the booking.

Many center activities occur regularly. A daily reminder file needs to be created to keep track of these items. For example, the newsletter comes out approximately the 20th of every month. Five days earlier we need all the materials in for typing and editing. One week earlier reminders need to be made to those persons who submit regular materials, etc. Thus when you come in to the center any morning you should check the file and find the activities required that day. These might include reminding the Chairperson that he has two days more before his newsletter column is due, checking with the finance chairperson about typing his monthly report to the board, preparing the monthly news bulletin for CCIC (our national contact, publishers of a monthly compilation of news from local agencies), etc.

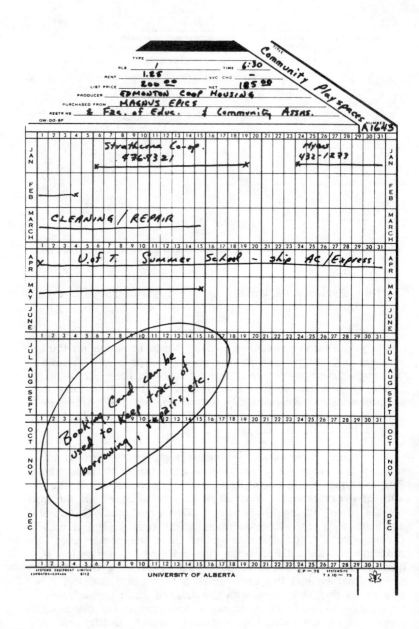

Film Booking Card

- Keep track of the time required for various activities and adjust the reminder file accordingly.

- Routinize activities and regularize their occurrence. It should not cause a major disruption of the library to prepare the newsletter. You should anticipate this and other regular activities, schedule meetings, etc., to avoid the times when you are engaged in them and encourage members, volunteers, etc., to maintain the required deadlines.

- Due dates, etc., for resource materials can also be placed in this file.

- Check the file every day for today's activities, and also for activities that may be coming up soon.

    Maintaining the booking cards, date calendar and reminder file may seem trivial. However, we exist solely as a service agency. If we "forget" to send out materials, or we "forget" to prepare materials, press releases, newsletter copy, mailings, etc., we lose our credibility and reason for existing: the community we serve ceases to need us.

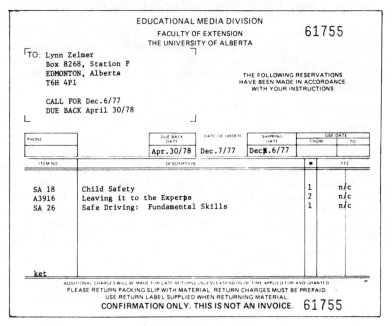

Film Confirmation Slip

Publicity

Publicity is an extension of our relations with our
volunteers and clients. Publicity consists of the letters,
news releases, newspaper articles, etc., that inform the
general public about our activities. Publicity, either the
planned type listed above or the unplanned word-of-mouth
variety, brings in our new clients and enables us to have
a public image that attracts funds.

- Staff changes and center activities should be communicated
  as widely as possible within our constituency. Board decisions will usually determine the policy and format of
  materials for circulation to the commercial media. Controversial issues should be approved by the Board, let the
  Board take responsibility for such issues.

- Cooperate with the commercial media if they request assistance. Refrain however, from discussing the projects or
  programs of our constituency or related agencies, especially on a controversial issue. Again, let the Board take
  the responsibility for unpleasant work. Refer media persons to a responsible (and available) Board member.

- The newsletter is our most consistent publicity piece.
  Staff shouldn't have to be responsible for content and production. Board member involvement will depend upon
  staff reminding them of their responsibilities and agreed
  commitments.

Finances

The constitution of the center leaves responsibility for
budget, purchases, etc., with the Board. You (staff) will
be responsible for helping prepare the budget, issuing purchase orders and paying bills. Leave the financial decision
making to the Board--they may delegate certain responsibilities to you--but they should remain the persons accountable to our granting agencies for the disbursement of funds--
let them take the rap for bad decisions.

- All purchases should be made by purchase order.

- All purchases require receipts and/or invoices.

- All income should be receipted--this includes donations,
  rental receipts, material sales, etc.

- The "books" must be kept up to date.

- The "petty cash" fund normally contains a maximum of $100.00. It should be used for purchases of small items only, and should not be a substitute for purchase orders and payment by check.

- Any purchase over $50.00 requires the approval of the Board. Emergency purchases over $50.00 must be approved, in advance, by the Chairperson of the Board or the Treasurer, and approval must be ratified by the next Board meeting.

- Purchases of resource materials should be made through the Resource Committee. You and the committee should preview materials (see preview form) before purchase and seek Board approval if the purchase is over $50.00.

Committees

The Board functions through a number of committees: Finance, Resources, Long-term Planning and Special Projects (the Labor Committee is one such special project committee). The committee should be available to you to assist in your job: interpreting policy, setting informal guidelines, soliciting volunteer help, presenting proposals to the Board.

- Help make the committees work. Remind Chairpersons of their deadlines, etc. Help keep various committees in touch by passing messages, cross-fertilizing ideas and prompt posting of notices and minutes.

- Committees will only function where a need is perceived. If the staff take upon themselves all of the functions of the Committee it will fail to meet and cease to be effective. The committee should be able to ease your work load, provide you with a sounding board for ideas and serve as your professional support system.

Files

There are files and there are "files." Some materials should be available to the general public at all times. This would include information on agency activities, newsletters and announcements. Keep these in the proper place, throw out outdated materials, and keep them neat.

Files on the operation of the center (budget, corre-
spondence, etc.) can be kept more confidential. They should
be made available to Board members, and sometimes to the
public. Use your discretion about how much supervision is
required for any person using the files. Refer problems to
the Board.

Board minutes must be kept up to date and complete.
Bind them securely in a looseleaf binder. They should be
available to anyone for inspection but should never leave the
office. Provide xerox copies if necessary to enable copies
of minutes to be taken away.

- All files should be kept neat and up to date.

- Be consistent in your filing, do not place an item in one
  file this month and a different file next month.

- Old materials should be disposed of, referral to the Board
  may be useful before you throw materials away. Do not
  destroy old minutes, financial records, etc. We are required to keep these by law.

The Board

The Board of Directors operates by consensus, and
by committee. Ideally a committee will discuss items referred to it and make recommendations to the Board. Long
discussions or consensus on philosophy should be taken care
of in committee. The regular monthly and annual Board
meetings should mainly ratify committee deliberations/deci-
sions, provide a forum for keeping various center groups informed, and formalize decisions and expenditures.

- Special committee or Board meetings will be called for
  items requiring extensive discussion.

- You, as staff, are ex-officio members of the Board, non-
  voting but certainly free to express yourselves. You
  should also be involved in committee meetings where appropriate.

- Our Board meetings are open to the general public, anyone may attend.

- The Board knows almost nothing about the regulations

governing your employment (Board of Industrial Relations regulations, Workman's Compensation, etc.). It is your responsibility to bring matters affecting your employment to the Board for action.

- We try and function as a team, don't be afraid to question the Board's decisions or center policy. We will try and be as supportive as possible to your work in carrying out the policy we set together.

2 COMMUNITY MEDIA PLANNING

COMPARISONS OF MEDIA

There is a hierarchy of status attached to the various media, and if a prestige presentation is what is desired the considerations of utility will never change the format of a production. Thus the organization that was described in the introduction is committed to the acquisition of a color television studio in order to lend status to its operations. Unfortunately this push for status can affect the selection of otherwise very useful media and the media users suffer. Why, for example, should we spend $2,000 on a short 16mm film or a videotape presentation if 6 or 8 color photographs (8" x 10" mounted in cardboard, costing about $30) would do equally well? Likewise, why should we spend the time and energy obtaining a sound film from a rental source, renting a projector and setting up the equipment if a short selection of locally produced slides and a simple slide projector will work as well? The list is endless, but if you know what each medium is capable of you can make your selection based on need.

Media Alternatives

This list does not exhaust the possibilities for your use, it gives the advantages and disadvantages of several typical community media.

The rough cost estimates of possible solutions to a sample problem (page 63) were prepared in 1972. Obviously inflation has increased the prices, but it is likely that the comparison is still valid (try doubling all prices!). You should obtain price quotations for solutions to your communication problem before you make a decision on a particular media type. The availability of expertise, equipment and services in your community will also affect your choice, as will the amount of interest within your own group. An interested group of members might well decide to borrow equipment and make a single copy of a simple 16mm film (using an amateur film like Kodachrome which is designed for projection) for local use rather than hiring a professional firm to produce a slick film requiring a distribution system to recoup the investment.

The Sample Problem

As a community we want to produce a short (10 minutes approximately) media presentation to demonstrate the variety and potential of the services of our community organization (sports, literary, day care, etc.). We hope to use the presentation to gain additional support in our own community and the city at large. Thus the presentation might be used with small groups, at public meetings and with City Council. We picked the five alternate ways of producing our program (see charts on pages 64-69) and find the budgets work out as shown in the price comparisons. While the figures shown would not be identical with those you might work out for a presentation on your problem, the relative costs are fairly representative.

Note that the labor for anything that could realistically be done by members of your group has NOT been shown. Educational wholesale prices are assumed throughout (sales tax exempt). In all cases you should plan on some additional costs for dry cleaning, gas for automobiles and assorted meals for your volunteer staffs. Costs might be lowered considerably if you could borrow equipment rather than paying rentals; however, you need to consider an insurance policy to protect the loan equipment.

16mm Sound Film: shows motion and may have synchronized sound; may be black and white or color; good for showing procedures, developmental activities; can show relationships between two or more ideas; close-ups, extreme magnifications, overviews, slow or fast motion, animation, etc., all possible; requires simple (but heavy) playback equipment and is suitable for large groups or television.

Films are expensive to produce well, difficult if not impossible to revise, and are not particularly suited to small group use.

Most 16mm films from commercial sources are available for either rental or purchase. Remember than a $100 rental charge is paying for a film that may have cost $100,000 or more to produce plus $500 per print for distribution.

SUPER 8MM FILM

Staff of three: Producer, Sound, Picture

10 min., magnetic sound, color (b & w same price), 24 fps.

*Requires a screen and Super 8mm Magnetic Sound Projector for playback.

NOTE: A far better quality Super 8mm release print could be made from a 16mm original for approx. $38.00 (plus the cost of preparing the 16mm film).

4 Rolls 1/2" Audio tape	$ 22.00
800' Super 8mm color film incl. processing @ $4.50/100'	36.00
800' Super 8mm dupe for workprint @ $.13/ft.	104.00
Splicing Tape	5.00
Leader, etc.	5.00
Sound mixing (2 hrs.**)	70.00
Creative editing & sound synchronizing (4 hrs.**)	48.00
Reels & Cans (2 ea.) 200'	3.00
Sound striping, 200' @ $.06/ft.	12.00
First Class Mail to lab and return	6.00
200' Super 8mm dupe for release print (one only) @ $.13/ft.	26.00
Sound striping 200' @ $.06/ft.	12.00
First Class Mail to lab and return	2.00
Production Sub Total	351.00
Viewer, rewinds and splicer (purchased)	100.00
Super 8mm camera rental, 1 wk.	50.00
Super 8mm magnetic sound projector rented for two months	210.00
Tape recorder rentals	50.00
Equipment Sub Total	410.00
Contingency @ 10%	76.00
TOTAL	837.00

1/2" VIDEOTAPE

Staff of three: Producer, Sound, Picture

10 min., black and white program prepared using portable 1/2" videotape recorder and edited on regular 1/2" equipment.

*Requires 1/2" videotape recorder and monitors for playback.

1 Roll 1/2" Audio tape	$ 5.50
Sound mixing (1 hr.**)	35.00
Creative editing and sound synchro-nization (4 hrs.**)	48.00
4 Rolls, 30 min. each, videotape	96.00
Production Sub Total	184.50
Videotape recorder, camera, microphone rental (estimated)	150.00
Editing recorders and monitors rental (estimated)	300.00
Equipment Sub Total	450.00
Contingency @ 10%	63.00
TOTAL	697.50

*Presentation equipment costs not estimated.
**Fees for professional assistance.

PRINTED BOOKLET

Staff of two: writer, photographer

1000 copies, 12 pages and covers printed in one color. Folded size 8 1/2" x 11". Printed on better than average quality paper. Approx. 620 sq. in. of photos and 4200 words of text.

Community photography and prints for selection	$ 80.00
Printing Services:**	
Layout and stripping (5 hrs.)	125.00
Typesetting	65.00
Press time and ink	60.00
Assembly	51.00
Negatives and Plates (offset)	125.00
Cover stock (100M)	68.00
Inside stock (70 lb. book)	62.00
Production Sub Total	636.00
Camera, lenses, light meter rental	100.00
Equipment Sub Total	100.00
Contingency @ 10%	74.00
TOTAL	810.00

TAPE-SLIDE SHOW

Staff of two: Picture, Sound

10 min., automatically controlled using two screens (150 slides per screen approx.)

*Requires four projectors, two screens and special control equipment for playback.

4 Rolls 1/2" Audio tape	$ 22.00
Sound mixing (2 hrs.**)	70.00
Creative editing and sound synchro-	
nization (8 hrs.**)	96.00
1200 original slides @ $.18 ea.	216.00
Production Sub Total	404.00
Slide trays	24.00
Camera, lenses, light meter, etc.	
rental	100.00
Tape recorder rentals	160.00
Projectors, controllers, etc. rentals	
(estimated)	200.00
Equipment Sub Total	484.00
Contingency @ 10%	89.00
TOTAL	977.00

*Presentation equipment costs not estimated.
**Fees for professional assistance.

Staff of four: Producer (overall responsibility), Sound, Picture, Helper

10 min., color, sound.

*Requires 16mm projector and screen for playback.

(No special effects or optical treatments such as fades, stop frames etc.)

4 Rolls 1/2" Audio tape (to get a wide range of sounds)	$ 22.00
15 Min. sound transferred from 1/2" tape to 16mm magnetic film –Labour**	15.00
(600' @ $.02/ft.) –Stock	12.00
Sound editing, synchronizing and creative picture editing (4 hrs.**)	48.00
Sound mix (combine narration and natural sound effects) (2 hrs.**)	70.00
1600' 7242 Ektachrome film	144.00
Processing @ $.085/ft.	136.00
1600' Color single light work print with print-through edge numbering @ $.135/ft.	216.00
5 Rolls splicing tape	12.50
400' Black leader @ $.04/ft.	16.00
100' White leader @ $.03/ft.	3.00
A & B roll conforming at approx. 40 ft. per hour (10 hrs.)	100.00
Sound transfer to optical positive (Labour**)	15.00

400' stock @ $.05/ft.	$ 20.00
A & B Composite answer print @ $.20/ft.	80.00
Reel and can	3.00
First class mail to lab & return	2.00
Release print (one only) @ $.145/ft.	58.00
Reel and can	3.00
First class mail to lab & return	2.00
Production Sub Total	977.50
Camera, light meter, tripod (1 wk.)	105.00
16mm Projector (2 mos.)	210.00
Tape recorder (2 mos.)	120.00
Tape recorder (2 wks)	40.00
Movie-scope viewer, rewinds, splicer, stop watch (2 mos.)	175.00
Equipment Rental Sub Total	650.00
Contingency @ 10%	165.00
TOTAL	1790.50

*Presentation equipment costs not estimated.
**Fees for professional assistance.

Super 8mm film: essentially the same as 16mm film
except that the film is physically narrower and in general
costs are less.   It is sometimes possible to add sound (normally on a magnetic stripe attached to the film or with a
synchronized tape recorder).   In both cases (16mm and 8mm)
it is possible to prepare a silent film and read a narration
during the presentation.   Super 8mm is the present "amateur"
film size and equipment may be found in many schools and
similar organizations.   Regular 8mm (a smaller picture)
equipment may still be available as well but normally the
films made for regular 8mm are not compatible with Super
8mm equipment and vice versa.

Sound film equipment is not readily available, and
8mm formats are not usually acceptable for television (many
cable TV stations and a very few independent commercial
TV stations will accept Super 8mm) or auditorium use.
Super 8mm is quite difficult to edit, special effects such as
fades and dissolves are seldom possible and the quality of
duplicate copies is terrible.   Professionally produced Super
8mm films are first prepared in 16mm and then photographically reduced.   This is the easiest and cheapest way of
making multiple copies.   It is not normally worthwhile to
revise individual films, thus old films are thrown away and
totally new films substituted.

Television: commercial television may reach a large
audience if the timing is right but is rigidly controlled and
expensive.   To show a 30-second commercial promoting a
particular point of view will require first of all the commercial itself (somewhere between $50 and $50,000) and then
"time" purchased from the station.   All television stations
run "public service spots" free of charge.   My local network
station seems to schedule these during the "late-late" movie
or Sunday morning--hardly useful times.   For personal ap-
pearances and longer messages we have to rely on the talk
shows and the news.   Cable television stations are more ac-
cessible but they have evolved from being local "access"
stations where anyone could drop in and ultimately get "on-
air," to "community" stations with programming controlled
more or less by legitimate community groups, to their present emphasis on being "local" TV competing for audience
with the network stations.   To get on TV these days you
must have a well presented message and be reasonably
"legit."   (See the sections on "Obtaining Access to the
Media," "The Press Release," etc., for additional information.)

Locally produced videotaped programs are also possible. Five years ago community groups were perhaps the second largest purchaser of 1/2" television equipment (schools were likely the largest). Today it is 3/4" cassettes and color. For only $10,000 you can have a minimal selection of equipment that is capable of recording and playing back your presentations. Immediate playback is possible and the recording has synchronized sound and picture. Magnetic tape is the recording medium, with cassettes the operation is very simple and tapes can be reused. Cable stations can sometimes use 3/4" programs directly but most videotape productions are played back to small groups directly.

Television playback equipment is heavy and bulky. At least two large TV sets are needed for classroom viewing and rental or loan equipment is not generally available.

For training community leaders in public speaking, interviewing techniques, human relations, etc., I still use the 1/2" black and white equipment. Since I am working with individuals or small groups the small picture is not significant. I need the immediacy of playback and convenience of picture and sound.

Tape-Slide Presentations: color slides, a projector and a cassette tape recorder with synchronizing capability form the basis of most of my current medium and large group presentations. The equipment is reasonably lightweight and simple to use but most of all I enjoy the versatility of being able to make changes in content easily. If I don't have time to prepare the audiotape and control track I simply play appropriate music in the background and do a live narration. The slides can be reorganized or reused infinitely for other purposes.

Disadvantages include the difficulty of showing motion and the possibility of spilling trays of slides all over the floor (they can be cheaply copied into a filmstrip format to overcome this). Individual slides can also "jam" in the projector causing embarrassment if nothing else (slides should be cleaned and repaired prior to every use).

Radio: often overlooked, but radio audiences are very loyal. If you can identify your audience and have lively verbal or audio material then radio may be a good possibility.

The disadvantages of radio of course are the lack of visual materials and the difficulty of having information repeated. I invariably seem to tune in near the end of an interesting program and once broadcast the program is usually gone forever.

Printed Materials: conventional and easy to design and prepare; inclusion of photographs, charts, etc., is very easy as well as limited color (full color is very expensive); can be used to promote an activity, to supplement a presentation, or for follow-up. Print materials are the only materials that the audience can take away after a presentation. Formats include newspapers, newsletters, posters, leaflets and flyers, booklets, information sheets, self-mailers, books, study prints, maps, magazine advertisements, etc.

Printed materials may not have the emotional impact of the other media and may lack immediacy, they cannot easily show motion and/or sound. High quality printing can be very expensive, therefore it is essential to know the size of the intended audience before printing materials (storage of 500,000 booklets plus mailing costs to all the residents of a medium-sized city are enormous, in this case a newspaper advertisement might be cheaper and easier).

IDEA PLANNING

Introduction

Everyone wants something for nothing, and this seems particularly noticeable in the media production field. Prospective customers are always appalled when they receive an estimate of costs for their proposed epic and are often aghast at the idea of cutting costs by shortening the production or perhaps changing from color to black and white. Needless to say, this situation also exists when the customer becomes his own producer.

Between 1969 and 1973 I was involved in the design and/or production of over a dozen low-budget films. Several of them never saw the light of day, one of them is in shooting script form, a couple of them are sitting in unedited piles of developed film, and about five of them exist as

finished films of varying quality. They all have certain
similarities: they were conceived to fill a particular need;
they were all slow to develop from idea to script (if a
script was even made); and they all took more time and
money than was originally planned. True, it can be said
that time can be used to replace money at some stages--by
doing one's own editing rather than hiring it out--but time
and money seem difficult to estimate accurately.

One characteristic of the finished productions was
that they required motion as part of the message. Several
of the films illustrated developmental activities: children
of various ages were portrayed attempting various physical
tasks in one film, in another changes in urban decision making was immediately reflected in the physical construction of
a simulated city. Conversely the uncompleted materials required neither sound nor motion for their message. At
least one of them would have been better conceived of as a
set of study prints. Today I would likely recommend that
many of my film and TV productions should better have been
done as tape-slide presentations: less glamorous perhaps
but certainly easier to use and probably less expensive.

At this point however, it might be wise to review the
basic procedure for planning a production in hopes of improving our next endeavor.

The Idea

Refining the idea--what is the production's purpose,
who is it for, when is it to be used and why it was conceived?--will be the most crucial step of the production.
If we can define WHAT, WHERE, WHEN, WHY, and WHO,
we can go on to the HOW with no difficulty.

At this point it is most useful to ignore any
particular medium. Once we have defined the goals
of our intended communication it might be more appropriate to use some other medium--slides or a
booklet for example. Do Not Allow Yourself to Be
Boxed in by Thinking Only of a Film or a Television
Program.

You may find writing dull, but it is extremely useful

to write a statement of purpose.   This is just a note answering the questions we asked above.   Then show this to other
people in your organization and discuss the feasibility of the
idea.   Remember at this point we are not talking about a
film, but rather about communicating a message to someone
on a specific subject to accomplish a particular purpose.
(perhaps we want to show the mayor and city council how
poor the playgrounds are in our neighborhood so that we can
get new playground equipment.)   Everyone who has an idea
should be listened to and their ideas used to refine our project.   Keep it simple.   A simple message is hard enough to
communicate; complicated messages usually get lost in the
attempt.

     Remember to be very specific about your audience
and your message.   An illiterate high school drop-out requires a totally different message and approach than does a
college graduate.   A production aimed at the school classroom or an urban family will not likely be suitable for a
farm audience.

     WHAT is it that you want to say?   Exactly
what action do you want the viewer to perform after
seeing the production?   Try to specify your message
in action terms.   "I want the viewer (or listener or
reader) to be able to grow a spruce tree from seed,
and I want the viewer to be able to explain three
reasons why reforestation often fails."   Do not use
statements such as "I want the viewer to know about
poverty."

     WHO will actually compose the audience?   It
might be helpful to think in terms of "The audience
will be elderly people like my grandmother.   She is
94, still lives in her own home, and meets regularly
with those of her friends who are still alive.   She
thinks that all young people are irresponsible and
that many of the young people are either drunks or
drug addicts.   She votes in elections but had trouble
at the last election operating the voting machine.   I
want to prepare a campaign to solicit her vote."

     If you talk to a number of people you should be able
to get a wide variety of ideas and suggestions about how to

communicate the message.   Try and sort them into two or three categories so that decisions can be made about what to keep, what to throw away, and what style should be adopted.   Typically, some of the ideas will relate to the wisdom of the message itself, some will be suggestions about additional messages, and others will be related to specific tactics for handling the message (be tough, make them so sick that they will have to act, scare them, sneak our program in without them knowing it, etc.).   Let these ideas guide your plans but ultimately you must decide the answers yourself.

The Script

Sort out the conflicting ideas; make decisions according to your organization's goals and begin preparing a script or "play-by-play" description of what you want to say.   Include thoughts on both visual treatment and dialogue.   A very useful form for this is the simple 4" x 6" card.   As changes are made, cards can be shuffled, new ideas put into the sequence and old ones deleted.   Don't be afraid to drop an idea if it doesn't seem to work.

Again, the materials should be shown to as many people as possible to ensure that the right message is being communicated.   When this has been agreed upon, it becomes possible to select the format of the presentation--will it be film? or slides? or photographs? or something else yet?

Summary

Before we go on the question of format, our activities thus far have been:

1.   Preparation of a statement of purpose, writing down WHAT it is that we want to communicate, to WHOM, WHEN, WHERE and WHY.

2.   Discussion of this with as many people as possible in an attempt to make it simple and clear.

3.   Preparation of a script on 4" x 6" cards which shows the words and the images we want to communicate.

Scene: 26   Job #

Description: Production: *Fire Control*

M.S. - hand
squeezing
trigger of
extinguisher

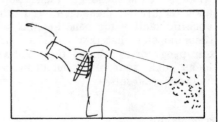

PAN to:

Dialogue:

... squeeze trigger and ...

Sample 4"×6" Script cards for
    short film.

Scene: 27   Job #

Description: Production: *Fire Control*

M.S. of foam
directed at
base of fire.

Dialogue:

... direct nozzle at base of
fire.

4. Further discussion to ensure clarity and agree-
    ment with the purpose of the communication.

In many respects the rest of the production is simple;
once a group or organization has agreed on the purpose and
content of the proposed communication, the project can be
completed by the group itself or can be turned over to an
outside body for completion. In any event, the ground rules
have been well prepared and our biggest task is to stick to
the prepared script. The work that the group itself has
done in preparing this script will make the task much easier
in the long run. This may be particularly important when
working with professionals who would rather do the planning
themselves and then submit it to the group for approval.
Their strategy may be simpler and quicker but will usually
result in the production of something that belongs to the professionals and not to the sponsoring group. (It is very hard
to criticize a completed script that someone has obviously
spent much time and effort on, especially if that someone
is an "expert" and we are poor amateurs.)

While we now need to make a decision about the format of our production (film, slides, videotape, printed,
etc.), our basic planning should ensure the success of our
venture.

WORDS AND VISUALS SHOULD COMPLEMENT EACH
OTHER.

DO NOT EXPLAIN SOMETHING THAT I CAN PLAINLY
SEE FOR MYSELF.

GET LOTS OF HELP IN PREPARING SCRIPTS FROM
USERS AND OPERATING STAFF AS WELL AS AD-
MINISTRATORS.

PRODUCTION PLANNING

Budgeting and planning for a production go hand in
hand. Remember that every individual action decided upon

in the planning stage will directly affect the budget, regardless of the media selected.   Also, it's usually wiser to wait
until after the production planning to make a final decision
on which medium you will use.

Start with an Idea Script

Redraw and retype your idea script into a two
column style--one column for content ideas and possible discussion, the other for pictures.   The producer can then go
over it shot by shot and ask questions like, "Do you realize
that you're calling for stock footage of an express train hitting a loaded school bus?"   He may get the reply, "OK,
I'll take any train hitting a school bus!" and finally ask,
"Would you settle for news shots of yesterday's train wreck?"
Eventually, everything can probably be worked out within the
budget.

One of the major problems with an idea script is that
it may read well but it can't be visualized.   An abstract
narration with "appropriate footage to match" is not fair to
the producer.   If the ideas are to survive, the visuals must
reflect them since the screen process puts visuals and words
into a relationship which says "these two things are connected."   If the mind can't grasp the connection, the product
will be a failure.

Radio Programs Belong on the Radio

Too often, it is easier to write good words, so that
you end up with a radio program rather than a visual script.
Then the producer has a tough time getting enough visuals
to fit without becoming stale.   On the other hand, a typical
script written after the visuals have been shot will read
"here you see," "now, as you can see."   In effect, the narration will describe the visuals, but most viewers have
enough intelligence to figure that out for themselves.   There
is no need for words that merely describe the picture; try
music or effects instead.

In developing a narration to go with a pre-shot picture the tendency is to use the words to overcome the picture's deficiencies.   These are exactly the deficiencies that
preplanning tries to eliminate by thinking of everything ahead
of time.

COMMUNITY X FILM: List of Shots

Scene

1.   PAN from house to street and cars

2.   TITLE: Community X CofC

3.   MS of traffic

4.   TITLE: Citizens for a better

5.   TITLE: Community X

6.   MS Post Office

7.   MS The Reprter, Red & White

8.   MS Openheimer

9.   PAN Bank of M. to Street

10.   CU Ladies and Childrens Wear

11.   LS Street Scene

12.   PAN Garden to lumber yard

13.   PAN Truck to street

14.   DOLLY Street scene to houses (Hwy.16)

15.   DOLLY Residential

16.   DOLLY Residential

17.   PAN Old house to men on bridge

18.   MS Boy on bridge

19.   MS Store

20.   LS Back of house

21.   MS House and log garage

22.   LS 2 story house and lumber

23.   MS 2 story house and lumber

It's difficult to tell where to start, but it's OK to
shoot ten times as much film as you need, if all the film
you shoot is potentially useful. ("Cut aways" are shots of
related materials that help develop the idea. You may be
showing the bus speeding towards the train and "cut away"
to shots of the driver's face, etc.) Mind you, it's a waste
to shoot ten feet on the assumption that nine of them will be
out of focus or otherwise useless. Everything that you do
should be related to the message to be communicated and the
final product. While it is sometimes possible to salvage
poor planning if you have a good editor, this usually becomes a compromise with your original intentions. Again,
preparing the "shooting script" (list of shots required, etc.)
must be done in connection with the budget; one of the reasons for not using that train hitting the school bus was a
matter of cost.

Improvised Productions

It's almost insane to make an improvised production.
Most documentaries (even those which seem to be spontaneous) have hundreds of hours of material shot and a common
thread is somehow found to edit around, but the budget is
immense and ordinarily impossible for the low budget producer, who must stick closer to the idea being communicated.

Community action materials are not as improvised as
they appear to be; usually the organizers have a particular
goal around which they go out and build a production. (Often,
this goal is to obtain people dialoguing via the media when
they wouldn't ordinarily have a means of communication.)
[For a description of this process refer to the article, "Community Development and Film-Making," page 246.] Your
main problem here may be to get all the required equipment
present and keep it working.

Visit the Location

Many of the problems of planning can be solved by
visiting the location where the shooting will be done, before
the actual production. Shooting angles, lighting and sound
problems can all be checked out in advance and the presentation modified accordingly. Even with an excellent script a
good director or cameraman may see other possible shots

The CHICAGO SKYLINE
   A tool for script analysis

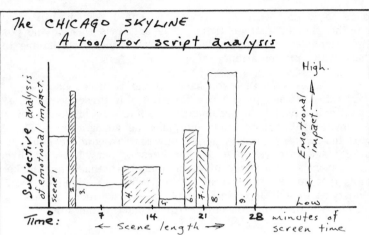

To help with the analysis of your script
estimate the emotional impact of each
scene and plot it on a graph with the
time required.
    In the "skyline" above scenes 3 & 5
are very low impact and in fact the
whole of the middle of the film is
weak.   Is this what you want?
    Variations in intensity are essential!
Use a large sheet of paper or a chalk
board for the skyline. A small group
of planners works better than one
individual. Useful for gauging the
impact of films, slide sets, video, etc.

    Characters, locations, emotional
moods, CU. us' LS. can all be graphed
and planned. Analyse your script to
provide continuity, variety, consistent
screen direction etc.

    Make your changes before you shoot!

once he is on location; however, he has a responsibility to
get the planned footage first.   The editor is then in the position of choosing between the two shots rather than having to
"save" the presentation.

Make sure that you have all the required shots--
particularly when people are involved.   If three people are
equally involved in a presentation, some way must be found
to cover all three of them--not just the young women who
will look cute.   This is not to say that a sequence couldn't
be devised to cover just the one person, but where all three
are essential, all three of them must be planned for (make
sure that you know their names and roles in advance, too).
You have to ask apparently stupid questions like "Is this
all?" "What's going on here?" or "What is that for?"

Look at TV Commercials

Anyone who is planning a media production should
look at TV commercials (look at the same one several times
until you know it backwards and can ignore the message)
and try to figure out what had to be done to achieve the
commercial:

- how many miles did they drive to find the site?

- how many people did they audition to get the "right"
  actors?

- where did the props come from?   (Just try finding a live
  baby elephant or an authentic mustache cup on short notice.)

- who was responsible for getting police permission to shoot
  the film?

- who was responsible for getting the helicopter or ladder
  for that aerial shot?

- where do you find trained animals who will act on cue?

- how did they check to make sure that everybody was wear-
  ing the proper costumes--without any wristwatches or other
  anachronisms showing--in historical scenes?

- how much did it cost to do all of these things?   What
  alternatives did the producer have?

Don't Despair

The commercial film-maker or television producer
must always be aware of production planning and techniques
which will save time or money.   Since most of your productions will not have lavish budgets you will not always be
able to use the most up-to-date time- and labor-saving devices.   You must however be equally aware of costs: both
time and money.

- stay within your community's resources, get grants, etc.,
  or raise money through community projects.   Only borrow
  money as a last resort.

- stay within your community's skills as well.   A few dollars spent to hire someone to do a complicated procedure
  may be money well spent.   Make contacts with the local
  radio and TV stations as well as newspapers; there are
  often people working there who can provide professional
  services inexpensively (watch out for phonies who can't do
  anything but talk jargon).

- rent equipment rather than buying if you only intend to
  make one or two productions.   However, if you intend
  using the equipment regularly, it will be cheaper to buy,
  even if you have to pay finance charges.

- often, you can save money through techniques which take
  time to set up or to accomplish the required results.
  Wherever possible do your experimenting ahead of time
  (including making a test roll) and don't force other workers
  to wait around while you try something new.

- a professional actor will re-do the same scene until it is
  perfect, even if this takes several days and a hundred re-
  takes.   The amateur will not have the discipline or patience (and you won't have the money).   As the amateur
  gets "cold" you might be better to put the shooting off for
  another day.

- some ONE person must be in charge; you cannot make a
  media production by democratic procedures.   Somebody
  ultimately must make the decisions and take the responsibility for them.

- there must be a fair amount of understanding between members of a crew so that each knows what the other person

means when he uses a particular term, or can anticipate what a person is likely to do.

- the cameraman and the soundman will determine how the final product will appear. Obviously then, it is quite possible for these persons to undermine the whole purpose of the production if they don't work to plan (on many small budget productions the cameraman is also the director or person who makes the decisions).

- if the director and the cameraman (or soundman) cannot get along with each other, you must replace one or more of them.

- decide upon how and where you will be using the presentation before you decide on a particular medium. (Don't make a film if you're only going to show it once; make a videotape instead.)

- retain control over your productions even when the local professionals are helping you; always have the right to veto the production if it doesn't do what your group wants.

- conversely, if you are doing a production for an outside group, make sure that there is a clear chain of command, a schedule for completion and payment, and that both parties are agreed on what your role is. Try to avoid starting a production where you can get caught in the internal politics of the organization for which you are working.

- assign someone to keep track of the running budget as the production progresses. This way you shouldn't run out of money or time before you get all the necessary shots. [See the article, "Simple Critical Path: A Tool for Program Planning," page 94.]

- if a production is going over its budget, either cut it way back so it will fit the money available, stop and raise more money, or stop completely and refund the remaining money.

- never get too enthusiastic about a shot before you see it on the screen. It's what is really there that counts, not what you think you've got (VTR's have an advantage here, since you can replay tapes immediately to check out a shot or a sequence); even the "perfect" shot sometimes doesn't work.

Non-media personnel can make valid contributions to the project in helping handle administrative details or by assisting trained crew members ("go-fors" are always helpful). "Extra" jobs include equipment security and simple maintenance; materials ordering; someone to line up personnel and schedule staff; clerical tasks.

While on location, small crews are easier to coordinate and help keep the production from becoming a three-ring circus.

Get simple "releases" from everyone who appears in a production. The release should give you permission to use their voice and/or picture. [See pg. 86.]

If you are going to be making a more advanced Super 8mm or 16mm film, you should get price schedules, time requirements, film marking systems and delivery instructions from at least one film laboratory. If at all possible you should also visit the lab and become familiar with their preferred methods of working. Since their work will determine the quality of your production, this time is well spent. Local professionals can tell you which labs to avoid.

BUDGETING

Budgeting for any media production is reasonably complex. Regardless of the medium that you choose, there may be hidden costs that are easily forgotten when preparing a budget, and other items that even the most experienced producer cannot anticipate. This article deals in some detail with the budget for a simple motion picture. In the earlier section "Comparisons of Media," several different media solutions to a communications problem are compared, with actual figures given for each step. The type of alternatives and considerations required for a film also apply to the other media.

In a community type of production, you must consider both time and money as expenditures (one of the easiest ways to lower the $$$ cost is to use more of your own time). Thus, you may have a choice between hiring a cameraman to shoot the film or renting a camera and

TALENT RELEASE

A. C. Lynn Zelmer, International Communications Institute,
Box 8268, Stn. F., Edmonton, Alberta, T6H 4P1, Canada.

Date: _____

I hereby give my permission to A. C. Lynn Zelmer, his agents,

successors, assigns, clients and purchasers of his products,

to use my photograph (whether still, motion or television)

and recordings of my voice, and my name, in any manner what-

soever.

Signed: _____

Address: _____

City: _____

Production Title: _____

Role: _____

Client: _____

(Standard Talent Release Form. 1969)

learning how to shoot it yourself. One of your main considerations will have to be cost versus quality: can you
learn enough and put together a decent enough production to
justify saving a few dollars? Of course, your own time
should also be considered as an expense (how much per
hour is is worth for you to work?).

Generally you can plot your choices according to the
following basic decision tree (see below).

In almost any organization you can find people who
will volunteer to assist with a production. Likewise you
can rent equipment and/or hire professionals or semi-pro-
fessionals to assist you. A small organization usually cannot afford to purchase all of the equipment for even the
simplest of film productions (remember, the purchase price
is not the only cost involved; there are also insurance and
maintenance costs as well as depreciation). Of course 8mm
(Super or regular) equipment may be less expensive than
16mm but the same considerations apply.

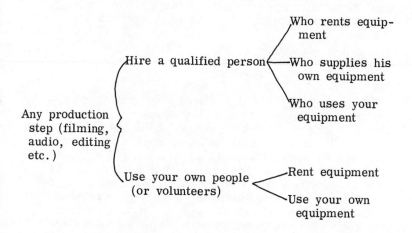

To be useful then, a budget should indicate the
amount of money that you have estimated will be needed for
a production, specifically where the money will be spent
(what categories and sub-categories), and the time schedule
required for completion of the project.

Cost Estimates

Today even the catalogues cost money. To effectively budget for any media production you will need to keep track of prices as advertised in the various magazines, write away for specialized catalogues and price sheets, and visit local suppliers for their prices. Since inflation will cause prices to rise from 5 percent to 200 percent each year, obtain current quotations from several sources before finalizing your budget or placing any orders. I recently tried to update my collection of equipment and materials catalogues: prices varied from $2.00 to $19.25. Of the 25 or so letters I sent out to suppliers about six of them were returned as "unknown" or "moved, no forwarding address." Another dozen firms just never responded--perhaps they are so busy servicing their regular customers that they don't need my irregular and sporadic business, more likely business is good enough that they don't respond to anything less than a purchase order for over $1000 worth of merchandise. (Incidentally one major manufacturer once told one of my previous bosses that the U.S. Government ordered several thousand cameras per year, since we only wanted one we had no right to expect service.) It pays to get to know your local supplier.

Staff

This category will be based upon your time schedule and will indicate what personnel you will require, for what length of time (number of hours, days, weeks, etc., beginning on what day and ending on what day), and the wages each will be paid. Use specific job descriptions where possible. This step and the time schedule must be completed whether you are hiring staff or not. You must know how many people will be required for each step, for what jobs, for how long, and at what cost. (If your volunteer sound man takes sick, you want to know how much work there will be for the man you will have to hire to replace him.)

Generally speaking, I would recommend that you keep your staff as small as possible. Too many people confuse things, particularly when they are unsure of their exact job.

Specifically, you must consider the staffing for the following steps (see the Glossary for an explanation of the film-making process):

- Planning: meetings with interested people; brainstorming sessions; consultants; scripting; budgeting; etc.

- Production: preparing the shooting script; organizing people and equipment, hiring staff; lighting; shooting the film; audio work; etc.

- Talent: actors; production advisors; make-up artists; preparing sets and props; musicians (royalties?); etc.

- Editing: rough edit of picture, sound; conforming original to work print; checking the answer print and corrections; etc.

- Distribution: previewing the film; showing it to its intended audience; sales and rentals; etc.

- Clerical: typing of ideas, script cards, scripts, budgets; handling expenditures; typing letters; etc.

        I realize that this is beginning to look quite complicated. Remember, however, that ONE person can do everything necessary to make quite acceptable films using very simple techniques and equipment (many really low-budget films do not use work prints, etc., but edit the original footage; this cuts expenses and the number of steps involved). If you are using this as a guide to producing a film, just omit the steps or categories that do not apply to your film.

Supplies

        These are the consumable materials that you will use in your production, everything from typewriter ribbons and postage stamps to film stock and splicing cement:

- Graphics: design, production and materials to produce titles, charts, graphs, special visuals, still photographs, etc.

- Stock Footage: film scenes purchased from an outside source to be included in your film. (An example might be a sequence of a rocket firing that you have no means of shooting yourself.)

- Canned music: musical sequences purchased for use in the sound track. May also include stock sounds (the

WORK ORDER

Project Title _____ Year: _____

_____ Docket: _____

Responsible Officer: _____

Date initiated: _____ Approved: _____

    completed: _____

Approvals:

Purpose:

Audience:

Description:

Budget Summary:

Evaluation:

Payment Record:

sound of a moose call during the mating season for example).

- Props, make-up: any of the special props, sets, costumes, cosmetics, etc., necessary to make the film appear authentic (borrow them whenever possible!).

- Lighting supplies: lamps, gelatins, filters, etc.

- Raw film stock and processing: the original film that you will use in the camera (may be positive or negative film).

- Audio tape: generally 1/4" tape (may be cassette in some circumstances) to record the original sounds ("Sound-on-Film" systems may use magnetically striped film).

- Work print and processing: if you check the original footage before you order the work print you may save $$ by not printing duplicate scenes or mistakes.

- Editing materials: splicing cement, blank film stock, cotton gloves, masking tape, film reels; 16mm magnetic stock; splicing tape, etc.

- Answer print: lab costs for answer print, processing; reels and cans.

- Release prints: lab costs for prints, processing; reels and cans, labels, etc.

- Stationery and office supplies: paper, envelopes, xeroxing (of scripts, etc.); script cards, etc.

- Postage and express: shipment of films to and from the laboratory; letters, etc.

- Telephone and telegraph: all calls related to the production should be budgeted (e.g., a panic call to the lab to make a last minute change).

Services

This would include hiring outside facilities when your own are non-existent, inadequate, or out of service.

- Photographic: to prepare special still photographs or

motion picture sequences that you cannot obtain on your
own (e.g., hiring a photographer in another city to shoot
a needed sequence rather than traveling there yourself).

- Editing: to hire an editing service to perform part of the
  editing chores such as the sound transfer from 1/4" tape
  to 16mm film or the conforming of the original to the
  work print.

- Darkroom: renting a darkroom to load film, etc.

- Recording studio, film studio: renting space and services
  to do recording or filming. Remember that even the
  school which is loaning its auditorium will expect you to
  pay the caretaker.

- Insurance: loss, theft or damage of equipment. Liability
  in case of accident or libel. (Insurance premiums are
  cheap compared to a lawsuit or other problems.)

Equipment

        Generally rented from an outside source by the hour,
day or week. Remember to include an estimate of the cost
of the use of your own equipment if you have any.

- camera, tripod, lenses, filters, batteries, film magazines,
  battery chargers, carrying cases, light meter.

- tape recorders, microphones, mixers, stands.

- lighting equipment: lights, stands, switching equipment,
  cords.

- synch sound equipment if required.

- Previewing: viewer, rewinds; or Moviola, or projector,
  or editing table.

- Editing: splicer and rewinds, viewer; or editing table,
  or Moviola.

Travel and Subsistence

        Will you have to do any traveling as part of your

planning, shooting, editing or approval stages? Don't forget transportation costs, vehicle rentals, motels or hotels, food, overweight charges for equipment, taxicabs, etc.

Remember that people who are working on productions like this will always be needing coffee, donuts, sandwiches, etc. Budget for them!

Overhead and Contingency

The overhead category might include the cost of the use of an office or editing room, etc., and the contingency category (5 percent to 30 percent of the total) is added on to cover any unexpected costs you may encounter (some organizations will not accept these categories in a budget).

Preparing Budgets

1. The budget should always contain honest notes and explanations of each anticipated expenditure.

2. Since the detailed budget will be fairly long and cumbersome, also prepare a budget summary to serve as the first page and introduction to the budget.

BUDGET SUMMARY

Staff:	$ XXX.XX
Supplies:	XX.XX
Services:	XX.XX
Equipment:	XX.XX
Travel and Subsistence:	XX.XX
Overhead:	XX.XX
Total:	$XXXX.XX
Contingency @ X%	XX.XX
Total:	$XXXX.XX

3. Add the Statement of Purpose, a brief timetable, and a short (very short) description of the final product to the budget summary on the first page. These four items will serve as a reasonably complete overview of the project and as an introduction to the complete budget.

4. The time schedule should allow enough time for
   delays due to difficulties with the lab, staff who
   fail to show up, weather problems, etc.

SIMPLE CRITICAL PATH: A TOOL FOR
PROGRAM PLANNING

In planning a project it is necessary to plan each
step in a logical order. The simple critical path method
which is described below is one tool for planning a project.
The critical path can also be used for keeping track of the
progress of the project, and will help in evaluating the
project at any stage of completion.

The term CRITICAL PATH refers to a planning technique that shows visually the steps in a project that will be
critical to the completion of the project. In other words,
it is a technique that allows the planner to identify the order
for completing the steps of a project, and to identify those
steps that will delay the project if they are not completed
in time.

The large chart (page 95) illustrates a CRITICAL
PATH for the preparation of a simple brochure. Each bar
on the chart represents a separate step and the estimated
time duration to complete the step. The bar can be moved
forwards or backwards horizontally within the limits of the
sequence of steps. If one step is delayed beyond the time
for beginning the next step, then all the following steps will
also be delayed. In the example shown it would be possible
to make up delays by working on the weekends (overtime),
or by using the extra or "float" time allocated to other
steps. The meetings on the Mondays, however, represent
a scheduling of executive time. These meetings would be
attended by a number of people from several government
departments and might not be able to be rescheduled.

Example: A delay in retyping the brochure draft
(step 5) would also delay the artwork preparation since the
artwork on the stencil cannot start until the typist is finished. There is enough slack time between the completion
of the artwork and the beginning of the pretest to allow for
several days delay in prior steps. A delay of more than

WORK PLAN: BROCHURE Design and Production (single field test only)

Work Days Reqd.	Week 1	2	3	4	5	6	7	8	9	10 MTWTFSS
1. 1ST Design Meeting (1/2)										
2. Typing Draft (2)										
3. Rough Artwork (2)										
4. 2ND Design Meeting (1/2)										
5. Retype Draft (Stencil) (3)										
6. Redraw Artwork (Stencil) (3)										
7. Duplicate 25 copies (1/2)										
8. Pretest in Village (3)										
9. 3RD Design Meeting (1/2)										
10. Type Final Copy (2)										
11. Prepare Final Artwork (3)										
12. Type setting (3)										
13. Layout (Final) (1)										
14. Proof/Corrections (4)										
15. DEADLINE for Final Approval (1/2)										
16. Printing: 5000 copies (1)										
17. Addressing Envelopes (15)										
18. Mailing (1 week in post) (1)										
19. DEADLINE for Receipt of copies.										

Notes: Project is small brochure

1. Work scheduled for 1 typist only
2. Completion requires approx 32 work days, over 10 weeks.
3. Solid Bars: work activities in sequence and estimated time to completion.
4. Dotted lines: "float" time
5. Vertical lines: sequence of dependent activities — one that cannot be begun before another is completed.

Notes: 7. No overtime scheduled. The timetable could be speeded up by about 16 days if staff worked Saturdays and Sundays. An additional 16 days approx. could be gained by removing all "float" time, however this would not allow for any hold-ups (delays) at all.

three days would require the duplicator operator, and possibly others, working overtime.

The partial chart below has been redrawn to show the changes in the chart resulting from a delay of four days in completion of step 5. The duplicator operator and artist worked overtime on Saturday to complete step 7. The project is back of schedule at the beginning of week 4.

5. Retype draft (stencil)(3)			4 Days	Delay
6. Redraw artwork (stencil)(3)			½ Day	O.T.
7. Duplicate 25 copies (½)			½ Day	O.T.
8. Pretest in village (3)				
9. 3ᴿᴰ Design Meeting (½)	Note: Step 17			
10. Etc.	Also delayed			Etc.

Changes in the plan are often made in colored ink. Delays could be shown in red. Early completions could be shown in green. Alternatively the lines could be drawn differently to show completions and delays more clearly.

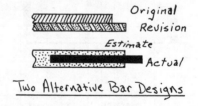

Two Alternative Bar Designs

This project could easily be reviewed every week. Deadlines are shown for each step. The work of each person on the production team can be determined for each week of the project. The delivery of materials (artist's materials, envelopes, mailing list, paper, stamps, etc.) can be scheduled. Weekly and monthly costs can be estimated and controlled. Vehicles and accommodation for out of station trips can be pre-booked and appointments arranged in advance.

In our example of the CRITICAL PATH, the series of activities that must be watched carefully, flows through a series of meetings, typing, artwork, etc. The path through the typing of the envelopes (step 17) does not become CRITICAL until the 9th week for completion. However, it would actually become critical for starting in the 6th week. If the addressing is not begun by the 6th week, completion will be delayed. A delay in completion will delay step 18. Note that step 18 does not have any "float time," and must be completed on the Friday of week 9.

Critical path charts are often made as wall charts A2 size, or larger. Colored wool or string may be pinned to the charts to show critical paths. Large headed tacks are often used to indicate steps, paste a code number to the head of the tack. Sophisticated planning boards with colored markers or tapes are available from office supply houses (very expensive).

Steps Involved in Developing the Graph

1. Determine each step involved in the project.
2. Estimate the time required to complete each step.
3. Establish the order or sequence of steps. It is essential that interdependencies be established. In other words, we must determine where the initiation or completion of one step depends upon the initiation or completion of another step.
4. Layout each step in sequence using a line to represent the time required for each step. Break steps into sub-steps. This is especially important if the project will be reviewed frequently.
5. Establish beginning dates for each step with float time for best use of manpower and other resources.
6. Prepare budgets, etc. as required with delivery schedules, meeting dates, etc.

Scheduling Resources

1. Plan for the ordering, arrival, and use of KEY RESOURCES. Then develop a schedule of weekly requirements, etc.
2. Plan for the best use of the minimum number of workers. For example, the plan may be modified to keep a key worker such as an artist busy for a minimum period of time. Alternately the plan might be modified to spread out the typing or translating to avoid hiring extra staff.

3. There are two constraints:
    a) Achieve a level demand on resources with
        a constraint on the total project time.
    b) Minimize the project time with a con-
        straint on the availability of key resources.
4. Budget control (labor, staff, materials, etc.) can
    be achieved by keeping a simple record of actual
    expenditures versus the budget estimate.

PRE-TESTING AND EVALUATION

Thus far we have presumably prepared a statement
of purpose, a timetable, a budget, and a script for our production. We have tried to select a medium suitable to the
audience and the content. Now we can prepare graphics, go
on location and obtain film or television footage, and generally work through the details of production. This section
provides some guidelines for pre-testing and revision of
those materials prior to their release to your audience and
some thoughts on evaluating the finished product.

Unfortunately a large number of the media presentations that are prepared every year are dismal failures.
Many hours of work have often gone into the production of
the annual school play, the camera club annual exhibition,
the monthly newsletter, or the community cable television
production. Yet nobody really reads, or listens, or watches.
Often, as a friend at my local cable station indicates, even
the friends and relatives of the involved performers are em-
barrassed to watch the program. Why?

- Most of the labor involved is voluntary, time is often very
  limited and budgets are small--unfortunately this often
  limits imagination as well.

- The biggest resource may be the "ego" involvement of one
  or more members who "know how to make a film" or
  whatever but who lack practical experience.

- The production fails to effectively communicate a message,
  sometimes there isn't any message to communicate, other
  times the message is lost in the complexity of several
  competing themes.

- Too big a production has been attempted. My feeling is
that it would be better to do a small, simple project well
than to louse up too big an endeavor.

Pre-testing involves preparing a draft of media materials (perhaps a mock-up of the final product) and doing a
trial run with a typical audience to refine and improve the
product. Pre-testing involves EVALUATION and REVISION--
unless you are willing to try to improve the product you
might as well forget any ideas of pre-testing. Typically
pre-testing a film might occur at several stages: first a
number of people are asked to comment on your script
cards, then perhaps several sequences are individually tested
for understanding, and finally the rough edit and answer
print stages are viewed. Ideas can be totally changed at
any stage but obviously it will be easier to make large
changes early in the process. In practice the answer print
stage is used only for correcting color and sound balance,
never major changes. Films are not the only media requiring pre-testing, we might follow basically the same sequence in testing any visual material. Print materials are
tested similarly but are often easier to revise and several
test methods are available to assist our work.

In pre-testing you are basically asking the questions:
"Can the intended audience understand my message?" and
"Does the intended message get communicated?" What often
happens of course is that the message is too complex for
the intended audience and/or the audience receives an unin-
tended message.

Testing Procedure

1. Obtain a written Statement of Purpose for the
    software being tested. The statement should be
    very explicit, i.e., a "general" audience is in-
    sufficient for test purposes. We must begin
    with a statement such as "The audience is The
    Tomahawk Town Council, a group of one female
    and eleven male rural adults...." Intended out-
    comes are perhaps the hardest to state and
    terms such as "to inform" or "to show" are
    inappropriate. It would perhaps be better to
    say "... should be able to list five reasons for
    unemployment in rural Alberta, and to write a
    campaign speech which explains the effects of
    unemployment on Tomahawk."

2. Obtain copies of the rough script, script cards, outline designs, sketches, photographs, text, or other material to be tested.

3. Show the materials or selected materials to a sample of the intended audience in either a structured or unstructured situation. Thus a draft copy of an environmental information brochure might be shown to 50 of the 2500 people on the final mailing list for the brochure. Their reactions would be solicited by questions such as "What is happening here?" or "What does this brochure say to you?" Alternatively a formal questionnaire might be prepared for answering by the test group. Keep a careful record of the answers to such questions, plus relevant information about the respondent (age, sec, education, etc.).

4. In some cases it is possible to gain an evaluation of the material more directly. If the reader of a brochure "should be able to operate a model R-13 mixer with no errors" then you merely have to select a number of typical readers, give them the brochure and a model R-13 mixer and watch for the results. If the reader fails to operate the mixer you are in trouble--you then need to question the reader quite carefully to try and determine the problem areas in the brochure.

5. Materials tested must be revised and retested until they do meet the objectives stated. Select new respondents for every test and select enough respondents to give a good evaluation (at least 10-20 people for most materials).

Testing Visuals

Figures 1, 2, and 3 showing the women at a well in Sri Lanka (Ceylon) are various stages of a drawing of pregnant women that was tested for use on a poster.

The drawings were prepared on 4" x 5" artist's paper and each successive drawing was shown to about ten persons selected as being typical viewers of the intended

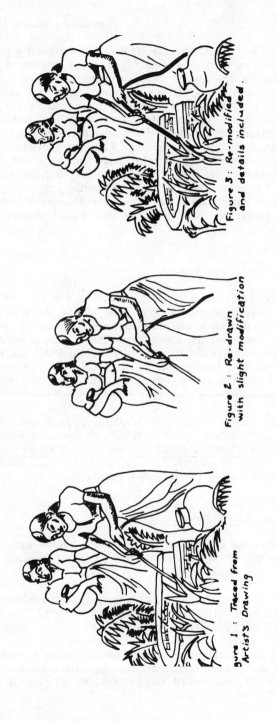

Figure 1 : Traced from
Artist's Drawing

Figure 2 : Re-drawn
with slight modification

Figure 3 : Re-modified
and details included.

poster. Figure 1 shows the drawing as originally prepared:
"two village women at a well." Figure 2 attempted to show
the woman on the left as being very pregnant, the one on
the right slightly so. Of seven respondents only one mentioned the pregnancy of either of the women. Figure 3, it
was hoped, showed both women quite pregnant, but only two
out of thirteen respondents mentioned the pregnancy when
asked "What do you see here?" From a discussion with the
respondents we decided that for most people in the test
group there was too much detail (clutter) and the angle of
view of the women was wrong. As well, pregnancy was so
common in the villages that several respondents failed to
mention seeing the pregnancy--it just wasn't important to
them.

Testing Print Materials

        Printed materials (and narration) can be tested in a
similar manner to visual materials. Type the text on a
card or record on a cassette recorder and let the respondent
read (or listen to) the message. The questions become
"What does this mean to you?" or "Please tell me in your
own words what this means." Directions can be tested
through trial and error testing as with the Model R-13 mixer
instructions discussed above.

        For more sophisticated testing to go a good book on
writing or technical report writing and learn to use such
tools as the Flesch Reading Ease Chart or Close Testing.
These tests help identify writing difficulties and writing that
is too complex for the intended reader.

Evaluating Existing Materials

        The use of any media materials begins with an iden-
tification of the objectives of your program, resources available and the audience needs.

        - WHAT exactly is it that you want communicated?
        - WHO is it that you are trying to reach?
        - What RESOURCES are available?

        Film catalogues, bibliographies, study guides, book
reviews and a host of other resource materials are available to point you toward audio-visual materials. If nothing

Name of Exercise				Subject Area
Publisher/ Distributor				
Cost	Date Developed	Age Level	Educ. Reqd	Language and level
Special Skills Required			Type of Activity	
No. of Players	Grouping		Playing Time	
Staff Reqd.				
Space Reqd.				
Equipment Reqd.				
Educational Objectives				
Preparation Time	Activities			
Participant Manual ( ) Instructor Manual ( ) Playing Materials :				
Summary of Major Events in Playing				
Related Materials and Activities				

User Comments (Include date and source):
How realistic is the exercise?
How complicated ?
How useful are the instructions ?
Adaptation suggestions :
Recommendations :
Evaluator :   Date of Evaluation :

Sample Evaluation Card

EVALUATION OF (Document Title):

Prepared by (Author, Agency):
Date Produced:

EVALUATION FORM
Handbooks, Manuals, Brochures, etc.

Directions:

Use this form to assist you in evaluating the utility of hand books, manuals, brochures and similiar materials.

_Training Materials:

procedures and background information. What to do, how to do it, where, when and why to do it.

—Reference materials:

a collection of all the useful information for a worker. Must have a good index since it will be used for locating specific information at time of need.

_Work materials:

step by step procedures. Used as a basis for work supervision and evaluation, very detailed, with examples of relevant forms, etc.

Some materials describe a new or ideal situation. Workers must be trained to perform the tasks.

Other materials describe actual routines and procedures. The worker has already been trained to perform the tasks.

Ask the Question:

If I were one of the people for whom the material was designed COULD I ADEQUATELY PERFORM THE TASKS DESIGNATED?

— is there enough information?
— is there too much information?
— is the information written so that I can understand it (language, reading level, etc.)?
— is the information illustrated so that I can easily understand the procedures (suitability of visuals quality of reproduction, co-ordination with text, etc)?
— is the material physically easy to use (size, index, titles and captions, etc.)?
— is the material durable?

DESCRIPTION

Document Title:

Prepared by:

Date produced:

Date evaluated: Evaluator:

_____

Format:

Size: Pages: Binding:

Language:

Illustrations:

Reproduction/Paper:

Special Features:

Synopsis of content:

EVALUATION

Subject covered: (   ) 1 (   ) 2 (   ) 3

Technical Accuracy: (   ) 1 (   ) 2 (   ) 3

Suitability for intended audience: (   ) 1 (   ) 2 (   ) 3

Co-ordination of Visuals to Text: (   ) 1 (   ) 2 (   ) 3

Layout: (   ) 1 (   ) 2 (   ) 3

Suitability of Physical Format: (   ) 1 (   ) 2 (   ) 3

Use fulness of Special Features: (   ) 1 (   ) 2 (   ) 3

Readability: (   ) 1 (   ) 2 (   ) 3
Test used:

Suitability of Visuals: (   ) 1 (   ) 2 (   ) 3

Durability: (   ) 1 (   ) 2 (   ) 3

Other Possible Uses:

SCALE: 1. EXCELLENT 2. NEEDS MINOR REVISION 3. NEEDS MAJOR REVISION

Background and other things taken for granted
(assumed) by authors in preparing materials:

General Comments:

Recommendations:

INTERNATIONAL COMMUNICATIONS INSTITUTE

is available that suits your needs and audience you may even
have to consider producing the materials yourself. Let me
warn you however that using a previously produced material--
film, book, etc.,--is far easier than producing your own
materials.

The sample evaluation cards (page 103) were prepared
to help the evaluators of materials. They provide a concise,
regular format for recording and filing comments on materials used (or previewed for use). Keep a file of all materials viewed by your center; staff changes and other disrup-
tions may otherwise make it impossible to remember whether
a specific film or videotape or book was useful several
months after its use.

Evaluating Program Effectiveness

It is becoming increasingly difficult to obtain funding
for any kind of project without an evaluation of the effects
of the project. Thus we write a sum of money into the budget and assume that somehow the project evaluation will take
care of itself sometime in the future. Finally, under pressure, we write a "case study" or "description" of effectiveness as the number of phone calls handled, the number of
feet of film distributed (many times more impressive than
the simple number of film orders processed), etc.

It is not within the scope of this Handbook to detail
more useful forms of evaluation. However, good evaluation
tools can help to improve the program offered, as well as
indicating whether the project was a "success" or not. Most
projects are developed to set in motion some events which
will lead to a desired goal. The failure to reach the goal
may be a result of the failure of the project (film or community service or whatever) to initiate the events (behavior
change or short-term effects) which would have led to the
desired goal; or we may successfully initiate the short-term
effects but find that they don't really lead to our desired
goal. Alternately we may in fact find that the desired goal
has been reached--the existence of our program, however,
may or may not have been responsible. A good evaluation
program can separate the wheat from the chaff, lead to a
better allocation of our resources and help us to a better ap-
praisal of our own abilities. Perhaps the reason why many
media producers and community services fail to properly
evaluate their programs is that they cannot face the thought

that they might be having either a negative effect or producing "no significant difference."

COMMUNICATING FOR UNDERSTANDING

Information cannot be presented too simply. It may
be very boring to read information that is written too simply but it can still be understood. Conversely, writing that
is too complex for the audience does not communicate.
Hopefully you will know enough about your audience to avoid
being either too complex or boring because of its simplicity.
Generally however it would be better to make your errors
on the side of simplicity.

- Write in the language of use. Translations almost always
  make the information more complex.

- Use sentences of less than 20 words if possible.

- Avoid technical terms, use commonly known words.

- Use the same word every time you describe an object.
  I know that bed and cot and sleeping place may all mean
  the same thing in your mind, but your reader may think
  differently.

- Make positive statements. The sentence "Change the
  baby's wet diapers" is better than "Do not leave the baby
  in wet diapers."

- Keep your statements active: "Wipe dirt off the VTR" is
  better than "Dirt should be wiped off the VTR."

- Explain steps in a logical order, explain every step, from
  the beginning to the end. Do not assume that your audience already knows how to do any step.

In most forms of communication the actual material
will be divided into at least three parts: the Introduction,
the Body (of the report or film, etc.), and a Summary or
Conclusion. Other sections are possible of course--a TV
program on a research project might follow the same format as a written report:

- Introduction and Statement of the Problem
- Background to the Study
- Procedures
- Results of the Study
- Analysis of Results
- Recommendations and Conclusion.

Other works would vary of course, but all have a logical format and a list of information that is required if the production is to be successful. Adopting a familiar and logical format will make your work easier to understand.

While the above paragraphs are mainly based on written communications we need to recognize that visual communications have the same demands. In addition, it is often possible for the artist or photographer to insert blocks or barriers to understanding. An award winning poster design may be "cute" or "pretty" and yet not communicate to its intended audience.

- Work with the artist or photographer from the beginning of the project. If the artist knows more about your message, audience and needs he will be better able to prepare effective visuals.

- Keep the illustrations simple and plain (avoid clutter created by unnecessary elements).

- Avoid detail, but if necessary use several visuals to show an overall view as well as details.

- Every illustration should have one theme, with only one center of interest.

- Choose common views of objects. We are all familiar with the side view of an elephant or the front view of a man. The rear view of either may be very confusing.

- Use familiar objects. Materials prepared for school children will not likely be suitable for adults, materials prepared for a suburban white community will not likely be suitable for rural use or for a black ghetto group. Visuals are very specific to the culture of use.

- Cartoon forms may often be used effectively. They are simple and convey a message graphically.

- Pre-test illustrations, photographs, graphic designs, etc.,
and reject those which are not absolutely clear.

**NEVER USE WORDS TO DESCRIBE SOMETHING THE
VIEWER OR READER CAN SEE FOR HIMSELF.**

A SPECIAL NOTE ON PLAGIARISM

Most everybody knows what plagiarism involves when
we consider written materials.   In effect we can make minor
quotations, enclosed in quotation marks and credit the
original author.   Any selection longer than one or two lines
however requires the permission of the original author before it is included in another work.   In my experience such
permission to reprint is easy to obtain and seldom refused.
There really is no excuse for a community group, school
or university which constantly flouts the copyright laws by
xeroxing thousands of copies of journal articles, etc., for
distribution (often "books of readings" are prepared this way
and distributed to students who have to pay for receiving
these stolen goods).   A short note to the author and/or publisher of a written article will usually obtain the permission
you require.

- Tell them who you are, why you want to copy the material, how many copies you intend to make, and costs, if
any for the finished item.

- Indicate that you will credit the original author with a
statement such as "Reprinted with permission from the
author: John E. Doe.   This article originally appeared
in the National Consumer News, Vol. IX, No. 17, pg. 43-
7, June 1977."

Plagiarism is also a concern when you are using
music (as in films, TV shows, tape-slide presentations),
photographs and illustrations.

**YOU CANNOT COPY, DUPLICATE OR TRACE ANY
CREATION WITHOUT PERMISSION FROM THE CREATOR.**

As with written materials there are obvious and not so obvious limitations to the use of illustrative materials:

- it seems quite permissible to use a magazine photograph pasted up as part of a collage. To copy the same photograph on a slide as part of a TV show is likely a violation of copyright (unless you seek and obtain permission).

- it is not really permissible to copy ANY musical recording into another medium. For example copying your friend's favorite records onto tape is not permitted. Using a normal record on a prerecorded radio or television program is not permitted. It seems possible however to play the same record "live" over the radio.

- TRACING an illustration or photograph is not permitted. My guess is that there would be no problems preparing one or two illustrations in this way for non-commercial use--such as for classroom teaching or for part of a community TV program. Regular, or excessive use of materials (whether from one or several sources) is not permitted.

The copyright laws are there to protect the original ideas of all of us. In our society it is not possible nor desirable to obtain government or other grants for all of our creative work. Many people therefore go to the market place with their ideas. Publication offers a chance (albeit a not very lucrative one for most authors, artists, photographers, etc.) to make a living off one's creative acts. At the very least it offers an attempt to help pay for the cost of writing or preparing creative materials. Every sale of this Handbook for example represents about seventy-five cents that will be returned to me, the author, to help defray the roughly one thousand dollars, and several hundred hours of work spent revising the original edition. Every xerox copy of an article, every traced illustration, every photocopied photograph represents a potential loss of income to the artist involved.

- Be sensible with your copying.

- Seek permission to reproduce materials whenever possible.

- Give written credit to the creator of any materials that you do copy.

3 COMMUNITY MEDIA TECHNIQUES

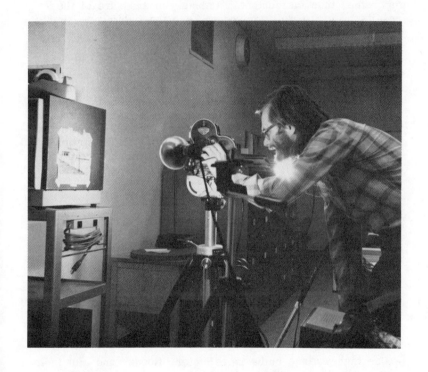

LIGHTING BASICS

The only lighting that is noticeable is poor lighting. A good lighting set-up contributes to the scene in such a way that we never notice any special lighting effects, and conversely, a poor set-up makes us conscious of the lighting rather than the content. Unless you are sure of the results, you are well advised to keep the lighting as simple as possible.

My own preference is to use the technique which is the least noticeable to the subject as well. Flash units can be quite distracting to a person being photographed and, in addition to being hot, extra lighting often makes the subjects' eyes strain. I almost always shoot with a fast film or a wide-open lens on the TV camera to avoid adding any extra lighting. This kind of work, however, has its limitations (often dull, "flat" images and dark shadows, and sometimes objectionable grain), and adding light may be necessary.

Raising the Light Level

Often, all that is required is to raise the level of general illumination to make an area suitable for shooting. This can be accomplished in several ways depending upon your budget and type of production:

- Replace normal light fixtures with higher wattage bulbs (500 watts) or special "photofloods." Removing the lampshade may help (it may also make harsher shadows).

- Use high wattage bulbs in reflector "floods" and aim them at the ceiling to "bounce" light around the room. This will result in a soft diffused light. The same effect can be accomplished by bouncing light off a reflector made from white cardboard, plywood painted matte white, or crinkled aluminum foil mounted on cardboard (smooth foil will cause some spots to be too bright--"hot spots"). When working with color film, remember that light bounced off a colored wall will give a colored tint to the picture.

114

- In still photography, flash units can be aimed to bounce light off the wall or ceiling for the same effect.

- Sunlight can often be bounced into a dark corner, using a large piece of white cardboard as a reflector.

- Sometimes the subject matter can be moved outside where the light is better; or moved closer to a window or other light source which can be bounced to add light.

- Professional studio or other photographic lights and amateur equipment such as "sunguns" can be used, but require experience and patience to set up for a good lighting effect (sunguns or flash units mounted on the camera almost always produce large ugly shadows behind the subject).

The need for a higher level of illumination can sometimes be eliminated by using a faster film stock (a film with a higher ASA number) which will record an image without as much light; a slower shutter speed (the length of time the shutter is open to let in light); or by opening up the aperture (thus letting more light into the camera). Ultimately, however, we come to a point where the material selected cannot record an image, and almost without fail a marginal image could have been improved with a bit more light on the subject.

Understanding Light

- Direct light is usually a harsh light, producing contrast and sharp shadows.

- Indirect or bounce light produces a softer image, open shadows and less contrast.

- Strong lights mounted on or near the camera often produce harsh shadows.

- A cloudy or overcast day has a softer light with no shadows that is useful for close-ups. Landscapes and architectural shots seem very two-dimensional because of the lack of shadows.

- The intensity of a light varies inversely with the square of its distance from the subject. $Intensity = \dfrac{1}{(distance)^2}$.

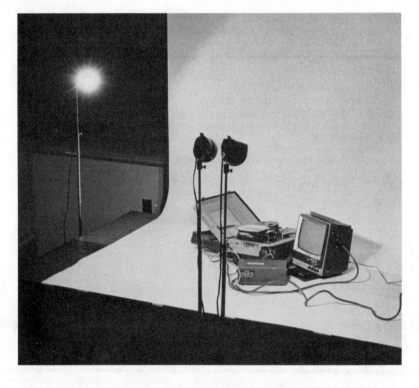

Lights and a white backdrop are used to produce
well exposed, uncluttered photographs.

Thus, a light four feet from the subject gives four times as much illumination as it would eight feet away.

- There are many colors of light as well as intensities; our eye can compensate for these changes but photographic films cannot, and thus yield "off-color" images (excessively blue or yellow are the commonest). Match film and light for best results. (For example, Type "A" film requires 3400° K bulbs, Type "B" film requires 3200° K bulbs. See the article, "Basic Photocopy Techniques," for a table of films, light sources and filters required.)

Conventional Lighting Techniques

Conventional lighting set-ups use as a minimum the following types of lights (on a large set more than one lamp could be used as a "light"; for example, it could require a dozen lamps to light the backdrop):

- KEY or MAIN light is the strongest or most noticeable light. This light determines the mood of the scene; back lighting being more dramatic than front lighting, side lighting being quite harsh.

- FILL light illuminates the general scene and makes details visible. It is usually placed near the camera and is of a lower intensity than the Key light.

- HAIR or KICK light illuminates specific details to provide visual separation from the background. Brightly lighting the subject's hair is a common use. Care must be taken to shade the light to ensure that it doesn't hit unwanted areas of the subject.

- BACK light illuminates the background.

The diagrams show the four basic lighting set-ups using these lights as seen from above. Remember that any light source can be used. Thus the sun might be used as a Key light, with a flash unit as a fill light.

Studio Lighting

If you are building a studio and have more than $500 to spend on lighting, you should hire a consultant or lighting

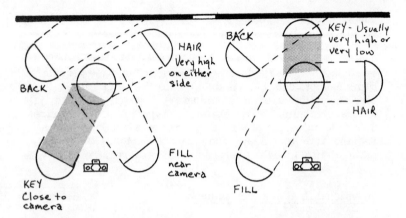

FRONT LIGHTING:
flat & uninteresting.
Similiar to on-camera
flash or movie-bar
lights.

BACK LIGHTING:
Very dramatic. Key
light is either hung
from ceiling or
hidden behind subject.

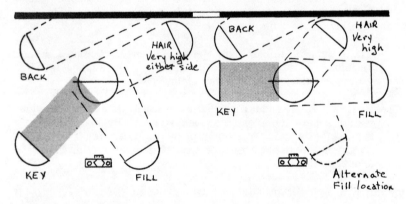

45° LIGHTING:
Key light is generally
fairly high so that the
nose casts a shadow
reaching to the lip.

SIDE LIGHTING:
Makes a harsh photo.

CONVENTIONAL LIGHTING STYLES

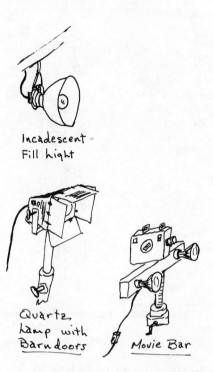

Incadescent
Fill light

Quartz
Lamp with
Barn doors

Movie Bar

engineer. While his rates will be high and he will have his own preferred way of doing things, you will probably end up saving both money and time. For those who are working on a low budget, all of the previous techniques will work, and you will also be able to copy some of the fixed lighting techniques of a film or TV studio.

- Keep your lighting simple. Just as with portable equipment, a studio set can get cluttered with too much equipment, the temperature can rise, and eye strain can become too much for your subject and crew alike.

- Keep your lighting flexible. A grid made of 1" pipe can be built near the ceiling to mount movable light fixtures with screw clamps, or surface mounted fixtures can be moved along the wooden ceiling joists by merely loosening a pair of screws. Lamps on floor stands can obviously be moved but the stands take up a lot of floor space.

- Have a set of "work lights" separate from your "shooting lights." All lamps have a specified life expectancy and this is usually fairly short for bulbs used in media work. In addition, incandescent bulbs get black as they get old, thus cutting down the light output. Having a separate set of lights for normal working conditions will save unnecessary use of the expensive bulbs. Fluorescents can be used for work lights but a bad ballast will often cause noise problems if they are used for shooting a scene which is being recorded on audio or video tape.

- Attempt to ensure that every duplex outlet is controlled

by a separate switch at a central
control location. This will increase costs but will allow lights
to be individually switched on and
off, and in some cases inexpensive
rheostats can be used for dimming.
(Commercial lighting rheostats are
too expensive for low budget use,
but "home type" rheostats can be
used for incandescent lamps if the
lamp wattage does not exceed the
rheostat rating.)

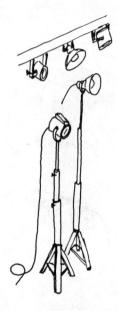

General Tips

Quartz bulbs are smaller and
thus can use a much lighter stand
and reflector than an incandescent
bulb. Most commercial equipment
bought today will use quartz bulbs,
particularly for portable lighting
situations. Quartz lamps also maintain the same light output
and color temperature for their full life. Incandescent lamps
turn black with use and both light output and color change.

Inexpensive barndoor units (to block light from hitting
unwanted areas) are available to fit PAR and "reflector"
bulbs. This type of incandescent bulb has a built-in reflector and will fit in a normal socket (also available with a
swivel base), thus making an inexpensive unit.

Bright reflections and glare can often be eliminated
by spraying the subject with "dulling spray" or spray starch.
Black masking tape, colored paper or cloth can also work.
Glare from non-metallic subjects (such as paintings or water)
can be reduced using a polarizing filter over the lens (additional control can be obtained with filters over the light
source as well).

Professionals use expensive photo umbrellas and re-
flective materials to bounce light onto a subject. An old um-
brella covered with white cloth or a large piece of white
cardboard will work just as well if you have someone to hold
it or can make some kind of stand (try styrofoam core art
board on a music stand).

Scrims are nonflammable diffusers which are placed in front of the light to reduce its intensity or soften its shadows (light rays are scattered). Scrims can be made from translucent fiber glass cloth, metal window screen material or mulberry paper stretched over a frame which can be held in place or clipped to the front of the light fixture (remember to leave space for air to pass to cool the bulb).

"C" clamps, suction cups and removable tape (Gaffer's tape) can be used to hold light-weight fixtures temporarily in place for a shot, and cost less than professional stands.

Inexpensive light fixtures can be "homemade" with good results if you understand basic electricity (use heat-proof cord and a three-wire grounding system) and are adept at improvising. A metal loaf pan with hinged metal barn doors riveted to the sides can be a very effective reflector for a quartz lamp mounted in a small socket. Use the "brushed" metal pans rather than the shiny metal type. A metal or wood and metal hanger/stand can easily be fabricated using wing nuts for quick adjustment.

Some photographic films can be "pushed" in processing to give an acceptable image under marginal light conditions.

Newer television cameras have special "low-light" vidicon tubes available as an option when purchasing the camera.

Buy a good light meter and learn how to use it properly.

GRAPHICS

The use of good graphic design serves to tie the elements of a media presentation together and to help explain its parts.

Add Interest: bright colors, strong shapes and large letters attract attention and give a forceful look to the

presentation. Posters, for example, depend upon these
graphic elements for their effectiveness. Books and other
printed materials use illustrations both to explain content
and to keep the reader interested. Soft designs and pastel
colors are used in slide shows to give the viewer a feeling
of calmness and relaxation.

Clarify Meaning: photographs, charts, graphs, drawings, tiles and captions are all graphic elements which help
explain meaning. Some, such as diagrams, often have other
graphic elements like arrows, captions and lettering to identify specific parts. Similarly, lettering can be superimposed
over still or motion pictures (including TV); typically, a person's name is superimposed on a TV picture so that the
viewer can more easily recognize the speaker.

Visualize Verbal
Data: charts and graphs
simplify masses of tabu-
lar data so that we can
more easily compare fig-
ures or understand com-
plicated relationships.
Flow charts, plans, and
other diagrams often
allow us to communicate
quickly where many
words would otherwise
be required (ever thought
of how many words it
would take to explain ver-
bally the location of the
various rooms in your
home?).   It has been
said that "one picture is
worth a thousand words";
pure visuals may be am-
biguous, however, and a
combination of verbal or
lettered information with
a visual can clarify meanings. (See "Flow-Charts,
Logical Trees and Tables,"
page 224.)

SYMBOLS

GAS STATION   RESTAURANT

PICNIC AREA   CAMPGROUND

R.C.M.P.   FARMERS' MARKET

SLEEPING SHELTER   GOLF

We are all famil-
iar with the person who

(from the Alberta
Motor Association)

looks at a book to see if it has any pictures before he buys it; however, when putting illustrations into your communications media you must remember to use graphic elements to advantage so that they will help attract and hold attention as well as helping to clarify your message.

General Guidelines

- simplify: complicated visuals are confusing and generally contain too much information to be understood.

- color: choose colors which will attract attention and emphasize the points you wish to make. Dark colors on a light ground (black on yellow) are more readable than light colors on a light ground (pink on yellow). Negative slides (white or colored letters on black) are often effective.

- line weights: use strong heavy lines, particularly for lettering.

- position: elements should be placed so that they direct the eye and allow a smooth flow from one element to another.

- lettering size: lettering must be large enough to be easily read from the back of your audience. (Five lines of five words each, completely filling the screen, is a general guideline.) Solid blocks of type are difficult to read. Block letters are better than fancy styles for most purposes. The Franklin Gothic letter illustrated is one of several such versatile styles.

- spacing of letters: set up headlines, titles, etc., so that they look correct--visual spacing is better than mechanical spacing. Leave about the same white area between each letter.

- shapes, texture, form: be careful not to clutter up your message, but special shapes (such as using a fish design for a poster about an aquarium) give non-verbal meanings to your message.

LETTERING

SU|T

Too much
space

SU|T

Try to keep an
equal area between
letters.

SPACE FOR NEATNESS & READABILITY

ABCabc

84 Point
Extra Condensed
Titles & Displays

ABCdef

60 Point
Condensed
Key Words

ABCabcd

48 Point
Condensed
Body type

ABCdéfg

24 Point Condensed
Still legible for overhead
transparencies but approaching
lower limit of utility for slides,
films, etc. Using STANDARD
ARTWORK FORMAT.

Note: This page
has been
reduced in
reproduction.

This is FRANKLIN GOTHIC — a good stock
of lettering for use with the standard
artwork format for T.V. Graphics, slides,
etc. About five lines of five words is
maximum. If you can hold a slide up
to the light and read it - lettering is OK.

Often, THE MEDIUM IS THE MESSAGE. A cast metal nameplate will always seem cold and formal (metal is cold and has a hard texture). A message printed on cloth moving in the breeze has an ever-changing form when compared to a painted sign on a billboard. Similarly, the audience gets a totally different feeling if they sit on the floor and are surrounded by visuals rather than sitting in a conventional theater.

Some Techniques

Layout: Use lots of paper and make several very rough sketches before you start. Select the best one as your rough design.

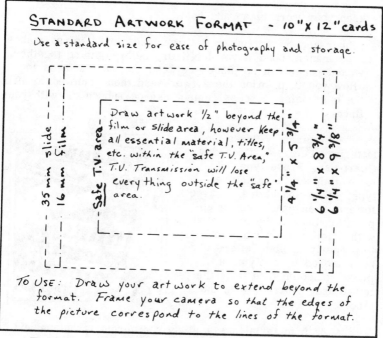

STANDARD ARTWORK FORMAT - 10" X 12" cards

Use a standard size for ease of photography and storage.

Draw artwork 1/2" beyond the film or slide area, however keep all essential material, titles, etc. within the "safe T.V. Area," T.V. Transmission will lose everything outside the "safe" area.

35 mm slide   16 mm film   Safe T.V. area

3/4" x 5" x 4 1/4"   8 3/4" x 6 3/4"   9 3/4" x 6 3/4"

TO USE: Draw your artwork to extend beyond the format. Frame your camera so that the edges of the picture correspond to the lines of the format.

- a T-square, drafting table, triangles and scales are indispensable to the artist. As well, 5H or 6H pencils make faint lines for laying out locations of elements or drawing guide lines. Soft pencils (4B or F) are better used for rough sketches. A soft eraser (art gum type) is necessary for making corrections. Masking tape is used to hold the paper down, and clear acetate tape (magic mending

tape) fastens prepared artwork or other materials added
to the final product (especially useful when you have to
cut out the page and rearrange it for a better appearance). Use scissors or a razor blade for cutting.

- keep your tools clean (wash regularly with soap and water,
  clean pens after every use).

- never use your T-square, triangles or scales as a guide
  for cutting. Get a metal straight-edge (cork backed steel
  rule).

- use a clean piece of paper under your hand as a shield to
  protect your drawing from getting dirty (your hand is
  greasy).

- keep your work clean and neat.

- rubber cement spread on both surfaces to be joined makes
  a permanent bond if you let it dry before joining together.
  Waxed paper can be placed between the two surfaces to
  allow you to position the artwork and then removed to affix
  the materials. Excess cement can be rubbed off with your
  finger.

Lettering: Press-On
lettering (Letraset, Deca-dry,
Chart-pak, Press-type, etc.)
is available in a variety of
type, sizes and styles. Large
letters often crack during application but can be corrected
with a felt pen or India Ink.
Improperly applied letters can
be removed by applying a
piece of Scotch tape over the
letter and then removing the
tape.

Each material has a slightly different technique and
pressure required to transfer letters effectively. Become
familiar with one brand as much as possible.

- keep lettering sheets clean.
- replace dried out sheets (or dirty sheets).
- burnish letters for maximum adhesion.
- use transparent colored letters for overhead transparencies.

- many stores do not stock odd sizes or colored letters-- these must be specially ordered.

Lettering tools (Leroy, etc.) and stencil type guides (Wrico, Stenso, etc.) are easy to use with a bit of practice. Once the tools have been purchased your only cost is for ink. You will, however, be limited to the sizes and styles of guides you have purchased.

Coloring:

- use colored card stock or paper as your first color.

- spray cans may be used for coloring localized areas, or if you use cut-out shapes you can spray around them and achieve a "reverse" effect (place the cut-out on the background, spray around the edges, let dry and remove; you are then left with an outline shape with the background color). Several light coats work better than one heavy coat.

- "air-brushes" are artists' tools for spray painting. Because they are usually delicate and require proper cleaning they should probably only be used by one individual.

- sheets of "press-on" colors are available. Some may be rubbed on, others require you to cut out a shape and press it into place.

- pastels and charcoal sticks are easy to work with if you use a rough surfaced paper.

- water colors (powdered or pre-mixed) are inexpensive and can cover large areas using a brush, a sponge, or an airbrush.

- colored inks are available in transparent colors for use on glass or acetate. Make sure that you buy inks designed for this kind of use--most inks form "bubbles" on acetate rather than forming a solid area.

- "press-on" tapes and special designs can make quick lines, shapes, shading, etc., which will appear professional with minimum effort.

High Contrast Photography: Printers use photographic

Press-on lettering materials are easy to use and
come in a large variety of type sizes and styles
(University of Alberta, Photographic Service)

materials that are valuable for the preparation of graphics since they are inexpensive and easy to work with. Most lithography materials are high contrast (they reproduce as black and white, no greys).

LITHO FILM ("ortho" or not sensitive to red) is available in sheet and roll sizes. A typical technique is to type a message on white cardstock, photograph it with 35mm roll film ("Kodalith" is available in 100-foot rolls), process and enlarge onto an 8" x 10" sheet of litho film, process this film, and you have a transparency ready for mounting. Total time elapsed: less than one hour.

- posters can be prepared using the technique discussed above; prepare the artwork on white paper with black press-on lettering, India ink, and self-adhesive printer's red masking film (the ortho photographic film sees red as black); photograph the complete artwork with litho film and enlarge to make a stencil for silkscreen printing or make a limited number of enlargements on photographic mural paper (it can be toned to give a colored poster).

- black and white slides can be made by mounting the 35mm litho negative in a slide mount. Color can be added with transparent color felt pens.

- the graphic arts dealer where you buy the materials can give you more complete instructions.

Diazo or Ammonia Processing: Drafting reproduction shops can make duplicate copies of drawings with dark lines on translucent paper using a "blue-print" process. Actually you will get blue or black lines on white paper, but the name comes from years ago when they used a "blue" printing process. Today's process uses ammonia as the developing agent.

- some dark pencils or India ink lines on a translucent "tracing" paper or film will reproduce. Obviously, India ink on clear film will give the best results (opaque lettering, flexible tapes and cut-out shapes will usually work too).

- colored transparencies can be made in a similar manner, using a specially treated film as the printing medium. (Using "diazo"-type colored transparency film.)

- an ultra-violet lamp (or the sun) will work to expose
  the image. Use a sheet of glass to hold the original
  or "master" in close contact with the printing medium.
  Process in a large jar containing a small piece of
  sponge soaked with concentrated liquid ammonia (from
  a drugstore). Do not let the sponge come into contact
  with the print.

Display and Presentation: The techniques used by the
graphic artist will determine the durability of the drawing or
artwork. If quick results are needed then shortcuts or temporary techniques can be used but these are often not durable. (Printers use a wax coating to hold artwork together
to make a photo-offset plate. Wax when heated, however,
will not hold, and pieces slip or fall apart.)

- matte and glossy clear sprays are available which will
  protect artwork, typing, etc., from smearing or dirt
  (varnish turns yellow).

- plastic laminating materials can be attached to a
  smooth surface with heat or pressure. They are
  washable and can even be written on with grease pencils or felt pens.

- special linen backings can be ironed on photographs,
  maps and similar items so that they can be rolled up
  and handled without tearing.

- cardstock is a good medium for charts, graphs, etc.,
  that are to be photographed since they will lie flat.

Graphics are not as simple to prepare as they might
appear. The illustrations for this article took over three
hours to prepare after the original design had been determined.

SKETCHING

Most community groups that I have talked with would

argue that the one "outside" skill that they lack--and would love to find (cheap!)--would be that of a GRAPHIC ARTIST or even just anyone to prepare some simple drawings.... Impossible? almost, since most graphic artists are busy making money--yet with a little effort and practice anyone who can visualize how a cube should be drawn can prepare credible sketches and drawings suitable for most community media work.

- PRACTICE, PRACTICE, PRACTICE.

- Buy some simple tools (or make them).

- Use good quality paper.

- Don't always use the first idea that comes to mind on a topic--prepare several rough proposals and select the best one for further development.

- Cheat if necessary by tracing from photographs or by

(cont. on p. 139)

<u>Sketching Materials:</u>

Pen & Ink :

Pencil :

Crayon:

Drafting Tape:

Masking tape: for holding down paper.

Good quality "rag" paper or smooth surface
   card for final drawings.

Newsprint (blank) or "tracing" paper for
   rough sketches.

Ruler, draftsman's triangles (30°-60° & 45°),
   eraser, rubber cement & thinner,
   paint brushes, household wax paper,
   razor blade (single edged if possible).

Use a 4H or 6H pencil for layout &
   rough sketches. Use HB pencil or
   Black INDIA ink (drawing ink) for
   final work. Make corrections with
   white drawing ink or typist's correcting
   paint. Add color with water colors,
   show card paints or "stick-ons."

Lettering can be by hand or press-on:

<u>Sketching</u>:
- Start with a rough
  sketch, place elements
  in approximate position.
- Try several rough
  ideas if possible.

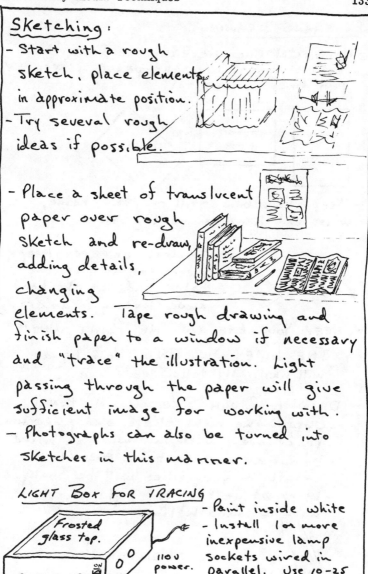

- Place a sheet of translucent
  paper over rough
  sketch and re-draw,
  adding details,
  changing
  elements. Tape rough drawing and
  finish paper to a window if necessary
  and "trace" the illustration. Light
  passing through the paper will give
  sufficient image for working with.
- Photographs can also be turned into
  sketches in this manner.

<u>LIGHT BOX FOR TRACING</u>

Frosted glass top.

110v power.
½ or ¾" plywood.

12"×18"×6" min.
1" holes for ventilation.

- Paint inside white
- Install 1 or more
  inexpensive lamp
  sockets wired in
  parallel. Use 10-25
  watt bulbs, keep at
  least 3" from glass
  to avoid cracking.
- Use glass or plexiglass
  for top.

FREEHAND DRAWING:

- Horizontal lines are easier to draw than vertical lines. Turn the page ... keep your lines horizontal.

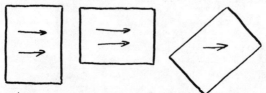

- Keep the elbow still on the table, wrist and hand move together.

- To draw an arc: Keep the wrist still on the table and let the hand move loosely in an arc.

- KEEP YOUR EYE ON THE POINT WHERE THE LINE WILL END. Your hand will naturally follow your eye.

- DRAW A ROUGH SKETCH IN PENCIL
  - Obtain the right shape and proportion.
  - Trace over with ink when satisfied.
  - Do not attempt to trace every line exactly ~ your lines will be shaky.
  - Work at getting the right shape with a smooth line.

- Maintain Proportion.
  Keep big objects big, small objects small.

Sketching:

Stick figures can be used on the
chalkboard, flipchart, for posters, etc.

Front views   Moving   Working

Use simple props: hockey stick, stove, etc.
Keep the IDEA & the DRAWING SIMPLE.

Simple Faces.

Sketching:

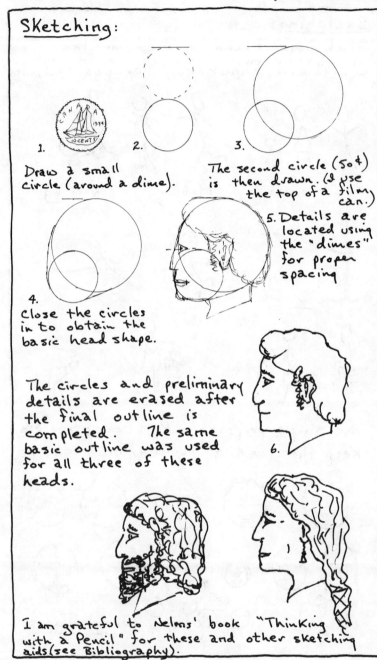

1. Draw a small circle (around a dime).

2.

3. The second circle (50¢) is then drawn. (I use the top of a film can.)

4. Close the circles in to obtain the basic head shape.

5. Details are located using the "dimes" for proper spacing

The circles and preliminary details are erased after the final outline is completed. The same basic outline was used for all three of these heads.

6.

I am grateful to Nelms' book "Thinking with a Pencil" for these and other sketching aids (see Bibliography).

Sketching:

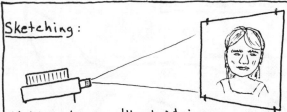

Making Large Illustrations:

- Project a negative or slide of the desired image onto a large sheet of paper.
- Lightly sketch the image in pencil, using the projected image as a guide.
- Complete the image with a heavy ink, crayon or felt pen line.

This is a very useful technique for posters, displays, etc. Avoid fine details — stick to broad outlines.

LETTERING takes practice and the correct size of pen.

A pen nib that is too broad will fill in the centres of "e" and "o". A nib that is too small will look very "shaky". The same factors are important when selecting a pen size for sketching.

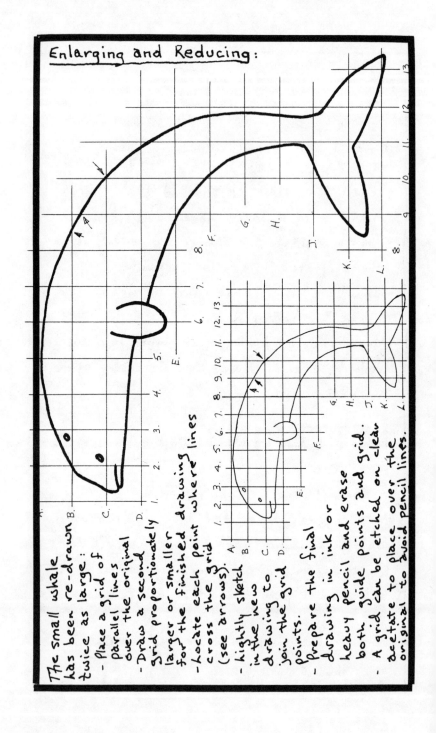

Enlarging and Reducing:

The small whale has been re-drawn twice as large:

- Place a grid of parallel lines over the original
- Draw a second grid proportionately larger or smaller for the finished drawing
- Locate each point where lines cross the grid (see arrows).
- lightly sketch in the new drawing to join the grid points.
- Prepare the final drawing in ink or heavy pencil and erase both guide points and grid.
- A grid can be etched on clear acetate to place over the original to avoid pencil lines.

copying successful designs in other media.   (See the note on "Plagiarism," page 111.)

Nelm's book (see bibliography) is the best aid to learning sketching that I have found.   Practicing the exercises and techniques that he recommends will allow you to prepare simple drawings and sketches easily.

LINE ILLUSTRATIONS FROM PHOTOGRAPHS

Photographs add interest to printed materials, and often provide useful visual clues to prevent misunderstanding the written material.   A good photograph can often replace several paragraphs of written explanation.   However, photographs are expensive to use.   They require good quality paper and may require expensive negatives and printing plates.

- Letterpress: requires special engraved blocks (cuts);

- Offset Printing: normally requires special camera work, screened negatives and metal plates;

- Stencil (roneo): requires pre-screened prints (photographs composed of tiny dots) and quality is poor;

- Spirit Duplicator ("ditto" process and hectograph/ gelatin process): requires specially prepared pre-screened prints or Xerox copies of pre-screened prints.   Quality is poor;

- Photographs pasted in place: very expensive and labor consuming.

Pre-screened photographs suitable for use on the offset, stencil and spirit masters can be obtained by cutting black and white photographs out of newspapers and similar sources.   There are a number of ways of making "screened" photographic prints if you have access to a darkroom.   Use a special pre-screened film in your copy camera or lay a printer's screen over the photographic print when you are making an enlargement with your enlarger (the screen must be held in close contact to the photo paper, a piece of heavy

Note changes from this photo to sketch on page 141.
(Courtesy of UNICEF water program, India.)

plate glass will work well to hold the two in close contact).
These prints may then be handled as line copy.

An inexpensive alternative with unlimited potential is
to turn the photographs into sketches or "line drawings." A
well equipped print shop can do this for you mechanically,
but it is also possible for anyone who can prepare a simple
tracing to make usable drawings very inexpensively. The
materials required are:

- a light box (the sun shining through a glass window
  will work),
- thin white tracing paper or airmail paper,
- sellotape or masking tape,
- hard pencil (4H to 7H),
- India black ink and one or more drawing pens or a
  straight pen and nibs.

1. Select a photograph that contains a view of the
   object that you wish to use.
2. Tape the photograph to the light box.
3. Tape a sheet of tracing paper over the

photograph and trace the outline of the object.
Add the major details. The light shining
through the photograph from behind (or underneath) will make the object easy to see and
draw. Use a sharp pointed pencil and trace
lightly.

4. Remove the photograph.
5. Tape a second sheet of paper over the drawing
   and repeat step 3. Trace the design onto the
   second sheet and make any required changes
   (changes of costume, repositioning of various
   component elements, etc.).
6. Remove the first pencil sketch.
7. Tape a piece of good tracing paper (ink quality)
   over the second sketch. Use black ink and a
   fine nibbed pen. Trace the sketch onto the
   third sheet with ink. Add details as desired.
8. This ink sketch can be pasted together with
   the typed or typeset written material to make
   an inexpensive printing master.

The final illustration may be very detailed or quite
simple. The same original can be used as a guide for a
stylized illustration which gives a general idea, or it can
be used to produce a sketch which has every detail from
the original photograph.

You can start from another sketch or illustration as
well as a photograph. The tracing technique can be used
to correct minor faults or mistakes, to reposition objects
in the drawing, to add variations for a local situation, or to
reduce the work needed to create a drawing. Good work
will come with practice. Any sketch made from a tracing
will be much easier and more accurate than working free-
hand.

- the drawing can be enlarged or reduced as required,
- omit all unnecessary details,
- add any details necessary to understand the drawing,
- keep your work neat and clean,
- keep the drawing simple.

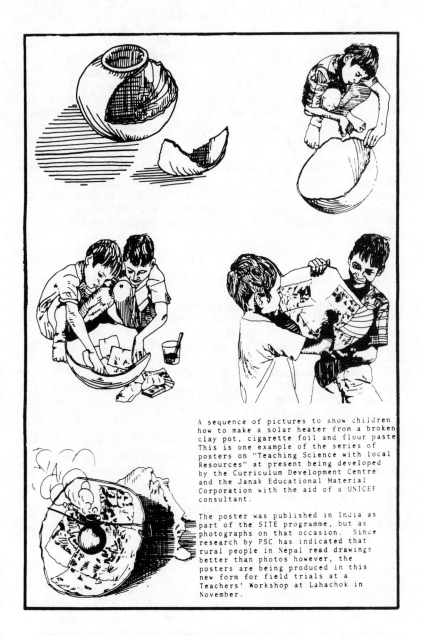

A sequence of pictures to show children
how to make a solar heater from a broken
clay pot, cigarette foil and flour paste
This is one example of the series of
posters on "Teaching Science with local
Resources" at present being developed
by the Curriculum Development Centre
and the Janak Educational Material
Corporation with the aid of a UNICEF
consultant.

The poster was published in India as
part of the SITE programme, but as
photographs on that occasion. Since
research by PSC has indicated that
rural people in Nepal read drawings
better than photos however, the
posters are being produced in this
new form for field trials at a
Teachers' Workshop at Lahachok in
November.

LAYOUT AND DESIGN

Most of us can vaguely recognize bad design in printed materials--a book where horizontal photographs should have been vertical, or where the lack of captions makes the printed page hard to read. Preparing well designed materials is very hard however. Unless we slavishly copy a good design prepared by someone else we are liable to either apply rigidly the rules of design, e.g., "S" curve layouts lead one's eye from point to point, or we unconsciously commit many of the same errors that we see every day. This latter category would include failing to leave sufficient "white space" to set off our main design elements, cluttering the design with too fancy an illustration (I believe in simple designs), or including more than one idea in a single illustration.

There are some elements of design that are crucial:

- parallel lines must be parallel.
- perpendicular lines must be perpendicular.
- straight lines must be straight.
- verbal elements must be large enough to be readable.
- artwork should be neat and clean.
- the design should normally tie the various elements together into a single unit.

When we look at an advertisement, a display, a poster, or something similar we immediately classify it as either amateur or professional. The poster that your child does in Grade III is amateur; the lettering is single line block or cut-out stencil and the coloring is usually either crayon or pencil. On the other hand the professionally prepared poster uses "fancy" lettering materials, bright colors, and has (sometimes) a design which directs your eye to the various elements included. The well laid out design using professional materials will usually be the most effective and eye-catching.

You can also prepare graphic materials which are attractive and eye-appealing: follow a few simple rules, practice a lot, and use the same materials that the professionals use.

- Before you start working, decide on the message, its audience, and the locations where it will be displayed.

- List all of the variables that you can think of regarding the topic, audience, and use. This might include interests of the audience, traffic patterns at proposed points of use, and taboos regarding the topic.

- Make a large number of rough sketch designs for solving your problem. Share them with others, get their ideas and comments. Each rough design should be 4" x 5" or larger.

- Select the two or three designs you think are best and prepare them in a better rough form using a large piece of cardboard (at least 8" x 10") for each.

- Show these designs to friends, associates and members of the intended audience. Don't explain the materials: Hold the sketch up--and ask: "What does this mean to you?"

- Make corrections as appropriate and prepare the final design. Get it checked for errors etc., before reproducing or distributing.

     In the example on page 146 we have listed the problem, audience, etc., and have given four possible design layouts. Two of the designs have illustrations, the other two use words only.

     Another advertisement had six design proposals for a lecture and workshop. The final design shown on page 147 was printed on white or yellow paper, 8-1/2" x 11", and was used as a direct mail advertisement. Because of a very low budget the text was prepared by typewriter and pasted up with rubber cement. The headline was done with press-on lettering and reproduction was done by offset and stencil duplicator (electronic stencil). Printed on only one side it could be displayed on a noticeboard or inserted into a newsletter.

BASIC PHOTOCOPY TECHNIQUES

When preparing materials for a slide presentation,

Design Problem: The Edmonton Learner
Centre wants to prepare posters to discourage
people from buying South African products.
Audience: high school students, shoppers.
Display Points: cars, schools, stores, pickets.
Budget: $100⁰⁰   (free labour)
Ideas: Racism - photos of S.A. people.
      "Boycott"

BOYCOTT
SOUTH
AFRICA

STOP
RACISM

BOYCOTT
SOUTH AFRICAN
PRODUCTS

SOUTH
AFRICAN
BOYCOTT

It may be that none of these ideas will be used!
What are your ideas??

Vanier Institute "Max Bell Lecture" by E.F. Schumacher.

Saturday, October 22nd, 9:00 a.m.

as a follow-up to the University of Alberta, and International Communications Institute

TECHNOLOGY with a human face: alternatives for alberta

Sponsored by Christian Farmers' Federation, Committee for Justice and Liberty,

A Lecture/
Discussion with
E.F. Schumacher,
author of
SMALL IS BEAUTIFUL:
Economics as if people
mattered,
followed by a workshop on
Alternatives for Alberta.

Registration: 9:00 a.m. at the
TORY TURTLE, University of Alberta
campus, Edmonton.

Cost: $ 3.00. Tickets at the door, limit of 500
people. Come early and bring your own bag lunch.

WORKSHOP SESSIONS

WORK, and the alienation of unemployment
LAND USE   URBAN DEVELOPMENT
POPULATION DISTRIBUTION   MARKETING
AGRICULTURAL METHODS AND PRACTICES   EDUCATION
ENERGY   COMMUNICATIONS and MEDIA
SPIRITUAL REVIVAL (Gaining a human faith)
FOOD   SOCIAL SERVICES
LABOUR   RELATIONS with the THIRD WORLD
ECONOMICS OF RESOURCE EXTRACTION   INDUSTRY
RURAL DEVELOPMENT (A sharing of experiences)
                                        HEALTH and MEDICINE

Each workshop will have a resource speaker and a person
to facilitate discussion. Workshop sessions will run from
1:00 to 3:00 p.m. in the Tory Building on the University
of Alberta campus.

Edmonton Cross-Cultural Learner Centre, Faculty of Extension at the

I.C.I. : 300/8/77

to illustrate a lecture or article, to produce film or TV
graphics, or to obtain multiple copies of visual materials,
we are faced with a common need: that of being able to
prepare photographic duplicates, with or without changes in
size and format. While Xerox and similar processes will
sometimes work for printed materials, and the commercial
photographer or graphic artist is in business to produce such
materials, you will often find that your time or money resources and quality requirements will combine to necessitate
your learning how to photocopy most normal materials.
This article will introduce the basic techniques and requirements for photocopying; expertise will come with practice.

What Can Be Copied?

Anything flat can be photocopied to produce slides,
transparencies and prints or to be incorporated into a film
or TV presentation; thus we can use prepared artwork (including painting, diagrams, charts, etc.), readily available
but difficult to use illustrations (such as photographs in a
book or historical prints in a museum), or even previously
prepared slides or transparencies. For training purposes
still photographs are often prepared with added captions to
identify various parts and are then photocopied to form part
of a slide set or for illustrations in a film. All photographs which appear in print publications have been photocopied at least once when the printing plates were being
made. Unwanted areas of photographs may be eliminated
by careful retouching and the result is then copied for distribution (Playboy does this with its centerfold photos).

Equipment Required

Most normal photographic equipment can be used for
copy work, although sometimes the more specialized equipment will be more convenient.

- any camera that will focus as close as 12 inches will
  work for larger materials, or

- any camera plus a close-up diopter lens (the diopter lens
  fits in front of the camera lens and is available in different "powers" which allow you to shoot from different distances), or

What you need for baby's bath

1. A large pan or basin will do.
2. Two towels and washcloths for baby only.
3. A large towel or bath blanket.
4. Mild soap and baby powder or oil.

Too light;
under
exposed

What you need for baby's bath

1. A large pan or basin will do.
2. Two towels and washcloths for baby only.
3. A large towel or bath blanket.
4. Mild soap and baby powder or oil.

Correctly
exposed

What you need for baby's bath

1. A large pan or basin will do.
2. Two towels and washcloths for baby only.
3. A large towel or bath blanket.
4. Mild soap and baby powder or oil.

Too dark;
over
exposed

- a camera with a "macro" lens or an extension tube or a bellows (only works with interchangeable lens cameras), and

- a copy stand or some other means of holding the camera steady (a tripod will occasionally work), and

- two floodlights, one for each side of the work; ordinary photo floods or flash unit will work, as will the sun if you choose your film properly, and

- an exposure (light) meter to measure the intensity of the lights.

- to copy slides and other transparencies a "light box" would be useful to illuminate the transparency from behind.

- in addition to the above equipment several manufacturers make specialized slide copy units; Kodak sells the Ektagraphic Visualmaker which uses a modified Instamatic camera and flash unit to produce 2" x 2" slides from flat pictures (very easy to operate); and graphic arts equipment can be converted to produce excellent results.

Lighting

    There are two lighting problems with photocopying:

- obtaining sufficient AND EVEN light of the right type (fast films may be some help but adequate light is crucial).

- eliminating glare, reflections and hot spots (shiny surfaced originals are worst).

    Two lights, one on each side, and positioned at 45° to the subject material, will generally eliminate reflections. Overhead lights, blinds and drapes, etc., must always be turned off or closed to eliminate stray light spots. It is also sometimes necessary to cut a hole in a piece of matte black cardboard for the lens to stick through, and to attach this to the front of the camera to guard against photographing the camera's reflection. A sheet of photographic-flat plate glass will serve to keep materials lying flat (prevents bumps and curls) and non-glare glass will work as well. A polarizing filter can help.

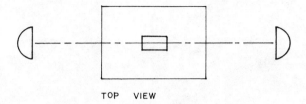

TOP   VIEW

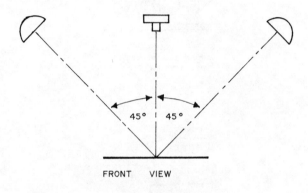

FRONT   VIEW

Camera   perpendicular   to   subject .

Lights   at   45 °   and   in   line .

Use a light meter to measure exposure.

- a "reflected" reading should be taken off of an "18% grey card" if possible. Do not read shadows. The grey card should be placed in the same location that the subject to be copied will occupy.

- an "incident" reading should be taken with the meter lying on the subject material. (Learn how to use your light meter properly.)

Film deteriorates with heat, and cameras will get very warm if the lights are left on too long; thus the heat of the lights can adversely affect the quality of the image obtained. Flash units are cool running but may require a reasonably long time between shots. Ordinary incandescent bulbs throw off an extreme amount of heat; quartz iodide

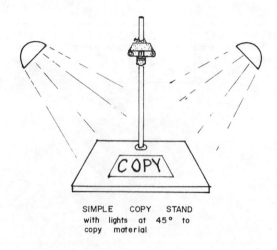

SIMPLE   COPY   STAND
with   lights   at   45°   to
copy   material

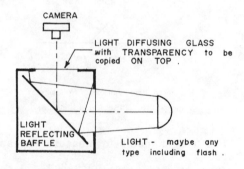

LIGHT   BOX   FOR   COPYING   TRANSPARENCIES

Paint   inside   of   box   matte   white .
A   small   focussing   light   inside   will   also   help
(turn   off   when   exposing   image)
Match   film   to   Exposure   Light   for   proper
color   rendition

bulbs are smaller in relation to light output and thus
run cooler.   A combination of incandescent light for
focusing and flash units for exposure are the basis
of several commercial copiers which work quite satisfactorily.

The same techniques can work for copying materials
which are placed vertically.

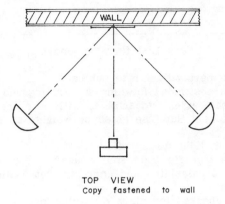

TOP   VIEW
Copy   fastened   to   wall

Filters

Mention was made of polarizing filters to control
glare and reflections.   These filters work by stopping most
of the light that doesn't come in a straight line from the
subject to the camera (light waves travel in all directions
but always in straight lines; the filter works like a set of
venetion blinds to cut out the stray light).   Polarizing materials are also available to use on the lights for further
control.   Since the polarizing filter cuts down on the amount
of light striking the film, an increase in exposure is necessary (see the instruction sheet that comes with the filter).

The best subject material for copying with black and
white films will be prepared with black India ink on white
cardboard.   Often, however, this will not be what you have
to copy and the contrast between the color of the illustration
and the paper may have to be increased.   Yellowed newspapers and old photographs can usually be satisfactorily
copied through a #8 (K2) (Yellow) or a #15 (G) (Deep Yellow)
filter.   To eliminate a color with black and white film choose
a filter that is approximately the same color (the yellow filters eliminate the yellow color of the old newspapers by making it appear white); to strengthen a color choose a filter
color which is opposite on the color wheel (red and green
will give almost equal shades of grey; using a red filter will
lighten the red and darken the green).   Again these filters
will require increased exposure.

Color correcting or conversion filters are used with

color film to change the overall color of a scene or to correct for the wrong kind of light for the film you are using.

Check List for Photocopying

- camera perpendicular to subject
- camera positioned for correct framing and focused
- two lights at 45° to subject, with no glare
- subject held flat (use glass or weights as required)
- all room light turned off
- correct film for light source used
- exposure calculated and correctly set on the camera
- image checked for glare or reflections
- camera steady when taking picture (use a cable release if possible).

Film Type	Light Source*	Filter Required
Daylight	Daylight	None
	3400° K	80B
	3200° K	80A
	Blue Flash	None
	Electronic Flash	None
	Clear Flash Bulbs	80C
Tungsten Type A	Daylight	85
	3400° K	None
	3200° K	82A
	Clear Flash Bulbs	81C
Tungsten Type B	Daylight	85B
	3400° K	81A
	3200° K	None
	Clear Flash Bulbs	81C
	Electronic Flash	85B

---

*PHOTOFLOOD BULBS have a color temperature of 3400° K and are available in most camera stores. 3200° K bulbs are not as readily available. Average daylight is 5500° K. Fluorescent light requires a special filter which has only recently become available.

SIMPLE SLIDES

Multi-media presentations, television and films have a certain glamour that is lacking in the simple still photograph. I know that a poor snapshot handed around amongst forty people is a poor substitute for a good film or other well designed and properly used media, however it seems to me that we could make much more use of a series of photographic prints displayed in the entrance hall or on the classroom bulletin board. Likewise the color or black and white slide is simple enough for almost anyone to prepare and the equipment for use is very simple.

At the present moment it is not very easy to use program materials prepared on portable 1/2" VTR's for broadcast or cable TV distribution. The best way of bringing outside materials into the TV studio is still probably sync-sound film shot on location. However this is expensive in 16mm and quite difficult to achieve in the less expensive Super 8 format because of equipment limitations. The inexpensive color slide remains the most feasible method.

- do not shoot very contrasty scenes as the TV system cannot reproduce these extremes of light and dark.

- use a light meter to get a good exposure; dark slides obscure details and too light a slide washes out on the screen.

- keep the material simple, avoiding fine details and complicated patterns since the slide is capable of reproducing more detail than the "lines" of a TV system.

- shoot lots of slides. They are relatively cheap and this will allow you to select the "best" shot, or to use several different shots of the same scene (35mm color slides will cost from $.12 to $.25 each).

- an overall shot and a close-up may explain your subject better than just one shot which covers everything.

- keep the important material in the center of the slide as the TV "format" cuts off the edges of the slide (see the diagram showing the relative formats of TV and slides etc.).

- make every slide "tell a story." The publicity shot of

someone presenting a check is an example of poor planning.
A better illustration of your story would be a photograph of
one of the activities that will be supported by the donation.

Slides can also be used to present other types of visuals such as graphs, charts and titles. A camera with a
close-up lens or attachment and a copy stand with adequate
lighting can be used with black and white "litho" film to
copy most flat materials (cost between $.05 and $.10 each).

- Kodalith Ortho film (other brands also available)
  is available in 100' rolls for 35mm cameras. It
  must be loaded into film cassettes for use. The
  film can be handled under a red safelight* and
  will keep for several years when refrigerated.

- with tungsten light I have found ASA 2 to work
  best for the exposure. Use a light meter. This
  often means an exposure time of one to two minutes.

- process in Kodalith developer until the correct
  density is reached, fix, wash, and dry. I have
  found that best results are obtained if I bracket
  my exposures and then develop the film until the
  middle shot appears done "by eye." Experience
  is a good guide here. More accurate development uses a "gray scale" card.

- under good conditions it is possible to photograph,
  process and mount a slide in less than 30 minutes.

- mounting is done in cardboard or plastic mounts.
  Cardboard mounts are heat-sealed with a hot iron.

- this kind of slide has no "middle" tones, only
  black and white. The clear (white) areas of the
  slide can be colored with transparent felt pens.

- the best originals will be clean black or red ink
  lines on white background.

*The proper safelight filter is a Wratten series 1A (light
red) with a 15 watt bulb at not less than 4 feet.

- limit the number of words on a slide to a maximum of five lines of five words.   The best height
for lettering would be about 1/4 of the total screen
height.

It is also possible to make simple title slides and
illustrations without a camera.

Materials for Making Slides Without a Camera

- India ink and a very fine tip map drawing pen (for sharp
  black lines).

- fine tip felt pens, for adding color, they must be the
  "transparent" ink type.

- clear or frosted acetate or stressed polystyrene (to draw
  the image upon).   Old X-ray film will work after the
  emulsion (image) is washed off.   Do NOT use cellophane
  or "saran wrap" as they burn too easily.

- cardboard or plastic 2" x 2" slide mounts for mounting
  your own slides.   The plastic mounts usually snap together, the cardboard mounts are sealed by the heat of
  an iron.

Procedure

1. Decide what you want included in the slide.

2. Locate a drawing or photograph that will fit within the boundaries of the slide (and which shows what you want to show) OR make a sketch of your illustration on a piece of paper.

3. Lay the sheet of clear plastic over the illustration chosen and trace it onto the plastic using the fine tip pen and India ink. If you make a mistake move the plastic over and start again. Taping the pieces to a work table will help keep the materials from slipping around.

4. Cut out the piece of plastic containing the illustration so that it will fit in the mount.

5. Follow the manufacturer's directions for sealing the mount.

6. Add color to the illustration as desired.

7. Write the description of the illustration on the mount.

The cardboard slide mount is 2" x 2", the image area is much smaller (see illustration). Any drawing or picture to be reproduced must be this size. Reduce your drawings to this size before copying on the film. (See the illustrations of "Tips for Better Pictures" below for an example of illustrations that would be suitable for hand-drawn slides or film-strips.)

2ⁿᵈ Stage of Labor. showing position of hands & holding baby.

PHOTOGRAPHY

Photographs can be good visual materials to enhance any graphic display, poster or brochure. As well good photographs are essential for a good tape-slide set, film, or TV program.

- keep your photographs simple. ONE TOPIC, ONE POINT OF INTEREST.

- avoid clutter in the background. Telephone poles do not really grow out of people's heads, keep them out of your pictures.

- get as close as possible to your subject.

- keep your equipment clean, use proper lens cleaning tissue for your lens and a soft bristle brush for inside the camera.

- protect your equipment--avoid extreme heat or cold, keep your equipment dry and away from salt spray.

- protect your film. Process film immediately after use, even if this means "wasting" a couple of shots. Keep film out of sunlight and heat.

The illustrations of common picture errors are simple sketches. These sketches are much cheaper than actual photographs for reproduction in your newsletter or instruction sheet.

Tips for Guiding the Photographer

- Get in as close as possible to your subject.

- Show people doing things. Try not to have people looking at the camera, give them something to do and take the photo of the activity. Informal photos of people at work will often be better than a posed photo. (The worst possible picture is the publicity shot of someone important making a donation ... it doesn't tell the viewer anything useful about the reason for the donation.)

- Eliminate unwanted details. The clutter in the background

Common Errors in Picture Taking

1. Heads cut off ... the camera was aimed too low. A similar problem arises if the camera was aimed too high or to one side. Correct by better aiming.

2. Subject too small ... move closer.

3. Near image fuzzy ... camera too close to the subject. Move back or refocus.

4. Image blurred ... the camera moved (or else the subject moved). Hold the camera steadier and squeeze the shutter gently.

5. Part of the image is covered by a blurred spot ... your thumb or camera strap is in front of the lens (or else someone's hat).

6. Bright stripe (often reddish) along one or more edges ... camera leaks light, or the roll of film was left out in the sunlight.

7. Image washed out (usually reddish or greenish) ... there was too much light. Check your light meter, and/or use a slower film speed. If using artificial light move further away.

8. Image too dark ... there wasn't enough light. Use flash next time or move the light closer to the subject. Use a higher film speed and check your light meter.

9. Bright flashes, like lightning ... caused by static electricity. Do not wind film too quickly, keep the camera and film warm in cold weather.

or a second center of interest in the picture is very distracting. It is possible to "block-out" unwanted background or to correct other details by "retouching" the photograph but this should be a last resort. Save yourself a lot of time and work by taking the picture correctly from the beginning.

- Assemble any required materials and people before the shooting session. Plan ahead so that time will not be wasted, making a list of the shots required, and the best order for taking (in motion picture work this is the shot list, often totally out of order compared to the final film,

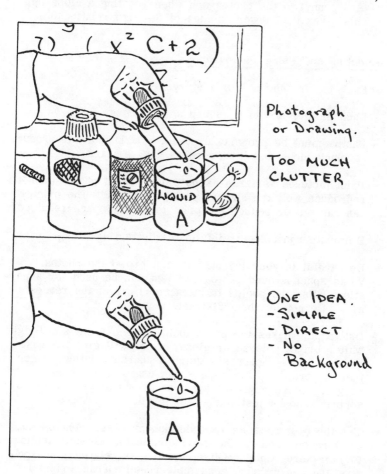

Photograph or Drawing.

TOO MUCH CLUTTER

ONE IDEA.
- SIMPLE
- DIRECT
- No Background

since it is easier to shoot some scenes before others that
supposedly happen first.)

- If you are photographing some activity ensure that the
participants can do the activity properly. I recently shot
some scenes for a slide set on operating a fire extinguisher, the operator/demonstrator had never used an extinguisher before and dropped it in the middle of shooting
as well as holding it incorrectly. Some activities should
be practiced before the shooting begins.

- It is sometimes useful to keep some common object (such
as a penny) in the photograph when shooting a close-up.
This gives the viewer an idea of the size relationship.

Selecting and Using Photographs

- Each picture should tell a story.

- Each picture should be sharp and in focus.

- Photos must be properly exposed. Dark photos reproduce
as black blobs and light ones as grey smears.

- Print pictures as large as possible. Most photos do not
reproduce well the size of postage stamps. The printer
can enlarge or reduce the print to fit the space required.

- Eliminate unnecessary details or distracting backgrounds.

- Be careful in your layout. Do not crowd the photos.
White space around photos and text can be used for separation. Use the photos to attract and direct the reader's
eye. Do not let them distract.

- Dull paper makes the photo look dull and lifeless. Bright
white, bright colored or glossy paper will give the best
results. Rough papers require a coarse printing screen
(newspapers), smooth papers can use a finer screen. Only
very expensive reproduction processes will print a photo
so that it looks just like the original.

- Use the best possible reproduction process. Photos do
not turn out well on the spirit duplicator, stencil duplicator, or xerography. Offset printing is relatively inexpensive and can produce acceptable results if the original
photo is good.

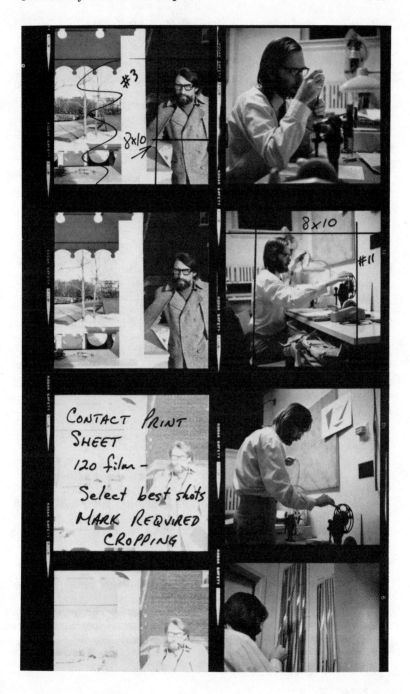

- Give the printer enough time to do a good job.

Note: Photographs, pencil sketches, paintings can only be
        reproduced from a half-tone or screened negative
        since a printing ink either covers an area or not.
        Graduations of tone are formed by breaking the area
        up into a field of tiny dots of varying size. Using
        colored photographs does not change the basic pro-
        cess, although a separate master or plate is required
        for each color (usually three colors plus black, with
        combinations providing the other colors).

AUDIO TECHNIQUES

        More people have trouble with audio or "sound" than
with any other aspect of media production and, while beautiful pictures may be necessary to make a film or a multi-
media show, the whole effect can be ruined by fuzzy or un-
intelligible sound.

        Viewers are skilled at filling in missing parts of
something they see, and are thus sometimes able to compensate for your poorer visuals; but people in our society
are not skilled at filling in or "guessing" about sounds.

        A distracting hum or unwanted background noise will
compete for your audience's attention; poor narration will
be "tuned-out."

        The quality of duplicate recordings deteriorates with
every copy step, due to the basic nature of magnetic sound.
Sound tracks (as on a 16mm film) are often copies of copies
of copies (4th generation), or even worse.   It is essential,
then, to make the best possible original sound recording and
to use extreme care on subsequent "dubs" (dubbing is a
term meaning copying).

        Your results will be no better than the equipment you
are using and, generally speaking, good audio equipment is
expensive.   Good techniques, however, used with medium
priced equipment, can produce sound as good as that achieved
by poor techniques on expensive equipment.

Microphones

Panel discussions and other events where several poeple will be speaking may require several microphones and a "mixer" to control each microphone separately. Often though, it is possible to work out a seating arrangement and microphone placement that will utilize just one microphone.

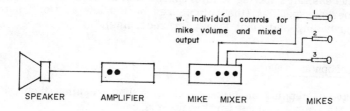

- keep the arrangement as simple as possible.

- for best sound, the microphone should not be more than 18" away from the speaker and should be directly in line with the sound waves.

- microphones that are hung around the neck (lavalier type) require special handling techniques and are usually specially designed for the purpose.

- use only specially designed microphones when they will be used closer than 2 inches from the mouth (some mikes will be damaged by the air pressure and most will "pop" or slur words).

- music reaches higher sound frequencies than voices do; some mikes have switches so they can be used for either, otherwise a special mike may be required.

- high impedance mikes are often used with less expensive tape recorders. They should never be used with mike cords longer than about 9 feet, as the noise from the cord will drown out the audio you require. Adapters are available to convert them to "low impedance" when you need a longer mike line.

- many expensive mikes can be switched from low impedance to high, to adapt to particular equipment, but are usually used on the low range. Amplifiers and similar equipment will indicate what kind of microphones they will work with

(low impedance mikes will not work through a high impedance input, and vice versa).

- a microphone usually "hears" all the sounds in a room or
other recording area (including the air conditioning or a
car going by on the street). To overcome the extraneous
noises we must lower the volume of the recorder. This
necessitates having a microphone placed quite close to the
person speaking (the volume can be too low as well, not
providing sufficient sound for recording).

Microphone Usage

- avoid stepping on mike cords or rubbing against them, as
this causes noises (or breaks the cable).

- tape mike cords down wherever possible to avoid tripping
over them and perhaps pulling a mike off the stand or
table.

- a "wind screen" cuts down on the noises caused by a person being too close to the mike or spitting into the mike.

- an old sock over the mike works outdoors to cut down on
wind howl.

- enunciate words carefully, varying tone and speed of
speaking for emphasis.

- watch recording or amplifier volume carefully to avoid
sound distortion or too low a level.

- keep equipment in good physical repair, especially cords
and connectors.

- bad habits include tapping the table or mike stand, "click-
ing" the on-off switch on and off repeatedly, "blowing"
into the microphone, and twisting the cord in your hands.

Microphone type	Relative expense	Characteristics and Use
Carbon	cheap	used in telephones, intercoms, not generally useful.

Microphone type	Relative expense	Characteristics and Use
Crystal	low cost	medium response, included in much older equipment, affected by temperature and humidity.
Dynamic	medium priced	reliable, good reproduction of voice and speech.
Condenser	medium to expensive	very good response, quite durable, good for situations with low sound levels.
Ribbon	expensive to purchase and repair	easily damaged by wind or vibration, should never be used by rock singers or equivalent, very good response.

Pick-Up Patterns

While the type of microphone determines the overall quality and response characteristics, the pick-up pattern determines the directions from which sound is received.

The lavalier mike (worn around the neck) is an omni-directional mike and picks up sounds equally from all directions around the top of the mike. Think of its pattern as being a sphere centered on the top of the mike. It must be used very close to the sound source.

OMNI - All directions

Cardioid microphones are directional and cancel out sounds coming from behind the microphone. They may usually be used up to 6 feet away from the speaker.

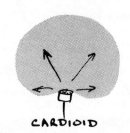

CARDIOID

A bi-polar micro-
phone picks up sounds
equally well from two
sides and is useful for
people sitting around a
table.

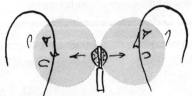

BI - DIRECTIONAL.

A "shotgun"
microphone has a very
narrow angle of accep-
tance in one direction
(another style resem-
bles a microwave dish).
Sports announcers some-
times use microphones
with special filtration
systems to eliminate
crowd noises (noise can-
celling mikes).

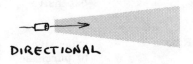

DIRECTIONAL

"Feedback" is usually the loud howl caused by having
a microphone directly in front of its speaker (the amplifier
increases the volume of small noises and the microphone
"feeds" them back into the system). Solutions: cut down
the volume, move the microphone or select a mike with a
different pick-up pattern.

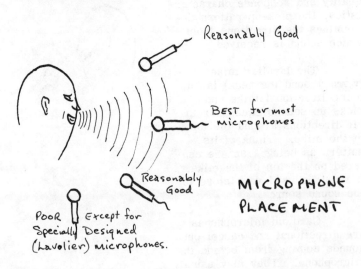

Reasonably Good

BEST for most
microphones

Reasonably
Good

MICROPHONE
PLACEMENT

POOR   Except for
Specially Designed
(Lavolier) microphones.

Sound Systems

Selecting a microphone and placing it properly is only half of the problem; we also need to have some form of amplification equipment and speakers for reproduction. Sound recording will be discussed in the next section so we will concern ourselves here with P. A. systems or their equivalents.

The amplifier's job is to increase the volume of a sound without distortion and is available in a variety of styles for different uses.

- portable Public Address (P. A.) systems use a battery-powered amplifier, usually designed to be lightweight and capable of reproducing only human speech.

- "bullhorns" contain an extremely lightweight battery-powered amplifier, mike, and speaker in a single enclosure.

- permanently installed P. A. system amplifiers are usually only capable of reproducing speech.

- musical groups need high-output amps that reproduce higher frequencies. Often special filters and attachments (echo units, etc.) are included.

- combination FM tuners and amplifiers are suitable for high-fidelity or "Musak"-style music.

- stereo systems contain two amplifiers which share some basic components. Stereo sound is more useful to multi-media presentations than any other form of community media. Even there the second channel is often used for programming the slide projector(s) rather than for stereo sound.

- an amplifier is too small for the room if it must be run at maximum volume (maximum distortion occurs at maximum volume).

- preamplifiers boost the sound level of some microphones, record turntables or tape recorders to a point where the amplifier can function.

- microphones are connected to "mike input" plugs; turntables, tape recorders and pre-amps are plugged into the "line-in."

- "line-out" is used when you want a tape recorder connected to record the program.

- hi-fi nuts often have far more audio equipment than is necessary for normal use and, since they desire wide range sound reproduction, their equipment is often more expensive than is necessary for audio-visual use.

- professional sound and recording equipment is engineered to be absolutely dependable as well as good quality. However, AM radio, television and film sound systems are not capable of reproducing a wide range of frequencies, and higher frequencies are thus not required for many uses.

The speaker converts electrical energy back into sound energy.

- several well placed speakers operating at a low level provide a better overall sound quality than a single speaker (the people closest to the speaker get deafened, those farthest away can't hear).

- always place speakers so that they will project their sound over the heads of the first several rows of your audience (do not place them down on the floor).

- extension speakers placed at the front of a room near the screen greatly improve the quality of film sound.

- the speaker used must match the output of the amplifier; e.g., using a 16-ohm speaker on an 8-ohm output will probably cause excessive distortion.

- basic electrical principles apply to speaker use; thus two 16-ohm speakers connected in parallel have an equivalent resistance of 8 ohms, and two 8-ohm speakers connected in series have a combined resistance of 16 ohms.

- "column speakers" are really housings for several smaller speakers and are very useful for auditoriums or meetings, particularly where microphones may be placed in front of the speakers.

- small speakers usually sound "tinny." Good speakers have heavy cabinets to ensure that cabinet rattle doesn't occur.

- split or torn speakers should be fixed at once with patching materials.

- all-weather speakers are available for outdoor work.

SOUND RECORDING

Good sound supports a media presentation rather than distracting from it, and requires good recording techniques on high quality, well maintained recorders. Since most recording is done these days on tape (usually a thin plastic-type material coated with iron oxide), using a magnetically induced signal, this article will confine its comments to this material. (In most cases optical "sound-on-film" or 16mm magnetic film recording will be done by professionals.)

Recording Narration

- if you have the opportunity, audition several people and choose the best speaker.

- use good clear diction, pronouncing all the words properly and making the words live rather than appearing to be read.

- keep the narration straightforward; do not assume a patronizing manner.

- try radio stations for possible narrators (and sound effects).

- don't record in a closet or other totally "dead" room; some echoes off the walls are necessary for the voice to sound alive.

Recording Groups

- be selective in recording meetings or conferences to save editing or transcription time later.

- identify voices in group conversations, interviews or panel discussions.

- repeat the question when recording a question period where the questioner does not use a mike.

- use several mikes placed close to each person speaking rather than one placed far away from most of the speakers.

- omni-directional mikes hung from the ceiling will cover discussions fairly well.

- have a skilled operator when using a "shotgun" type mike, or you may miss part of what the speaker says.

- do not allow the microphones to intrude upon the discussion (be inconspicuous).

- obtain written permission from individuals to allow you to use the recording.

Sound Effects

- commercial records are available for most common sound effects (doors slamming, sirens, guns, birds, etc.). Try your local library, radio station, or movie club.

- background noises add realism to reports or narration. Some radio reporters record live sound inside a meeting room and then play it as background when they make a telephone report to their station from a nearby phone booth.

- sound effects can be used instead of music to fill in gaps between segments of narration.

- effects can be recorded anywhere (e. g., traffic noise).

- record effects with a good 1/4" battery-operated tape recorder for best results.

- general noises don't need exact synchronization the same way the sound of a hammer might if we could see the carpenter using it.

Music

Most music for amateur productions is probably stolen from records, from tapes of live performances or from off-air radio recordings. More professional "thefts" include taping records at speeds other than normal and then playing them backwards (a rhythm still exists but the melody is unrecognizable).

- copyright regulations require you to pay a royalty for the use of recorded music. European records, or music from countries outside of the copyright regulations, are often assumed to be fair game but royalty rights may still exist.

- TV and radio stations expect you to have taken care of all releases and will assume that all music has been cleared.

- buying music from recording libraries is expensive.

Recording your own music can be fun, and inexpensive. Specially composed music is uniquely your own (if the prospective musicians can read music).

- jam sessions where musicians and friends improvise can provide useful mood music.

- folk songs with specially composed lyrics often require only enough music for chords and beat.

- royalties may have to be paid on recognizable tunes from sheet music.

- professional musicians will require royalties and often charge union rates.

- hit tunes go out of style too quickly for most use.

- classical music is often in the "public domain" (royalties are not needed) unless you use an arrangement that has been prepared fairly recently.

- one person playing a single instrument can provide enough music for background sound (you usually don't want absolutely quiet spaces in a film or other work). Try a guitar, a mouth organ, melodica or accordian.

- you must use trial and error techniques to set up microphones and levels for recording live bands. A good rule
of thumb is to provide one mike for each instrument (or
group of instruments in a large band) and one for each
vocalist. Volume levels are then balanced "by ear."

Equipment Operation

- when recording from a record, radio or television set,
always use a line connection rather than just placing a
mike in front of the speaker unit.

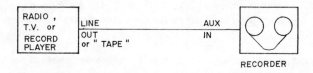

- alligator clips fastened to the two terminals of the speaker
will work if a regular output is not provided.

- always make sure that equipment is plugged into the
proper connectors. Mikes will not work on line inputs,
and most other sources (record players, etc.) will not
work through the mike input.

- duplicate recordings can be made by connecting two recorders together, "playing" one and recording on the other.

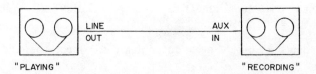

- make sure that the "record" button is properly engaged
when you start each recording period (the use of the
"pause" switch does not normally disengage the record
function).

- automatic level controls make it unnecessary for you continually to monitor and change the volume on some

machines. However, they cause a fairly distracting hiss to appear during quiet periods.

- tone controls work only on playback.

- the "line-out" connection bypasses the tone and volume controls and is useful for making duplicate tapes. The "external speaker" jack is affected by both controls.

- reel-to-reel tape recorders usually have better quality and speed control than cassette recorders.

- cassette tapes are smaller, harder to damage and easier to handle than reels of tape.

- cassette tapes longer than the C-60 size tend to jam in some types of use.

- cassette tapes are difficult to edit or repair if broken.

- long thin tapes take less storage space but tend to imprint sounds from one layer to another in storage (causing an echo-like background noise) and stretch easier.

- shorter, thicker tapes are more dependable and resist the print-through mentioned above but cannot be used for long continuous recording sessions.

- many commercial stations will not accept radio programs or similar materials unless they were prepared on professional quality recorders (expensive). These are often faked by rerecording cassette interviews onto 1/4" half-track recorders during editing.

- if you intend to make synchronous sound motion pictures, consult some local professional about equipment and techniques.

- become familiar with the controls and operation of your equipment so you will be relaxed and inconspicuous.

Equipment and Tape Maintenance

- keep your recorder and other equipment clean (weekly at least) and have it checked periodically for alignment and speed.

- never use metal tools for cleaning the recording heads.

- keep cleaning solvents off the rubber rollers unless they have been specifically designed for that purpose.

- cotton swabs and alcohol will remove most magnetic oxide deposits.

- a "head demagnetizer" should be used regularly to remove the permanent magnetism that builds up in the head and causes background noise (follow carefully the instructions that come with the unit, and cover the metal end with tape to prevent damaging the recorder head).

- magnets or magnetized tools must never be brought near tapes (will cause "clicks").

- tape should be stored in a cool dry place in dust-proof cases (placed upright).

- never use pins, scotch or masking tape to repair tapes. Invest in a small splicing block, razor blade and proper splicing tape: splices are easy to make. (Splice only on the shiny side of the tape, not the oxide side.)

- keep batteries fully charged as weak batteries will cause the recorder to slow down and operate erratically.

- keep batteries warm in cold weather as cold batteries lose their strength quickly.

Label tapes properly, the label should read the same as the catalogue title and the same as the program title on the tape itself.

INTERVIEWING TECHNIQUES

There are many occasions in working with media when it is useful to know how to conduct an interview

properly. For instance, you may need to interview a member of your community to obtain information for a project,
or a local personality for a television or radio program, for
a news release or as part of a fund raising campaign.

An interview may have one of three purposes: to
elicit information, to predict behavior or to change the actions or behavior of the person being interviewed (as in a
counselling or disciplinary interview). While the characteristics of all these interviews are similar we shall deal
only with the information-gathering type.

- first, as an interviewer, you should have clearly in mind
  a very specific set of objectives that you want to accomplish in the interview. You may even want to write these
  objectives down to help you remember them.

- next, you should plan just how these objectives might best
  be reached. This might include some of your thoughts or
  impressions about the particular individual you are interviewing.

- or, you might want to make notes on the particular aspects of the person's background and experiences you want
  to explore.

- next ... and most important ... it is necessary to establish rapport with the person you are interviewing. This
  means the setting of a climate that will allow for getting
  information as well as giving it (many interviewers, particularly on television and radio, monopolize the conversation and do not allow the guest or interviewee to interact).

Establishing Rapport

- being determined to listen to the other person is the first
  step in establishing the right atmosphere for discussion.

- step number two is to let the person being interviewed
  know that you are a fair person and will try to understand
  the situation regardless of the issue at hand.

- the "climate" we are talking about is often established by
  some preliminary conversation. The interviewer will
  choose a location and a topic which will put the person

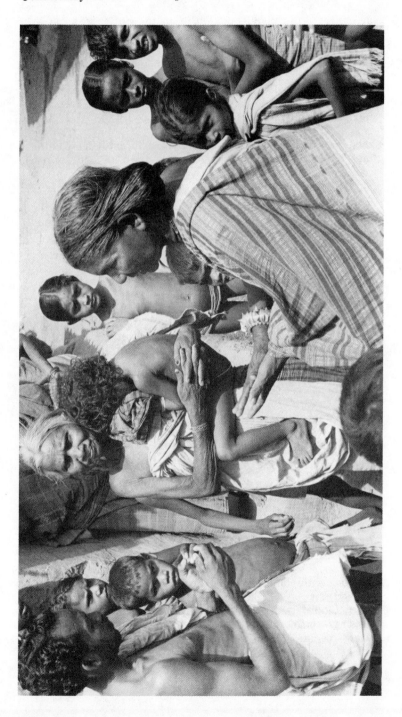

at ease. This could take place in the coffee shop and
shift to the studio once the guest is at ease.

- the main purpose of the interview should be made very
clear early in the conversation. The preliminaries should
not drag on so long that the person you are interviewing
(or the audience) begins to wonder just what it is you intend to discuss.

- then the conversation should move right into the points
that are important to the main purpose of the interview.

Helping the Conversation to Move

- choose words and phrases that are likely to have the same
meaning to both you and the person being interviewed. For
example, some people think of commercial radio and television when you use the word "Media," others think of
films and slides. Words do not mean the same thing to
different people!

- avoid showing a bias towards any point of view if possible.
Often your tone of voice or even the selection of words
you use will indicate a dislike or prejudice which may
insult or inhibit the interviewee.

Avoid multiple questions or ones that can be answered
"yes" or "no." Keep your questions short and concise, and ask only one question at a time. Try to
make the questions open-ended so that the answer ex-
plains "why" or "how."

Don't put words in the mouth of the interviewee; a
good interviewer lets the person being interviewed
answer honest questions rather than only saying what
the interviewer wants to hear.

- set a comfortable stage: have the person being interviewed sit in a comfortable chair facing the interviewer without having to strain in an awkward position.
Ashtrays and coffee also help. Of course, there is a
limit to comfort; a person who is too comfortable may

not be able to concentrate on the subject of the interview.

- see that there are no glaring lights or reflections in his eyes. You shouldn't be giving the impression of an inquisition.

- see that he gets your complete attention. The person (or persons) being interviewed must feel that this is the most important thing you have to do at this time. Have someone else answer the phone and avoid looking at your watch. (You can always handle any messages or business later, and the interview doesn't seem very important if you ignore it to do other work.)

- summarize the important points of the interview when you conclude it. The summary should be meaningful to both of you (and your audience) but doesn't need to cover minor points.

To conclude, an interview shouldn't be something to be afraid of (either for you or the person being interviewed). Proper planning and the establishment of an open, honest climate will ensure the success of most interviews without requiring elaborate scripting, rehearsals or acting.

EDITING: THE UNIQUE SKILL

Of the many skills required to produce a motion picture, film editing is the most difficult to learn and master. Cutting or editing has the distinction of being unique to the motion picture. It was "born in and of the film," and its combination of skill and art has no other precedent. Cinematography has much in common technically with still photography. Film writing is related to play writing or technical writing. Direction also has its theatrical counterpart. Editing skills, however, can find a place only in film making. [Editor's note: also television].

There are few opportunities to learn editing formally.

Almost without exception editors learn by observing others.
Books on the subject are limited to discussions of film
grammar, analysis of films or technical instruction in using
equipment and materials. Having struggled through a few
films on an editing bench and watched some of the top editors work, I have developed a few theories that you might
find helpful (or at least interesting) in improving your technique.

Theory Number One: Editing is a discipline that can be
learned by anyone of at least fairly
normal intelligence.

This does not mean that anyone will make a top
creative editor, but most people can learn to do a crafts-
manlike job of putting a film together. This discovery came
as a great revelation to me because I had always considered
this field as a sort of art form, like painting, that required
some supernatural gift as well as skill.

Theory Number Two: There are two distinct and different
functions that must be accomplished
in the editing process.

First, in order of importance, is the creative contribution the editor makes. He will select the shots that
tell the story best and put them together in the order that
will give the film its continuity or cohesiveness. He will
determine the length of time that each shot will play, which
gives the film its pace.

The second job an editor must accomplish is the
mechanical handling and manipulation of the work print and
sound track. This is not as interesting or satisfying as
creative decision making, but it is a large part of the total
editing job. In fact, the actual time spent in editing breaks
down to about 80-89 percent mechanical and only 10-20 percent creative.

It is reasonable to assume, then, that the largest
area open to improvement of editing skills is in mechanical
film handling. This will not necessarily improve the creative editing job you do, but improving efficiency in mechanics will net you more time to do creative work and make
the whole editing task more pleasant and efficient.

Separating the editing job into its mechanical and

creative functions will make the job easier. This can be
done in a number of ways. The best approach is the one
used by large studios. Some men do the mechanical work
(assistant editors, splicers, cutters, etc.) and others do
the creative thinking (supervising editor or director). Most
small units simply do not have the volume of editing for
this approach. More logically, one man will do the entire
job. Separating the two functions is still possible, however,
by doing all of the layout and setups before trying to join
scenes together.

Theory Number Three: Efficient and organized editing me-
                      chanics will result in a better over-
                      all editing job.

     The place to begin is with the editing table and equip-
ment. Statistics compiled for an "average" one-half hour
film for industry or television show that this hypothetical
film has about 100 to 150 scenes. The uncut printed picture will average 5000 feet; plus voice, effects, and music
sound tracks. During editing the picture is viewed about
10 times and rewound each time. This amounts to about
100,000 feet of film that passes through the editor's hands.
Add the sound tracks, which are handled approximately five
times each, and the total footage wound and rewound in editing approaches 250,000 feet for each half-hour film. Splicing statistics are equally impressive: about 1,100 picture
and sound splices are made in the editing phase. The point
is that with this volume of film being handled you should use
efficient equipment designed for professional production.
Saving a few dollars on equipment can cost many hours of
time in loss of efficiency.

     Specifically, use the best equipment available, and as
much as necessary. For example, I use differential rewinds
rather than straight shafts. The initial cost is repaid in
time saved on one or two productions. I also use a pair of
single-shaft rewinds on the same table for searching. Mylar
tape splicers are used for both work print and magnetic
track. Cement splicers are used only on original. Also
on my table are a viewer, sound reader, and a four-hub
synchronizer. I have spent many hours working out the best
placement for each piece of equipment. The table itself is
larger than average. I have also played with the idea of
two tables side-by-side or front-and-back.

     Some of the equipment is slightly modified. The

viewer and sound reader are one unit.   Multiple sound heads
can be added as necessary for music and effects tracks.
The viewer and readers are used mostly for searching and
mechanical setup of rolls before they are edited.

With good equipment efficiently arranged on a table,
the job of handling the film can be organized and planned as
a routine.   Three ideas that have saved me a lot of time
are:

(1) Break down the picture and track by shots.   Break-
     down of large rolls into individual scenes can be ac-
     complished by hanging strips into bins, spooling onto
     small reels or cores, or re-arranging scenes into
     script order on rolls.   The purpose is to lay out the
     film so that you can judge and decide where cuts will
     be made.   I usually do this by sequences.   The 100
     or so scenes end up in 10-15 small rolls.   At this
     stage duplicate and alternate scenes are sorted into
     a "hold" pile, which is easily available if needed
     later.

(2) Mark scene numbers and slates (of sync frames) on
     both picture and track for quick visual reference.
     Marking shots and tracks with white grease pencil
     during the breakdown will save searching on the
     viewer and reader in later stages.   While assembling
     these sequence rolls it is a good idea to put some
     additional sync marks on picture and sound rolls that
     will remain after the slates are removed.   One easy
     way to do this is to copy a few edge numbers from
     the picture work print onto the sound track.   Select
     edge numbers well into the scene so they will not be
     trimmed off.   This adds a safety factor to prevent
     losing sync in later cutting stages.

(3) Don't splice during this mechanical breakdown; use
     masking tape.   Splicing should and can be avoided
     until the film is in the creative phase.   Taped care-
     fully, film will run through a synchronizer, viewer,
     or reader, and taping is much faster than making
     even a sloppy splice.

Segregating this purely mechanical work from decision-making simplifies the job in the long run.   Another plus factor is that all of your available brain-
power can be concentrated on the important job
ahead--creative editing.

Theory Number Four: Creative editing is largely a matter
of common sense.

Many profound statements have been made by great
men about where and when to join two scenes together or
make a cut. The one that has impressed me most was
made by John Sims, a one-man film unit for the Canadian
Department of Agriculture. Although not verbatim, it went
something like this: "Never make a cut unless you have a
reason." He goes on to explain, with his dry sense of
humor, that there are many reasons. One may be that the
client wants you to cut there, or that the scene was shot
too short, so you have to cut here. When he gets into a
serious explanation, his rule makes a lot of good sense.
For example, when someone in the scene looks or points
to something, cut to it. Cut the way your eyes would move
if you were observing the action in person. When a scene
begins to drag, cut in or cut away. When the narrator ex-
plains a process, show what he is explaining. If the narration is short but the picture is interesting, put in some
track spacing. Another way of expressing this same idea
is to put yourself in the viewer's place and cut the film in
a way that will make the story clear and interesting to him.
If you do this, creative editing loses its mystery and becomes a matter of common sense and good taste.

These "theories" are not meant to end all further
thinking, but as guidelines to begin thinking further on the
subject. Editing is truly an art in that change, improvement, innovation, and progress will always be possible,
limited only by the imagination and skill of the individual
who does the job.

For your general motion picture education, here are
a few more statistics compiled in the editing survey referred
to earlier. Editor's time on this "average" film was 160
hours or four working weeks, depending on the deadline.
In one case the 160 hours were used by three men working
20 hours each per day for about two and one-half days on
the calendar. The cost of editing time and materials averaged 10 percent of the total budget. Supplies for editing the
one-half hour film averaged $50 (not including coffee and
cigarettes).

Editor's Note: In the years since Harry Paney wrote this
article, videotape has become an important
medium requiring editing. The same skills

are required for both film and videotape
editing, and in general the same thought
process is required for editing a tape-slide
presentation.

EDITING NOTES

The basic skills of editing are not just those of how
to operate a splicer or how to run a videotape recorder.
Editing for any medium requires a sense of timing, a thor-
ough knowledge of the content matter and an ability to communicate both visually and aurally, for a well edited presentation is a series of closely interrelated pictures and sounds.

If the editor of a production and the film maker/
photographer/cameraman are different people, much more
organization will be needed than if the cameraman both
shoots and edits.

- all scenes must be well identified. Keep a list of shots
  during the actual shooting to provide the editor with
  "what," "who," and "when." (This should be the responsibility of one person only.) Any errors in a scene must
  also be listed.

- the editor must keep a list of all scenes (never erase or
  throw anything away until after the production is finished).
  The editor's shot list is used to check continuity.

The editing process starts with the scripting to develop a series of preconceived ideas which get converted
into film, videotape or slides. There are always changes
between the conception and the shooting. It is the job of
the editor to take the shots and create a flow of ideas.

- use the best grade of editing equipment you can afford,
  work in a clean room, and keep everything super clean.

- for films, use fresh film cement. It's cheaper than a
  broken splice.

- use fresh clean-edged splicing tape for audio work; most
  other kinds of tape ooze adhesive from the edges.

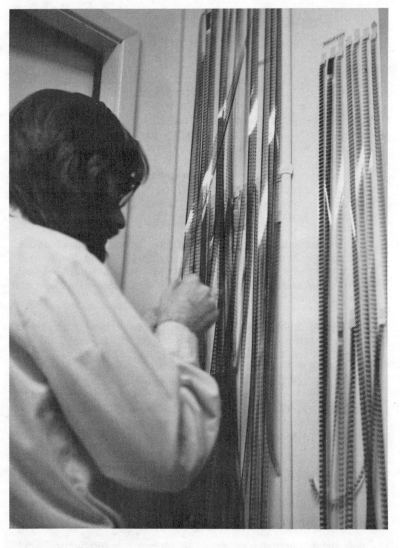

Care must be taken to keep film materials clean during editing.

- audio tape, like motion picture film, can be edited physically (cut apart and spliced back together again). Video tape, however, must be edited electronically (excerpts from one tape are assembled together on a second tape). Hook two vtr's together and record the image from one onto the other.

     In working out the flow of ideas think of your audience and try not to leave the viewer hanging. This usually means having a beginning, a middle, and an end.

- look at all the footage shot, view it at normal speed on a large screen.

- if working in film, break up all the shots into individual lengths of film and hang them up in a hanging bin or on a wall.

- keep a log of all shots, their locations (i. e., where you can find them--reel and footage numbers for video tape, peg location for film) and your comments (lousy exposure, too much sky, etc.).

- edit on paper. String all of the shots and narration together in a logical order on paper first. This saves wear and tear on materials as well as lessening the editor's frustrations. This "conceptual edit" will only work if you have a good description of each shot.

- scenes must be long enough to identify the image. Use short scenes only in a sequence of short scenes; very seldom use one short scene between two long scenes.

- perform the physical edit paying particular attention to timing, pacing and continuity. Check each scene for rhythm and continuity of movement before actually making the edit.

EFFECTIVE PRESENTATIONS

     The glamour jobs of the media world generally belong to the film director and the television producer, so that the techniques of effective audio-visual presentation are often

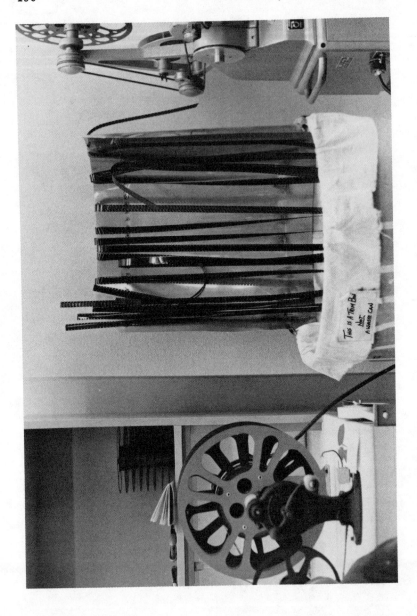

ignored. Thus, we have an otherwise good television production shown on a small screen to an audience that is too
large, or a motion picture that is badly framed being projected with a squeaky projector that drowns out the sound
track. If our original objective in using the media was to
present a message that would accomplish our organization's
purposes, then we must ensure that every step, including
the actual presentation, is carried out to the best of our
abilities and resources. Since the presentation stage is
relatively simple and straightforward we have no excuse for
a poor "show."

Setting the Stage

The charts below show basic information: room layout, distances from the projector to screen of common projection equipment, and the distances the audience should be
away from the screen for effective viewing. These distances
have been developed through actual testing with audiences and
represent optimum viewing conditions.

As you can see, a 70" screen would be quite adequate
for a normal classroom-size room for any media, but a
large auditorium would require a much larger screen (8' x
10' at least). Likewise, while a single TV set works adequately in your living room a group of 20 to 30 people would
need at least two large monitors, and an auditorium would
require strategically placed sets for about every 12 viewers
(a single TV set at the front of an auditorium is worse than
useless).

Sound is one of the major problems of media presentations. Film projectors with built-in speakers become totally inadequate and in larger rooms even the extension
speakers need assistance (put the extension speaker at the
front near the screen and high enough that it projects over
the heads of the audience). Be careful with speakers, to
avoid "blasting" the eardrums of persons sitting close, yet
not having the sound too low for those far away. Remember,
several speakers spread out at lower volume will give better
sound than one speaker at high volume ("Sound Columns" are
especially designed sets of speakers that help overcome this
problem; placed to radiate over the audience's heads, they
will usually also reach the last row).

Arrange the seating in the room so that everyone can

PROJECTION LENS DATA
Approximate lens size for same size image at various distances.

Screen Size	50" x 50"			70" x 70"				8' x 10'			
Projection Distance	10'	20'	30'	14'	18'	32'	42'	22'	48'	65'	90'
35mm slides	3"	6"	10"	3"	4"	7"	9"	3"	6"	9"	12"
Super 8 mm film	½	⅞	1⅝	½	¾	1	1½	½	1	1½	2
16 mm film	1	2	3	¾	1	2	3	1	2	3	4

It is often practical to place several projectors together at the rear of the room. This table gives the projector lens size required to operate 35mm slide, Super 8mm, or 16mm film projectors from the same location. With these lenses the image size will be approximately equal for each medium at the projection distance specified.

- 35mm slide projectors commonly have 3", 4", 5" lenses or a 4-6" zoom lens.

- Super 8mm projectors have a 1/2" or 3/4" normal lens.

- 16mm projectors usually have a 2" lens.

Overhead projectors are used at the front of the classroom and do not follow the above data. Use a WIDE ANGLE lens to get a bigger image.

Note: The main difficulty in using this table is that even if the images are the same size the image brightness may be quite different. Use the brightest bulb possible in your projector under these circumstances, or the HI setting for your projector.

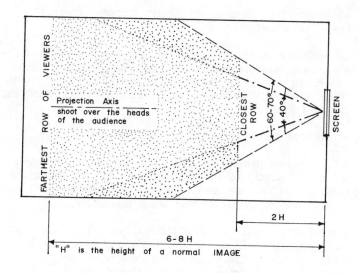

"H" is the height of a normal IMAGE

GLASS BEADED SCREENS have a viewing angle of about 20° on either side of the projection axis.

MATTE and LENTICULAR SCREENS have a wider viewing angle (30 - 35° to either side.

VIEWERS SHOULD NOT BE SEATED BEYOND THE RECOMMENDED ANGLES AND DISTANCES.

NOTE:- These standards assume that the image will fill the screen when selecting a screen size.
- Keep stray light from windows, hall lights, exit lights, etc. off the screen.
- Use the matte screen standards for T.V. monitors and use several monitors (I for every I2 people).

see and hear effectively (see optimum viewing angles of screens). Provide aisles for access by the audience and so that you can reach light switches and equipment. In more sophisticated viewing rooms there may be a sound-proofed projection booth; however if all the equipment is behind the audience the operating noise should not be too bothersome.

Once the room is set up, do a dry run of the presentation as a check.

- all projectors aimed at the proper screen, correctly framed and focused.

- all software correctly wound on reels and ready to operate (films, video tapes, slide sets, etc., in the right order, right side up and oriented correctly left to right). Make sure all the take-up reels are the correct size and mounted properly.

- sound levels correctly set.

- all equipment projecting over the heads of the audience; no viewer should be able to block out the screen image (also try to arrange aisles so that late-comers don't walk in front of the projector and block the image).

- electrical circuits adequate for maximum load (turn on all equipment that will be on at the same time to check circuit). It also helps to locate the electrical outlets in advance and bring extension cords if necessary.

- know the location of circuit breakers (or fuse boxes, and spare fuses) and light switches.

- will the blinds or drapes adequately darken the room? Locate screens in the darkest corner of the room if complete darkening is not possible (or use a rear projection screen).

- spare reels, bulbs, etc., near at hand and ready for use when required. A pocket flashlight is particularly useful for emergencies.

- extension cords for power supply, extension speaker systems or remote control of equipment taped to floor or otherwise protected from damage or being tripped over.

     As an operator you should plan on being present and alert during the presentation. Equipment and materials seem to delight in malfunctioning just as soon as you slip out for a smoke, and the time that it takes you to correct the condition will have distracted the audience and possibly damaged either machines or your media materials.

Preventive Maintenance

Properly maintained equipment will work better and cause less damage to your message-carrying software.

- projectors, recorders and other presentation equipment should be kept clean and free from deposits of dirt, film, tape oxide, etc. Dust covers will keep general dust off the equipment but dirt will also accumulate through use (the gate of a film projector should be cleaned after every film for best results, but weekly cleaning of most machines should suffice if they are used regularly).

- over-oiling a machine can cause as many problems as under-oiling (oil splattered on a bulb will cause it to bulge when heated), so follow the manufacturer's recommendations.

- audio cords and their connectors are particularly prone to damage. Loose connections should be repaired promptly (a soldering iron should be used).

- inspect equipment regularly for weak tubes, run down batteries, switches and bulbs that won't work, burrs or scratches on surfaces which film or tape will touch; and replace or repair.

- a good operator will have a small "first aid" kit containing a flashlight, cleaning materials, splicing materials, spare parts (bulbs, connectors, etc.), and basic tools which he takes with him to every media presentation. See also the article on Basic Repair Kits in the Community Media Center section (Chapter 1).

Even the most experienced operator will have trouble occasionally, but with well maintained equipment, software in proper condition and advance planning, he should be able to handle any emergency. Nobody notices the good operator because he never becomes the center of attraction. Planning ahead will keep you from being a distraction from the main purpose of the Audio-Visual presentation.

Providing a Context

Knowing that the room is arranged, the equipment

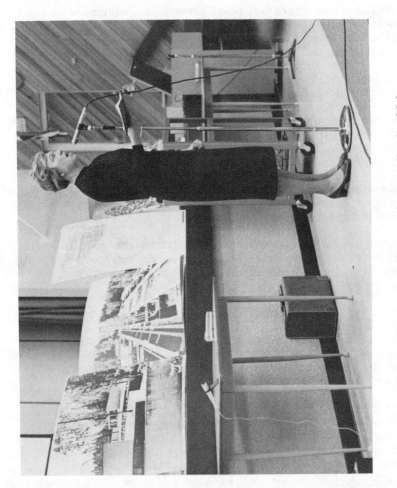

Materials that a speaker uses for a talk should be
made available for browsing later.

working, and the materials in order leaves you free to help
the audience participate.

- be aware of the audience needs and choose both media and
  content to fit these needs.

- introduce the presentation when appropriate (something like
  a spontaneous street theatre act may not be appropriate)
  and let them know what you intended them to discover as
  well as how to accomplish this discovery (this requires
  pre-viewing the materials before use when you are using
  new or unfamiliar materials). For example, if you are
  using a thirty-year-old film you might caution them to listen closely since the sound track is poor (don't apologize--
  be positive in your explanations).

- have an alternative plan in case something does go wrong.
  The show must usually go on; don't let occasional mishaps
  throw your plans off, but attempt to continue to your predetermined goal (abandoning the media if necessary).

- plan for a follow-up activity; a discussion, a work session
  or other means of making the media an integral part of the
  audience's world rather than just an "aid" or a "show."

- have a hand-out or other materials for the audience to take
  home. For example, the film "Diet for a Small Planet"
  talks about protein complementarity. When I use the film
  I always try to have printed copies of the complementarity
  chart and a couple of sample recipes. If possible the
  meeting concludes with a social hour to sample several
  dishes prepared using the recipes.

4 PRINT MEDIA

REPRODUCTION PROCESSES

Printing is the process whereby your typed or drawn materials are reproduced in quantity. Obviously if you only wanted a few copies you might use carbon paper and extra sheets on your original typing (1-5 copies) or an office copier (1-10 copies). Many office copiers will also produce a "master" for use on a duplicating machine to produce more copies (20-500 copies).

- Thermocopier: Spirit master (20-100 copies)
- Xerography: Paper offset "plate" (10-500 copies)

Stencils for the roneo type duplicator can be prepared with a special electronic stencil maker (e.g., Gestafax). Alternatively, masters can be typed directly in your typewriter (stencil/roneo, spirit, direct image offset). For larger quantities, special type faces, or better quality you might want specially prepared graphics, typesetting (handtype or photographic) and proper printing processes:

- letterpress with hand or machine set type.
- offset from metal or plastic plates.

For small quantities (20-100), especially of color posters you might use silk screen printing.

Your selection of a process will depend upon the quantity desired, availability of equipment, budget, and quality needed. If you are using equipment within your own organization the major costs will likely be paper and supplies. If you go outside your organization your costs will include labor (typesetting, printing, collating, folding, binding, etc.), paper, blocks or plates for illustrations, machine costs, and profit to the printer.

- check in your community for sources of low-cost or non-profit printers, e.g., schools, religious orders, community groups.

- a small printer if often cheaper than a large commercial press because his labor and overhead costs are lower.

- rush work always costs more.

- carelessly prepared work always costs more.

Many printed materials will be quite acceptable with typewritten text. Illustrations can be added and press-on lettering used for headings. There are a number of type-writers which have a "golf ball" style interchangeable type element. You can add variety and emphasis without any extra cost simply by changing elements.

More expensive typewriter style machines can also "justify" the right hand side of the page by changing the spacing between letters and words. When copy is justified both the right and left margins are even. (Normal typewrit-ing leaves the right margin uneven because of the different lengths of the lines.) These "Vari-typers" can be rented by the month or you can take your text to a commercial service for typing. Vari-typers can change the size and style of type. Inexpensive photographic "Headliners" can be used to prepare extra large type for posters and large type headings.

On occasion you may even want to have your text set photographically for offset reproduction or in solid type (by hand or typesetting machine) for letterpress. Modern news-papers and magazines have their type set by computer. These services are expensive and time-consuming. Go to several printers for price and delivery schedule before you commit yourself to any printer.

Paper: commonly sold by weight. Heavier paper is more opaque and generally is more durable. A "ream" used to be 516 sheets of a particular size and weight, however, paper is now supplied in a ream of 500 sheets. When speci-fying paper the most reliable method is to give the weight by grams per square meter (gsm). Board is usually specified by thickness.

Paper quality and finish can vary considerably within a given weight. Generally newsprint and other uncoated papers are used for inexpensive duplicating. Special papers are available for offset duplicating and fine photographic work.

Getting a Quotation: Before a printer can give you a

QUANTITY

Use this chart for selecting the appropriate reproduction process when you know the number of copies required.

Copies	1-10	10-20	20-100	100-500	500+
Hand drawn	x				
Typewriter	x				
Photographic Print	x				
Office Copier	x	x			
Sign Press (1)	x	x	x		
Silk Screen	x(2)	x(2)	x		
Spirit Duplicator		x	x		
Stencil Duplicator		x	x	x	
Offset Lithography		x(3)	x	x	x(5)
Letterpress			x(4)	x	x

Notes:

1. A simple flat-bed letterpress machine with large type for making display signs.

2. Can use block-out and paper stencils as well as commercial materials: silk-screen film and photographic stencils.

3. Direct image master.

4. Very expensive, used for business cards, wedding invitations.

5. Metal or plastic masters.

quotation on price or delivery, he will need some basic information from you.

- copy of the final draft of your publication, cleanly typed.

- any illustrations, photographs, tables, charts, etc., you want included.

- size: number of copies? physical dimensions?

- print: style and size? typesetting done by him or you? color?

- paper: weight? quality? color?

- illustrations: photos, sketches, or what? who will prepare final copy? does he need to change sizes? photographs, size of screen?

- layout: who does it?

- proofs: how many? how soon? who does proofreading?

- binding: folding? stapled, glued, stitched? collating and gathering? cover material?

- delivery: when? how? payment?

    With this information he can recommend a reproduction process (almost always offset in North America) and give you a price and delivery schedule. He may also be able to give some tips on cutting costs, improving quality or speeding up the process. Your quotation should include samples of paper, cover stock, etc. Quotations should always be in writing and will often give a time limit beyond which the printer will not guarantee his price.

    The ownership of your original materials should always be specified. Unscrupulous printers will keep your artwork or photographs and will use them for other customers.

    Compromises: The cost of typesetting or preparation of illustrations and plates (blocks for letterpress) will be the same regardless of the number of copies. The cost of the paper will obviously increase with the number of copies, as will the cost of printing (machine time) and binding. A decrease in the size of type can reduce the size of the

PROOF READER'S MARKS

Mark	Meaning	Mark	Meaning
⊙	Period or Fullstop	⌐ or ⌐	Move up/down
,/	Comma	tr	Transpose
H/	Hyphen	Ϥ	Delete
:/	Colon	⊗	Broken letter
;/	Semi colon	wf	Wrong font
ᵛ/	Apostrophe	Caps	Capitals
⸂⸃/⸂⸃/	Quotations	s.c.	Small caps.
#	Space	ital	italics
ჶ	Turn	l/c	lower case
⌒	Close-up	rom	Roman
ʌ	Caret - left out, insert	[/]	Brackets
↧	Push down	(/)	Parentheses
⊢⊣	Dash	@/	Superior
[↔]	Move to left or right		

nnection is recommended ; otherwise the
y service not keeping pace with the quick
uraterstic of developing countries whether

i/i/i/i/
c/i/i/i/i/

iterprises Bureau : Operations

ncy attending to and responsible for up
te Corporation Division of the Treasury
idenced by the new provisions relating to
nce Act No. 38 of 1971.

u/o/
#/

terprises Bureau be entrusted with thi
Public Corporations, Ministries and othe
vernment policy move amendments and
porations.

⊥/
⊥/

Sample
Corrected
Proof

policies adopted with respect to Publi
f the State Enterprises Bureau. Incon-
y, it could be due to a change in govern-
the existing government ; thirdly due to
vernment ; fourthly differences of views
finistries who interpret policy. In most
ition itself or for the relevant Ministry to
i it. The Bureau is better equipped for

⊔/

Get to know your
printer and the
exact style of
proof readers marks
that he prefers.

publication but may also decrease the readability. A compromise must always be made between size, quality and
quantity to produce an economic yet attractive and readable
publication.

Proofs and Corrections: Proofs are produced by the
printers from the final draft. The textual material is often
produced on long sheets rather than separate pages. Illustrations will also be produced as proofs but they will not
likely be joined together at this point. The final proof (if
requested) will show the text, illustrations, layout and paging
as it should appear in the final document.

Accurate proofreading is necessary. A well typed,
well written final draft will give a better proof, however,
any proof will have to be carefully checked.

- are all the pages there?
- is the text complete?
- are the references, section numbers, etc., correct
  and in the right place?
- are words properly printed, correct size of type,
  italics correct, etc?
- are there spelling mistakes, upside down letters,
  words run together, mixed-up lines, etc.

Every error must be marked, corrected by the printer
and reproofed, then re-checked. Your printer can supply
you with a list of proofreader's symbols. Illustrations must
also be proofed:

- are they the correct size?
- color correct, block-outs or other manipulations
  correctly done?
- are photographs the right way around? (The negatives often get flopped so that the original scene is
  reversed. This is often only crucial if there is
  some form of lettering visible in the picture).

Errors in the final draft, or changes that you think
should still be made often appear at the proof stage. They
are expensive to correct at this point but it is obviously
cheaper to correct now rather than after the publication is
printed. Any corrections have to go back to the printer and
new proofs made. The printer will charge extra for revisions in the text or illustrations, unless they were caused
by the typesetting.

The Publishing Process

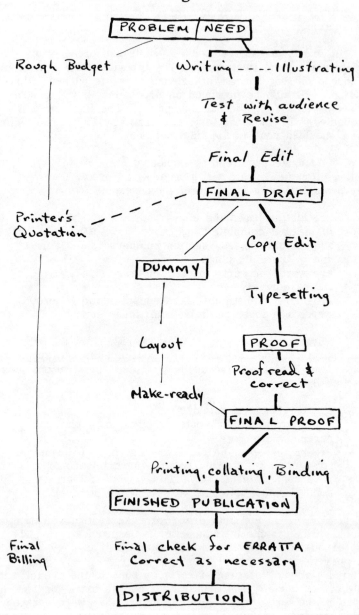

PROBLEM | NEED

Rough Budget

Writing ---- Illustrating

Test with audience & Revise

Final Edit

FINAL DRAFT

Printer's Quotation

Copy Edit

DUMMY

Typesetting

Layout

PROOF

Proof read & correct

Make-ready

FINAL PROOF

Printing, collating, Binding

FINISHED PUBLICATION

Final Billing

Final check for ERRATTA
Correct as necessary

DISTRIBUTION

Always check the printed document again before it is distributed. It may be embarrassing to include an errata sheet but that is cheaper than recalling copies after distribution or attempting to make changes to copies that have been distributed.

TIPS FOR TYPING MASTERS

Spirit

- Clean your typewriter keys before typing stencils.

- Type with a steady even pressure. If the center part of an "o" or a "p" or similar letter is cut out of the stencil during typing your pressure is too heavy.

- Erasures can be made by scraping the "carbon" image off the reverse side of the master with a razor blade. Retype corrections with an unused area of the carbon transfer sheet.

- Illustrations can be drawn with ball point pen.

Stencil

- Clean your typewriter keys before typing stencils.

- Use the "stencil" position for the ribbon or remove the ribbon from the typewriter before beginning.

- The wax coating on the stencil must be completely cut. Hold the completed stencil up to a light to check for a completely open printing area.

- Type slowly to minimize corrections.

- Let the correcting fluid dry completely before retyping corrections.

- Illustrations can be drawn with a special stylus on a hard surface (e.g., sheet of glass). A ball point pen which has run out of ink may be used as a stylus if necessary.

- Special shading plates are available for backgrounds and fancier illustrations.

Offset

- Clean your typewriter keys before typing masters.

- Use the special offset master ribbon for your typewriter.

- Use a carbon acetate ribbon rather than a cloth ribbon if possible.

- Type with a light even pressure. The paper master must not be cut by the typewriter keys. An electric typewriter works best.

- Illustrations can be prepared using special offset master (direct image) ink, direct image pencil or grease pencil.

- Errors can be corrected by erasing with a special offset master eraser and retyping or redrawing.

PHOTOGRAPHS FOR PRINT REPRODUCTION

Usually, when we think of community media we think of video tape recorders, cable television, films and the like. We often forget the role of the humble still photograph printed on a "hand-out," poster or brochure. Yet a single photograph can immeasurably increase the value of an information piece of any kind. Properly chosen, a photograph or series of photographs can capture attention and add both excitement and emotional impact--attributes lacking in many printed papers.

However, the inclusion of photographs is quite often hampered by a lack of knowledge about what kind of photograph will reproduce well with the printing process being used. "Blah" photos reproduced poorly will not enhance any message. The photograph must undergo several changes between the original photography and its appearance on a printed page, and these changes affect the final result.

1. The original scene is photographed with black and white or color film and a photographic print or transparency (slide) is made.

2. The image on the print or transparency is then copied through a fine screen to make a "screened" or halftone negative image. The size of the screen used varies with the printing process or paper to be employed (compare the large dots on a photograph in your daily newspaper with tiny dots on a photograph in a high quality magazine). The color process is similar except that several negatives are made using various colored filters.

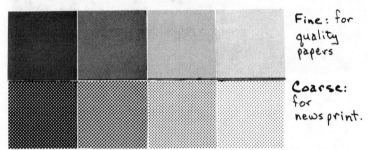

Fine: for quality papers

Coarse: for newsprint.

Mechanical Screens: Used to give shades of gray for illustrations or photographs.

3. The negative image is then transferred to a printing plate. In the case of offset lithography the plate may be paper, plastic or metal and is thin enough to bend around the printing cylinder. For silk-screen printing the image will be transferred to a gelatin-like masking material which is then affixed to the screen.

4. The image is then transferred to paper through the mechanics of the printing press. Because black ink is usually printed on a white page, we achieve a representation of our original scene. (In color work each color is printed separately, one on top of another to give a composite colored image.)

Since the photograph on the printed page is composed of tiny black dots (white areas have very small dots, grey areas larger dots, and black areas quite large dots) the reproduction range is limited. It is often impossible to get both a "white" white and a "black" black; usually we end up

RECORD OF
CONSTRUCTION
PROGRESS

with various shades of grey. (In low cost offset reproduction a crisp black is impossible.)

Choosing a Photograph for Reproduction

        Printers used to request a contrasty print on a
glossy paper since this facilitated their work.   Today, however, it is generally agreed that the photograph used should
have image details in all areas of the print, and that it be
less contrasty to better fit the paper-to-ink density range of
ordinary paper.   This doesn't mean that the photo will be
washed out or grey, merely that the print is balanced to
avoid excessive white areas or extreme black areas (a
washed out photograph will reproduce badly using any reproduction process).

        Small negatives blown up to large prints will not re-
produce well, since the natural grain in the negative will
tend to dominate.   Large prints reduced very small tend to
become very contrasty and also lose details.   "Drugstore"
prints also tend to be too contrasty for normal use.   For
best results, become familiar with the photographic materials you are using and their limitations.

        Blemishes in a photograph can be corrected before
reproduction.   This includes removing unwanted details from

Good promotion requires photographs that show

agency activities and service recipients.

a photo (such as street lights or wires) or improving a person's appearance (removing freckles or a double chin) but this requires experience and may be best left to a professional. (Any photographic studio can recommend a retouching artist.)

Almost everything on the print will be reproduced, especially dirt marks, scratches and writing. Torn or cracked prints must be repaired or replaced before reproduction is attempted, and any marks on the surface of the print removed (use a soft art gum eraser). Writing on the back of the print may ruin its usefulness if the writing has embossed the front surface.

Note: A good art fixative in a spray can will protect the surface of a matte print if applied when the print is clean. A sheet of white tissue paper will similarly protect the surface and can be used to indicate which portions of the print should be cropped (removed) by the printer. Fasten the tissue to the back of the print with masking tape and fold over the front.

Cropping

Often a photograph can be improved by eliminating distracting or inessential areas--this is known as "cropping."

The easiest way of cropping is to use scissors or a knife and cut the photograph. This doesn't allow you to change your mind, however, and is usually discouraged.

Another method is to indicate to the printer what is the most important subject matter of the photo and leave the decisions up to him. Invariably, he will sooner or later make a mistake because of your lack of responsibility.

The best way is to mark each print with the exact cropping you desire (and the amount of enlargement or reduction required). Since most photographic prints have a white margin, this can be done here without destroying the image itself, and this gives the printer definite directions.

In the example shown we have started with a 4" x 5" print and have marked the cropping desired. Since the cropped area is too small for the final use desired, it is also marked for an enlargement of 10 percent. In its final use there will also be a caption set in 12-point gothic type.

Children's Animation Workshop

Choosing a Screen

If a continuous tone photograph is not screened, it will reproduce as harsh black and white. This process is sometimes used for special effects and some kinds of posterization.

Photographs to be printed on glossy (expensive) paper will use a screen of 150-250 lines per inch. The high gloss paper allows reproduction of the widest range of details.

Non-glossy or uncoated papers will probably use a screen of 100-150 lines per inch. The matte surface of the paper obscures some details and dulls the white tones.

Newsprint will need a screen of 50-100 lines per inch. High speed daily newspapers generally use a rough screen (about 85 lines) while newspapers printed by offset may use a 100-line screen.

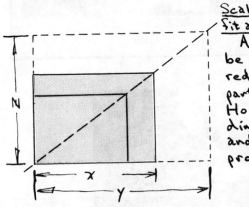

Scaling Photos to fit a specific space:
A photograph can be enlarged or reduced to fit a particular space. However both dimensions change, and in the same proportion.

Draw a diagonal line through the photo. "Y" is the new dimension, determined by your space. "Z" is scaled from the diagonal and is the second dimension. The photograph must be marked with the new enlarged (or reduced) length:

|← Enlarge aa % →| or

|←— Make y" —→|

Billboard and silkscreen poster printing may use even rougher screens depending upon the quality of the work.

Since the screening process is relatively expensive it is crucial that the final reproduction method and materials be selected before ordering the screening. If you are using a commercial printer, he can provide you with the require-ments of his equipment and may do all the steps involved himself. In any event it is wise to supply him with a cor-rectly sized, clean, properly printed original photograph for the reproduction process.

PRINTED REPORTS, BROCHURES, MANUALS, ETC.

Printed materials are technically the easiest media materials to produce. Anyone with a typewriter and access to any of the common printing techniques can become an author and publisher. Most offices, schools, government departments, and community associations have at least a spirit duplicator or a stencil duplicator (roneo). Increas-ingly they are likely to have an offset duplicator which will print A4 or foolscap size sheets. A local job printer will have letterpress and offset machines from A4 size to A1, or even larger. In addition, a silk screen press is so simple to make that any group with a small amount of space can print posters, wall placards and newspapers.

The ability to reproduce the spoken word does not automatically mean that people will read or understand the material. I have set two piles of leaflets at the back of a meeting room for follow-up to a discussion. One pile was typed and duplicated. The other pile had several simple illustrations on the front page and was more attractive visu-ally. Most participants picked up the leaflets with the illus-trations and left the typed text. On another occasion, I handed out a printed brochure that had been supplied by the sponsors of the meeting. Since I knew the subject area of the brochure fairly well, I had no difficulty understanding the content. After the meeting however, several individuals told me "I couldn't understand a word of that brochure. How does that machine work?"

Good writing can do a lot to overcome these problems:

- Know your audience needs, what it is that they need (want?) to know.

- Organize your writing to be clear and logical.

- Write using language that the audience will understand.

Several of the articles in this Handbook can help you with your writing.

Reports

Reports may be general or technical, a single page or several volumes. Almost every report, whatever its kind, style, length or use will have some common elements.

Title
Author (or evaluator, testing agency, etc.)
Purpose (why it is written, and to whom it is
    directed)
Background information
Procedures used in gathering information
Results obtained
Conclusions and Recommendations

Often reports are prepared on special forms which provide the writer with an outline and specific order of information. The evaluation form for training materials on pages 104 to 107 shows one such form. The equipment list, page 250 is another, but several of the above elements are implied and not explicitly stated.

Reports are usually prepared in response to a specific request. Some reports are once only events, others occur on a regular basis. The report must be tailored to the needs of the individual requesting the report. A report which doesn't contain the requested information is useless, no matter how beautiful and well written it may be.

Since reports are often lengthy, a short summary should be used to present the most important information. Summaries may need to be prepared individually for different readers. Thus, a two hundred page report on water pollution might have four or five separate summaries prepared.

Water Pollution Report

Original:	200 pages, 150 copies to Water Board and Government Agencies.
Water Board Summary:	10 pages, 20 copies to members of Water Board emphasizing policy implications.
Government Summary:	2 pages, 500 copies to local, regional, and national politicians emphasizing decisions recommended.
Popular Summary:	4 pages, leaflet, 10,000 copies to residents of affected area, soliciting comments.
Press Summary:	10 pages, 100 copies to all media for background briefing.

Brochures, Leaflets

Materials for popular distribution take many forms. They may be single sheet reminders after a demonstration, a single page of instructions, a nicely folded political campaign brochure or direct mail advertisement (look in your mailbox for examples), or a multi-page booklet on a single topic. This Handbook was originally prepared as a series of leaflets and brochures, each one covering a single topic, and different versions were often addressed to quite different audiences (e.g., school teachers, service clubs, youth groups). In this case all the materials had a consistent size (8-1/2" x 11" or approx. A4) and followed a general theme.

Brochures

- title block or one panel with title.

- one topic, short.

- specific audience.

- designed for hand or mail distribution (usually foldable for mailing).

    Booklets are longer, may have several topics and resemble small versions of a book.

- Cover page.
- Table of contents, pages numbered.
- A4 or A5 size.

Manuals or Handbooks

    You have an expensive camera, the manufacturer has provided an operating manual; the manufacturer of your car has provided your mechanic with a repair manual; a petro-chemical plant has a manual of procedures which takes about six feet of shelf space; the local crèche attendants want a small handbook on games for toddlers.

- What are they?
- How do we use them?
- How can we prepare them?

    Paperback books are "pocket" books which are now too big to fit in your pocket. Likewise manuals are perhaps "hand" books which are too large to fit in your hand. A handbook is a simple reference tool, a printed publication on a single topic or a series of related topics. No one ever "reads" handbooks or manuals. You buy them (or have them issued to you), you glance at the table of contents and place them on your bookshelf. The best ones go in your glove compartment or sit very close to your work (machine, desk, repair bench, order book, etc.). You refer to them when you have a question.

- What size lens do I need for projection in this audi-torium? (page 192, Projection Lens Data).

- How can I make inexpensive illustrations? (page 130, Sketching).

    Sometimes information needs to be taken out of a "book" and kept even closer at hand. The projection lens data might be typed on a card and taped inside the lid of the projector case. The hook-up diagram for a VTR, camera and microphone is duplicated on cardstock, plastic coated and included in the VTR package, or enlarged as a poster to go on the wall of the equipment storage room. In each case we have the handbook/manual to refer to for further information.

Longer publications need tables of contents, indexes, checklists or procedures and perhaps flow-charts of procedures (see the following section).

- If you need to remember the material use short sentences arranged in note form as in this section.

- Be consistent with your sub-headings and page format.

- Keep your sub-headings and numbering system simple. (Do not use systems like iv, v, vi or 7.34.1, 7.34.2, etc.).

- Use numbers like 1, 2, 3, ... for numbering sections.

- Use boxes around important sections.

- Use dashes to provide emphasis.

Writing Instructions

Write instructions very carefully and clearly. Describe each step. Don't assume that the reader knows some steps. Don't put in unnecessary information. Try to test your instructions as you write them. Do the task. Ask yourself, exactly what do I do next?

Divide instructions into two parts. What to do, and how to do it. Don't mix these two sorts of instructions up in one set. For example:

What to do:

- Put the food and water in the pressure cooker.

- Put on the lid.
- Put the pressure cooker on the fire.

How to put on the lid:

- Look at the grooves on the lid and the pan.
- Hold the handle of the lid to the right of
  the handle of the pan.
- Put the lid on so that the grooves meet.
- Turn the handle of the lid to the left, so
  that it meets the handle of the pan.

Pictures will often help with instructions.
Make sure they are clearly labelled.

Make sure the instructions agree with what
really happens. Try to test all your instructions in
real conditions. If, for example, your instructions
talk about steam hissing from a pressure cooker,
boil a pressure cooker yourself, and see exactly
how the steam hisses.

Try to give people exact amounts of time to
wait, or exact places to look, or exact things to
hold, to help them. Test the instructions by giving
them to several members of the intended audience
to see if they can perform the task properly (see
Pre-Testing, page 98).

Layout

One column layout   - long lines
                                 - good for typewriter
                                 - good for small pages

Two column layout   - shorter lines
                                 - easy to read
                                 - good for larger pages
                                 - easy to layout illustra-
                                   tions

Three column layout   - very short lines
                                 - harder to read
                                 - good for very large pages
                                 - good for small type

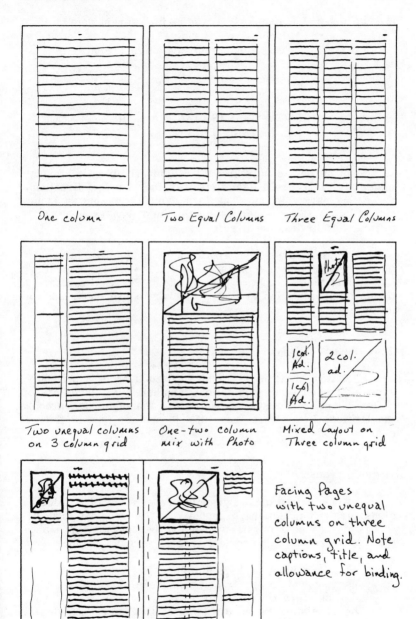

One column   Two Equal Columns   Three Equal Columns

Two unequal columns   One-two column   Mixed Layout on
on 3 column grid   mix with Photo   Three column grid

Facing pages
with two unequal
columns on three
column grid. Note
captions, title, and
allowance for binding.

Two unequal columns   - useful for margin notes,
                             headings
                           - an attractive layout

FLOW-CHARTS, LOGICAL TREES
AND TABLES

Many people have trouble reading complicated textual
materials. We are all familiar with the complex directions
for filling out an Income Tax form, or for making an Insurance Claim. Even an expert in the field may experience
difficulty following the directions.

Some of the recent research in readability suggests
that for some information the use of flow-charts, logical
trees, and tables is more appropriate. These alternate
forms of presentation are often quicker to use and result in
fewer errors.

Flow-Charts

A flow-chart is a graphic presentation of a process,
especially where one step follows another. A typical use of
a flow chart is to show the steps in a manufacturing process,
the Critical Path Chart (page 95) is another type of flow-
chart.

Logical Trees

A logical tree is a graphic presentation of the decisions involved in solving a problem. The simplest form of
a logical tree uses questions that can be answered Yes or
No. The design of the logical tree is very important:

- questions must be kept simple,
- use several trees for complex ideas,
- do not allow flow lines to cross,
- be consistent in the direction of flow, for example,
  keeping all the "Yes" responses going to the right.

Loading of the tape can only be done in the wind or wind back position after lifting up the head cover and the loading diagram ...

Illustration 1

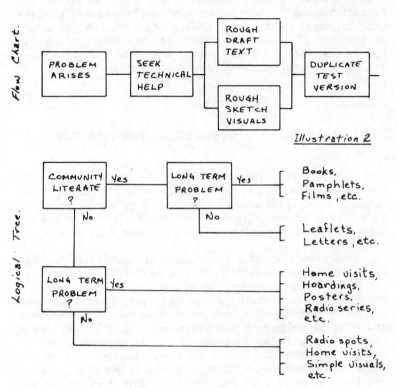

PROBLEM ARISES → SEEK TECHNICAL HELP → ROUGH DRAFT TEXT / ROUGH SKETCH VISUALS → DUPLICATE TEST VERSION

Illustration 2

COMMUNITY LITERATE ? — Yes → LONG TERM PROBLEM ? — Yes → Books, Pamphlets, Films, etc.

No ↓ / No → Leaflets, Letters, etc.

LONG TERM PROBLEM ? — Yes → Home visits, Hoardings, Posters, Radio series, etc.

No → Radio spots, Home visits, Simple visuals, etc.

Illustration 3

Conversion Table:
Typed Draft* to Printed Page

Typeset:	A4 Page	A5 Page
8 point	1/4 pg.	1/2 pg.
10 point	1/3 pg.	2/3 pg.
12 point	1/2 pg.	1 pg.
14 point	3/4 pg.	1½ pg.

* Original Draft is typed, double space, A4

Illustration 4

Tables

A table is a presentation of numerical or textual information using a grid-like arrangement of vertical columns
and horizontal rows.   Each column and each row has a label
or heading.   The label organizes the information in the table.
Use tables when the reader knows what information he requires and merely needs to check for specific details.

NEWSLETTERS: THEIR DESIGN AND FUNCTIONS

It is a very rare individual today who doesn't receive
some form of a regular newsletter, whether from his local
church, union, professional organization or social group.
This article examines some of the major types of letters and
suggests ways to obtain the maximum benefits from them.

A newsletter is a continuing and inexpensive publication (regular or irregular) which is published by an organization to inform members and/or the general public about
specific aspects of the organization's operations.   This could
include "gossip sheets" designed to keep members informed
about the happenings of other members, bulletins advertising
organization activities or products, or information sheets
issued to disseminate factual material compiled by members
(such as the occasional bulletins issued by some engineering
and law societies).   By our definition, this does not include
monthly magazines or journals, books, newspapers, or
single-topic booklets issued in a regular series.

In terms of physical appearance the newsletter can
be equally varied.   Some groups use a typed letter reproduced on their own mimeo or spirit duplicator, others go to
commercial print shops (at an increase in cost) or have the
publication printed as a favor by a friend or member who
has access to low-cost or free printing services (which are
unpredictable because they cannot be controlled very easily).
Large organizations often have their own print shop, capable
of producing most of the organization's publications (newsletters, magazines, letterheads, envelopes, etc.), but a
small organization is usually advised to stick to a process
it can control directly (mimeo or ditto) or use a commercial job printer.

IMAGES ALBERTA CAMERA CLUB

Volume 2, No. 3   November/December 1977

PSA Connecticut Tops 1976 November 24	The Photographic Society of America's Connecticut chapter 1976 competitions tops will be featured at the clubs November 24, 1977 meeting. The club's own competitions that evening will include the categories of moods (colour slides), pictorial (colour prints) and portraits (black and white).
Alberta . . . A Nice Place To Live	If you're not already convinced that Alberta's a nice place to live or if you'd just like to see some photography on the province you might be interested in a slide show taking place at the Provincial Museum November 24 and 25, 1977. The presentation is entitled "Alberta . . . A Nice Place To Live" and starts at 8 p.m. Admission is $2.00.
Photographer In The Grasslands December 8	Clifford Wallis of the Alberta Recreation, Parks and Wildlife Department will give a slide presentation on what he found photographic in prairie grasslands at the club's December 8, 1977 meeting. Members will have a chance to view and evaluate each others work also as this meeting will feature a 'Members Night'. In order to participate just bring along whatever slides or prints you wish to display. Later in the evening the Prairie Region of Photographic Arts (PRPA) 1977 travelling salon will be shown. Members are asked to remember December 8 is the deadline for the club photo-essay competitions. The theme is social comment and you may submit as many as ten slides or prints which tell a story. You may submit a written narrative but no tapes.
Images Places 13 out of 44 In NAPA Competition	Images Alberta came in 13th out of 44 club entries in the recent National Association of Photographic Arts (NAPA) Hancock Trophy competitions. The club entered six colour slides in each of the Hancock Trophy (pictorial) and Nature Trophy quarterly competitions as well as two prints to the print pictorial contest.
December 8 Bring Your Pictorial Slides	NAPA club representative Helen McArthur would like club members to bring their pictorial colour slides to the December 8, 1977 meeting. She will choose six to be entered in the next NAPA Hancock Trophy quarterly competition early in 1978.
Unicolor Print Seminar December 14, 1977	Anyone wishing to attend the Unicolor Print Seminar, December 14, 1977 at the Executive Inn on 105 Street should act fast. A registration form and details on the course can be found in the September, 1977 'Popular Photography'. The cost of the colour print processing course is $15.
And The Winner Is!	Congratulations to the following first prize winners in the September 29 and October 27, 1977 Images Competitions:

September 29, 1977 |

OXFAM-CANADA

Western Region

P.O. BOX 12000 • WINNIPEG R3C 3A4 • REGINA S4P 3M6 • CALGARY T2P 2M7 • VANCOUVER V6B 4T3

December 1977

Dear friend,

What's your next cup of tea got to do with an OXFAM-supported development project halfway around the world? Well, there's a good chance that cup of tea came from the island nation of Sri Lanka.

Sri Lanka (known formerly as Ceylon) is a teardrop-shaped country the size of Vancouver Island suspended beneath India in the Indian Ocean. In pre-colonial times, Sri Lanka's kings ruled a lush and prosperous island. A highly-organized and elaborate system of irrigation and water control enabled its people to be self-sufficient in food. When the Portuguese, Dutch   then British colonizers came, they introduced coffee, rubber, and finall'   'ations for the export market in Europe. Tea estates flourished un~   ' administration, taking over a quarter of the arable lan~   the irrigation works fell into disuse, large tracts of th`   d for the first time rice began to be imported. Dom~

Note: Newsletter: Offset Printed. Unscreened Contrast Photos High

By 1948, when Sri Lank^   ~endence, it was left with an economy still heavi'   ~e from tea exports. Worse, it was no longer able to p~   . its own people. In the twenty-five years that followed,   ~e food and machinery that Sri Lanka had to import increased more   ~imes, while tea prices only doubled. Sri Lanka was in continuous econ~   ~isis. Wages on the tea plantations declined to starvation levels, unti. in 1974 low wages and high prices for imported food together resulted in a doubling of the death rate among the tea pickers.

Two kinds of agriculture in Sri Lanka: Left, picking tea for export at starvation wages; above, growing rice for local use. (WFP photos)

When starting a new newsletter, it is wise to collect a wide variety of publications from other organizations and try to determine what you like or do not like about each. Try to model your own publication upon the best elements of each to meet the unique needs of your own audience (Who is your audience? What are their needs?). Prepare two or three "dummy" issues of your publication, each in a different style (the way that the content is written up) or format (physical layout and appearance). This will help the members of your advisory board or executive to make effective decisions about the publication.

Advisory Board

Most organizations will want a part in determining the policies of their publications. Advisory boards should be representative of the membership and should be kept informed and consulted. They should not be set up to oversee the day-to-day operations of the publication (this is the editor's job) or to insure that the editor doesn't say anything "wrong" (if you don't like what the editor writes, then fire him). In small organizations the advisory board should be willing to pitch in and help with the collating or to stuff envelopes.

Style

Adopt a style and stick with it. If you want to be folksy that is OK, but don't be all efficient and technical in one issue, then folksy in the next. Readers will feel more comfortable with a consistent policy (this doesn't preclude having several different writing styles or types of content in an issue--just be consistent and include the variety on a regular basis). Editorial and reader styles will change with time, but this is usually a gradual process.

Format

Check out various methods of printing the newsletter and adopt a style and duplicating method consistent with the organization's resources. It is easy to upgrade the printing quality at a later date if budgets become more liberal; discontinuing too ambitious a publication because you have lived beyond your means will earn black eyes all around.

Name

Letting the membership choose a name is an easy means of involving them in their publication. Have a graphic artist (or art student) prepare several possible logos (or mastheads) and select the best one. The newsletter's name and logo will be a prime factor in keeping your identity with the reader. (Other factors are the reproduction quality and the layout of text and illustration--is it easy to read?)

Copyright

Most newsletters are not copyrighted, nor need they be. It might be useful, though, to print a statement saying that materials may be reprinted on condition that credit is given to the publication or the organization. An address should always be provided, indicating where the editor or some other responsible party may be reached for additional information. It may also be useful to indicate that opinions expressed in the publication are those of the writer and not official policy of the organization (this is one of the ways that an organization keeps the editor from usurping the power of the executive). Materials which have previously been published should never be reprinted without obtaining the permission of the author and the original publisher. Likewise, extensive editorial changes in an article or letter should always be checked with the writer before publishing.

Advertising vs Public Relations

Calendars of upcoming events are a very useful part of any newsletter, and it is usually possible to subtly pro- mote the organization or a product without blatant advertis- ing. A photograph with a caption or short note can indicate new arrivals or changed responsibilities in an organization without the disadvantages inherent in the "paid political an- nouncement" type of article. Marriages, births, etc. should also be handled with good taste and generally should occupy a subordinate position in the publication.

Mechanics

It's the little problems that get an editor down....

- establish a system for building a mailing list and keeping it up to date. The system should not require retyping address labels every issue.

- get a number of individuals regularly involved to share the work load; e.g., one person can handle the mailing list, another the gathering of news items from members, another the writing of a regular column.

- budget realistically, do not overspend your allocated budget, and try not to depend too heavily upon free or borrowed services (the person who is getting your newsletter printed free may get transferred or company policy may change and the resulting loss may force the discontinuance of your publication).

- announce deadlines for regular publications and stick to them; nothing is worse than a late publication.

- reject materials that do not logically fit the content or style of your newsletter. Most people understand if you tell them that another place would be more appropriate (also be careful that there is a balance of submissions-- encourage other people to write if it seems that only one or two authors are exclusively represented).

- keep editorial opinions clearly labelled as such.

- review the publication, its objectives and its intended audience constantly. An up-to-date and relevant publication attracts readers.

POSTERS

Posters have often been used to announce meetings or to make people aware of a particular campaign. You shouldn't forget, however, that posters are easy to produce, inexpensive, attract considerable attention, and can present a short message or stimulate action.

- keep posters simple and uncluttered, one idea only.

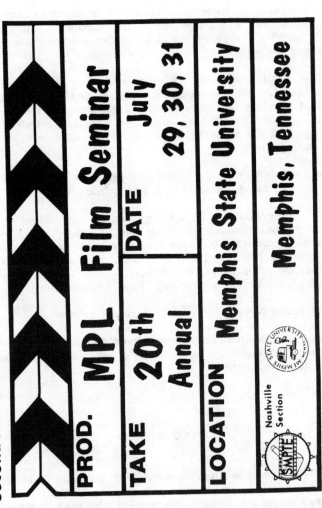

Second Announcement

PROD. MPL Film Seminar

TAKE 20th Annual   **DATE** July 29, 30, 31

LOCATION Memphis State University

Memphis, Tennessee

Nashville Section

→ Meeting to be held at the University Center building. ↓

- bright colors, block letters and distinctive graphics (use of lines, shapes, etc.) attract attention.

- POSTERS ARE VISUALS; use as few words as possible.

- a family of posters can be created on the same theme by using a consistent style, and similar layout, color or lettering.

- photographic posters are relatively expensive.

- don't try to copy "comic book" characters, create your own design.

- silk-screen printing is a simple, effective means of making several identical posters, and equipment for screening can be constructed for under $20.00.

- very simple posters are often most effective. A black felt-pen drawing with a neat slogan will out-draw a complex four-color extravaganza.

- simple cut-out stencils can be made from cardboard or sheet plastic. Draw the required words or "shape" on the stencil material and cut out using a razor blade. Remember to leave small "bridges" to hold the elements of the design in place. Place the stencil on top of your poster paper and splatter, brush or spray ink or paint through the stencil. (A toothbrush dipped in paint can be rubbed on a comb to splatter paint, an insect spray gun can spray paint, or the stencil can be used as part of a silk screen operation.)

- posters to be glued onto a surface can be printed on newsprint but usually they should be done on fairly heavy card stock.

- posters can also be used to visualize the discussions of a group. The illustrations on pages 236-239 were the outcome of a public health workshop and were used to inform participants about the discussions of other groups meeting simultaneously.*

*Drawn by Ms. Judy Steele, reproduced courtesy of the artist and Northern Medical Services, Department of National Health and Welfare, Canada.

- stealing posters is a form of flattery; while it may be an-noying to continually lose posters that may have cost $1 each, they will be getting circulation in places you can't ordinarily reach.

- posters don't need to be large to be effective; where peo-ple can get close or are able to stop to look they may be as small as 8-1/2" x 11".

- billboards are merely large posters, placed where passing motorists will see them. Smaller posters should also be placed where people will see them--too many distractions will cause potential viewers to ignore them.

- logos and trademarks are posters too--they are used to identify products or ideas when people's eyes are moving too fast to take more than a quick glance (on freeways, escalators, or in crowded grocery stores). The less time a person has to see a poster, the simpler it must be.

- newsletters and brochures have extended use if they are designed to be attractive as posters when posted on bulle-tin boards (see the following section, Wall Newspapers and Bulletin Boards).

WALL NEWSPAPERS AND BULLETIN BOARDS

A poster is a single sheet visual--an announcement of a meeting, motivation for change, general inspiration, etc. The poster might be as small as a postcard and mailed to potential viewers, or as large as a billboard. A poster attracts attention but is transitory--most people view-ing the poster do so as they are traveling from one point to another--they do not stop to read the fine print (if any).

A newspaper is a regularly issued collection of cur-rent events and activities. A newspaper often uses very small print, may have photographs and other visuals, and usually takes some time to read.

A wall newspaper is also regularly issued, and dis-plays news of current events and activities. Hand printed

(cont. on page 240)

Reading 'all about it'
on Copenhagen's walls

11/5/77 Ed. Journal

By ANTONY TERRY
London Sunday Times

COPENHAGEN — Thousands of people in Copenhagen have become accustomed to setting their alarm clocks half an hour early so that they can keep up to date with the news. They set off to work early and queue up to read what have been nicknamed "Chinese wall newspapers" — single-sheet editions of one of the city's dailies, *Politiken*, posted up at more than 800 sites.

These minimal news-sheets are printed secretly in a Copenhagen suburb and stuck on the walls by hired schoolchildren. They provide almost the only source of printed news; and for Danes living out in the country the famine is even worse. The reason is that a printing dispute that began three months ago at Copenhagen's largest daily, *Berlingske Tidende*, has spread throughout Denmark.

The only newspapers still appearing are a Communist daily and two small trade-union journals. Radio and TV are not much help, for in normal times they largely depend on the papers for their news, and now their small staffs have actually had to cut down on newscasts.

Danes are finding that without newspapers to keep a proper eye on the government, important public issues are going by default. In a bitter editorial *Politiken's* wall newspaper said the news blackout had prevented the proper airing of a row over the appointment as a senior judge of a man convicted of drunken driving. The absence of public debate, *Politiken* said, had saved the minister of justice "in the nick of time" from having to resign. It had also enabled the government to play down another affair concerning the appointment of judges with fraud convictions.

The spread of the strike has been especially bitter for some newspapers, such as *Politiken*, which began going over to computerization five years ago as a means of survival, having negotiated redundancy agreements. Now even the terms of those agreements are in dispute.

Danish editors and journalists come into their offices each day and try to look busy. Some newspapers are filling in time by planning "shadow" papers to appear when the dispute ends. Herbert Pundik, chief editor of *Politiken*, said: "We go through the motions for a bumper end-of-strike tabloid, but it's hard to persuade journalists to concentrate on meeting deadlines several weeks or months ahead."

or type set sheets are posted on fences, walls, etc. and are located in places where people can stop and read every line. In some countries wall newspapers can even be displayed on a chalkboard.

A bulletin board on the other hand contains a number of discrete items which may or may not be changed regularly. Viewers will stop and read the items--however most items may need to be posters or other such visual "attractors"--particularly since items may not change regularly.

Well read newspapers and bulletin boards need a lot of supervision:

WALL NEWSPAPERS and
BULLETIN BOARDS:

- keep the boards clean, throw away all old materials.

- perhaps one person should be responsible for approving all materials posted--this will keep obvious trash from being posted and may help keep materials relevant to the major viewers.

- a wall newspaper will require reporters, editors, layout artists, printers, distributors, etc.

- a number of locations will be more useful than a single location.

- in a low literacy area every effort should be made to use cartoons and drawings about the news.

- if the material is changed regularly the readers will make a habit of coming to look at the new "news."

CHALKBOARDS, FLIP CHARTS AND FLANNELGRAPHS

The chalkboard is still one of the commonest visual aids, and unfortunately, one of the worst used. Properly used, the chalkboard serves as a useful place for recording the ideas of a group or for organizing a talk. The flip chart is smaller and uses paper and some form of writing tool but is essentially the same medium as the chalkboard. The flannelgraph is a formalized version which uses previously prepared graphics.

- the chalkboard is cheap, easy to use and is reusable.

- the flip chart is usually fairly small, requires paper and a special writing tool (heavy pencil, crayon, wide tipped felt pen, etc.).

- the flip chart pages can be saved and used to produce a record of what went on in a session.

- the flannelgraph cannot easily record ideas from the group.

- the overhead projector is a mechanized combination of these tools. Visuals can be prepared ahead of time or materials can be developed during a session as on the chalkboard.

For all of these techniques of presenting information we need to keep visuals simple and lettering large. People sitting 12-20 feet from the board or screen will need lettering at least 4 inches high for good reading. Use the tools for summarizing a talk, for listing the most important ideas or for developing a process which requires visualization to be understood.

- face the audience when talking. Do not talk and write at the same time.

- use large clear lettering and simple illustrations.

- clean a chalkboard before use.

- use contrasting colors and materials: white chalk on a green board, black ink on white paper, etc.

- use handouts if required for large amounts of written material, use slides for photographs and similar visuals.

Flip Charts are suitable for small group use.

- Flannelgraph materials can easily be prepared in quantity by silk screen printing onto cloth.   The individual graphics can then be cut out for use.

5 VISUAL MEDIA

COMMUNITY DEVELOPMENT AND FILM-MAKING

In the past few years there has been a growing interest in the use of film-making as a technique for community and group involvement. One of the best known of these projects was the National Film Board's Fogo Island Project, part of the Challenge for Change program, but numerous projects have also been attempted by other community and youth groups.

This type of project may make use of simple or elaborate equipment, a few or many people, and continue for varying lengths of time. In general, however, each uses the film medium, sometimes with accompanying sound, to "say something" about a community as seen by a particular group. There is generally no script and, in the beginning, often no clear idea about the type of production which will result. The development of a cohesive presentation is an important part of the group learning process. It grows out of the sometimes seemingly endless discussions with the community group and also out of their observation of the results of their own efforts. It is helpful if the people involved have the opportunity to see the results of their efforts as soon as possible, so that omissions can be corrected and the new suggestions which will almost inevitably result from this process can be utilized. Although this article refers to "film-making" the same principles apply to the use of videotape productions and tape-slide productions. Videotape has the advantage of providing instant playback so that community groups can see what they have produced now. The flipside of this is that the process of deciding what should be filmed, or who should be interviewed and how, may be pushed aside by the premature taping. Repeated taping of the same person or situation in search of perfection may also lead to staleness and a loss of spontaneity and "life."

This use of film-making differs from standard film production in that the film as an end-product is usually less important than the involvement of the community or group in the film-making process. This emphasis on involvement has several purposes:

246

- it provides a situation in which sometimes disparate elements can learn to work together. The novelty of the film-making process is generally an asset in this situation since everyone in the group will be on an even footing; i.e., there are no ready-made experts. It provides a new motivation for working together.

- it helps groups and individuals take a fresh look at their situation. (You can't use the excuse that the film-maker presented a distorted view of the community if you are the film-maker.)

- it introduces groups and individuals to a new mode of communication--often a particular help to those who are not skilled with written communication.

A typical project might progress through the following stages:

a) initial idea that "making a film" would help this group with a particular problem. The idea might originate with the group itself, a photographer or, perhaps more likely, a community development specialist.

b) introduction of technical personnel to the community, and initial exploration of the process. There will probably be some false starts, wasted film and general disorganization at this stage, but it is of crucial importance that the photographer or other technical consultants not impose their ideas on the community.

c) initial viewing of materials produced and decisions about their use. This is often a two-step process: the decision about whether the materials will be used will be made by the persons filmed and the community group.

d) editing and gathering of further material. This process may continue for some time depending on the complexity of the issue and resources available. It is well for the whole group to be aware of the effective time and budget limitations so that they will not be left with a partially completed project.

e) utilization of the completed film. At this point the photographer and other technical personnel are usually withdrawn from the project, but it is a most important step in the communications process for the community as they continue to discuss and perhaps take action on the issues they have raised, and possibly release the film for use in other similar communities.

In actual practice this use of film-making as a technique means that the film-maker has much less control over the situation and the product than he would, in say, the making of a documentary. It should be made clear from the beginning that this is not the type of project in which a budding film director can expect to make his reputation. He must rather be prepared to act more in the role of technical advisor to the community group.

Although circumstances vary from project to project, the community group should generally have the final decision on what is filmed or recorded, how it is edited and whether or where the final product will be shown. For some groups this may mean participation by physical operation of the equipment, for others it may be sufficient to take part in the decisions about these matters. In either case, the film-maker must be ready to suggest without imposing his ideas on the project.

Lest this somewhat negative viewpoint discourage any reader from taking part in such a project, I should add that the photographer or television producer participating in such a project will be helping a community or group to take an important step in its development by sharing his expertise with them. Tape-slide productions are usually easier for a community group to handle from the point of view of cost and availability of equipment--almost everyone has access to a 35mm camera and cassette recorder. A well-planned tape-slide production can have as much impact on viewers as a slick film or television production--it can also be changed more readily and updated easily to reflect changing circumstances. Of course, there are concomitant drawbacks:

- since the process is apparently simple and not as glamorous as film production the initial novelty effect cannot be counted on as a catalyst to draw people together.

- since the possibilities for changing the production are more open it may be more difficult to have a community group come to one decision about what they wish to portray. But is it a disadvantage to have more than one view of the same reality?

FILM EQUIPMENT

This list represents the minimum equipment and services that I feel are necessary to produce a simple low-budget film in either Super 8mm, regular 8mm or 16mm. Note that the starred (*) equipment may be deleted if the film does not have any sound.

Shooting

- camera with lens (single focal length or zoom).
- light meter (preferably a hand held meter).
- *tape recorder and microphone (for wild sound).
- lights (depends upon location and type of film used).
- clip board, pencils, felt pen, paper.
- lens cleaning tissues and camera cleaning brush.
- batteries for camera and/or lights if required.
- *batteries for recorder if required.
- extension cords (110 volt, grounded) for recorder and/or lights if required.
- black changing bag (in case film jams in camera).

Editing

- two (2) rewinds, securely fastened to baseboard or editing table.
- two (2) reels (at least one of them a "split" reel). The reels should be large enough to hold all of the film you intend to edit.
- white cotton gloves (to keep film clean).
- film viewer.
- film splicer, and splicing cement or splicing tape.
- bare wall or film bin (to hang up individual shots during rearranging).
- masking tape (for temporary splices), and marking crayon.
- black leader, white leader.
- *tape recorder (at least one).
- *tape splicer, stop watch, and splicing tape.

Outside Services Used

- *sound transfer (required to end up with an optical

INTERNATIONAL COMMUNICATIONS INSTITUTE

EQUIPMENT CHECK LIST

___ ___ Camera, Arri 16S   ___ ___ Matte box

___ ___ 16mm lens & lens cap   ___ ___ Film changing bag

___ ___ 25mm lens & lens cap   ___ ___ Shoulder pad

___ ___ 50mm lens & lens cap   ___ ___ Sync pulse generator

___ ___ 100mm lens, shade & cap   ___ ___ Extension tube

___ ___ 200mm lens, shade & cap   ___ ___ Camera/magazine cover

___ ___ 500mm lens, shade & cap   plate (to use 400' mag.)

___ ___ Variable speed motor   ___ ___ Practice film

___ ___ Constant speed motor   ___ ___ Spare 100' reel

___ ___ 2.6 Ah Battery   ___ ___ Spare 100' can

___ ___ 5.2 Ah Battery   ___ ___ Spare plastic film core

___ ___ 6 ft. Battery cable   ___ ___ Lens cleaning tissue

___ ___ Coiled battery cable   ___ ___ Tape measure

___ ___ Light meter   ___ ___ Notepad, stickers, marking

___ ___ Gray card   pen

___ ___ 400' magazine & torque motor ___ ___ Masking tape

___ ___ Two (2) core adapters   ___ ___

___ ___ Small metal case   ___ ___

___ ___ Large metal case   ___ ___

___ ___ Filters (specify) _____

          _____

___ ___ Other equipment (specify)_____

          _____

Date checked out_____   Date returned_____

Production_____

Photographer_____

Remarks (Damages etc.)_____

_____

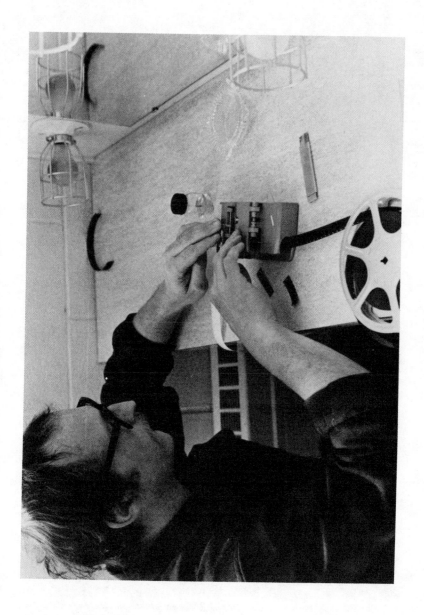

EDITING BENCH:
A similiar design
could work for T.V.
Control Room by
substituting equipment,
ie: VTR, controls,
monitors, etc. Also
makes a good repair
bench. Note: 110 volt
power outlet, and
fluorescent lamp
under shelf unit.

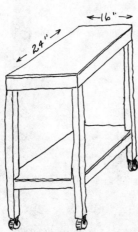

← 16" →
← 24" →

Mobile Projection
Stand - 4'6" high.
1x2, 2x2, Masonite.

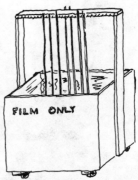

FILM ONLY

Film Bin - lined with
a clean cotton bag. Film
is hung on small headless
nails.

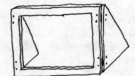

Rear Projection Screen.
3 pieces plywood, hinges, cover
opening with translucent paper.

Filmstrip Copy Box

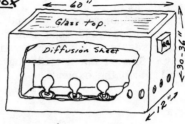

- With front cut away to show interior.
- Diffusion sheet is frosted glass, clean white cloth or paper.
- Ventilation holes for use as light box.
- Negative and unexposed copy film taped to glass top, cover with a weight to ensure tight contact. Initial exposures determined by experimentation.
- Uses four 25 watt incadescent bulbs spaced along bottom plus one red safelight.

- sound track film). Magnetic track films can sometimes be transferred by the user.
- processing of film stock.
- preparation of work print.
- preparation of composite or answer print.
- preparation of final release print.

This list of equipment represents a financial investment of perhaps $500 for used equipment (maybe less for
used Super 8mm equipment) and up to several thousand dollars for new equipment. You can usually rent all of the

Paper Cutter:

- Make from straight metal bar stock on a masonite or hardwood base.
- Hold paper or card stock and cut with a knife or single edged razor blade run along the bar.
- Several light cuts are better than one heavy cut.

necessary equipment but I have found, in my area at least, that purchasing equipment wisely will save me money. Based on local rental fees, minimum length of rental (including transportation time) and shipping expenses, I only need use my $3,000 used 16mm camera for about four shooting sessions per year for five years to be saving money. Since I am not filming regularly the convenience is well worth the expense.

1/2" PORTABLE TV EQUIPMENT

Today, the simplest tool for obtaining a combined sound and visual record is the portable 1/2" video tape recorder. While tapes made with this machine can not be broadcast easily, they can be replayed on most 1/2" video recorders and with some luck can occasionally be used on cable television systems.

Sony manufactured an early 1/2" portable system which is not compatible with current models (but which was often more dependable). Most manufacturers now conform to the EIAJ (Electronics Industry Association of Japan), Type 1 standard which supposedly guarantees interchangeability of tapes between any 1/2" machine. This interchange is possible if both machines are correctly adjusted, otherwise the picture will roll or "flag" (one side flops down like a flag waving).

Recording

- check the tape threading carefully; use the threading diagram as necessary. The tape must sit in the grooves around the drum (the drum contains two heads which spin at high speed); get it around the two posts and it will fall into the tape path.

- the tape can only be threaded when the recorder is in the STOP position and OFF. Since the heads spin at high speed they can shear oxide (brown metallic material) off the tape or tear the tape into shreds if you attempt to thread with them moving.

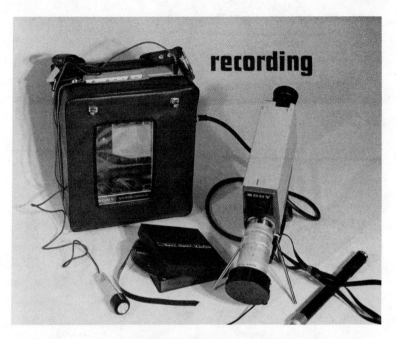

recording

- put the machine into the "play" position (FWD or FOR-
  WARD) and let about 30 seconds of tape run to check that
  the recorder is threaded properly. Set the digital counter
  at "000" and close up the case for use. The counter can
  be used to help indicate how long your batteries will last,
  as well as providing an indexing system for locating segments within the tape.

- to record a picture, hook up the equipment, set the
  CAMERA/TV switch to CAMERA, turn the record lever
  on RECORD and the other lever to FWD. Adjust the
  camera to obtain a clear picture and press the grip switch
  on the camera handle (or the start button).

- the red indicator lamp in the viewfinder indicates the tape
  is running.

- if you didn't get an image in the viewfinder you either
  forgot to remove the lens cap or the batteries are dead.

- the batteries may operate for 45 minutes in warm weather.
  The 45 minutes include the time when the camera and recorder are powered, whether you are recording or not.

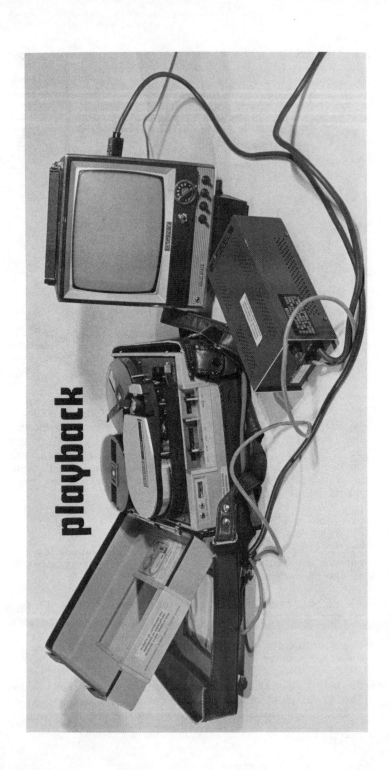

playback

- an auxiliary mike should be used wherever there are traffic sounds or other distracting noises (get it within 12" of the mouth of the person speaking).

- read the instruction manual.

Problems and Solutions

- most operating problems are caused by poor threading or handling.

- keep the tape clean, dry and free of dust and grease (keep it off the floor and keep greasy fingers off).

- any physical damages to the tape should be cut out. Use video splicing tape, or throw away short lengths of tape.

- dropouts show up as snow or "noise" or blips across the screen, and sometimes as static on the audio track.

- a clogged head usually means that there will not be a usable picture. Follow manufacturer's directions for cleaning.

- a crinkled edge on the tape will cause the picture to roll (the sync track is affected).

- pieces from several tapes can be combined onto one tape in a smooth presentation using the SONY AV3650 or a similar machine. Editing is simple and easy if you follow the directions with the machine (SONY has an Editing Guide which summarizes the directions).

- the recorder and camera will not work if the battery is weak--keep it properly charged. (Some people have reported that their battery has a "memory." If it was used for 15 minutes and then recharged, the next time the battery thinks it is only good for 15 minutes and it gets weak after that time. Apparently, the remedy is to fully charge the battery, fully discharge it, and repeat several times. The life of the battery should increase on each discharge.)

- keep the batteries warm in cold weather, and carry a spare set inside your coat to use when the first set is weak (cold weakens batteries quickly).

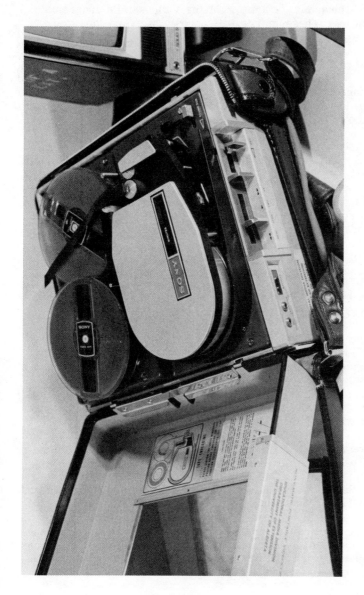

Threading the 1/2" Portable VTR is simple.
Tapes can be replayed on conventional 1/2" recorders as well.

- never point the camera at the sun or other bright light.
  Black burn marks appear on the vidicon tube and remain
  forever. These marks will appear on every tape you
  make thereafter.

- remove a minor burn by turning the camera on and aiming
  it at a well lit but completely blank wall or grey cardboard
  for one or more days. (Leaving the camera aimed at a
  high contrast subject for a long time will also burn the
  vidicon but usually not as badly as the sun.)

- the most fragile part of the camera is the eyepiece; it
  breaks easily if banged or dropped. However, the camera
  will work without it.

- don't put any weight or other pressure on the head cover
  (the circular cover over the spinning heads), as this will
  cause the cover to "pinch" the heads as they revolve.

Maintenance

        Careful maintenance of the recorder will literally add
hundreds of hours of life to your "heads."

- do not improvise head cleaning swabs from cotton batting.
  The manufacturer recommends a swab which is basically
  a piece of chamois glued to a plastic stick. Several types
  of solvent may be used with the swab: video head cleaner,
  film cleaning solvent, alcohol. Let the solvent dry before
  rethreading the tape recorder (most solvents will dissolve
  the oxide off the videotape).

- there are now aerosol cans of video head cleaner which
  can be used while the recorder is running.

- the electrical contacts inside the cover for the video heads
  also require cleaning.

- follow the manufacturer's directions completely for cleaning the heads. The heads themselves are very tiny pieces
  of metal which are easily broken off their supports (and
  are expensive to replace).

- the audio and erase heads also need regular cleaning; use
  the solvent to clean carefully every part that touches the
  tape.

- a cloth dampened in solvent can be used to wipe the deck.

- send more complicated repairs out to the service representative.

Shooting Tips

- don't pan too fast (a pan is a horizontal movement from one side to the other) since the picture will be blurred.

- don't keep zooming in and out like a yo-yo.

- shots from a long distance away do not show very much; get in close to your subject.

- talking heads are not very inspiring; try to include other images.

- do not use the built-in microphone unless you have no other choice, as it usually cannot get close enough to the speaker to be effective.

- edit out unnecessary material before showing it to an audience.

OPERATING 1/2" OR 3/4" HELICAL SCAN VTR's

A video tape recorder (VTR) is a machine which will record the sound and visual portions of a television program for later playback.   The video signal is recorded on a magnetic oxide coated tape as a diagonal track. (Also called a slant track recorder.)

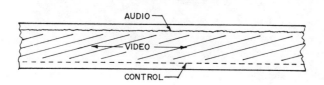

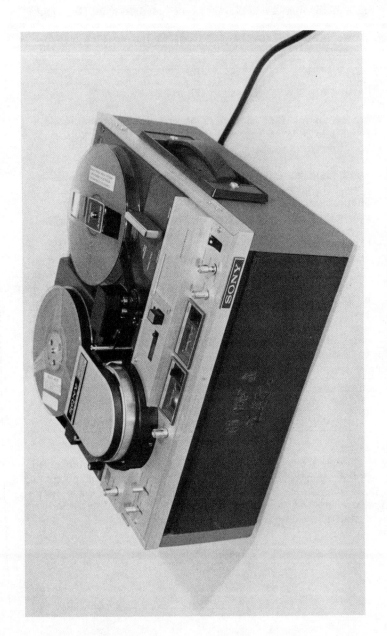

A 1/2" Videotape Recorder with editing capability.

Synchronizing signals are also recorded on the tape to keep the picture steady. (Expensive commercial television recorders use a video track recorded directly across the tape, called Quad or Quadraplex recorders.)

      The most popular helical scan video tape recorders for our use are manufactured to the EIAJ Type 1 standard and use 1/2" magnetic tape on reels.   This article will deal primarily with EIAJ Type 1 equipment, although general information is applicable to all slant track recorders.

NOTE: Prior to the introduction of this standard it was not possible to record a tape on one machine and guarantee playback on another.   While this is still not possible with 1" and 2" recorders, all recent 1/2" recorders use the EIAJ standard, and all 3/4" recorders are compatible.

Auxiliary Equipment

      To use the video recorder you will always need some additional equipment. For recording "live": the VTR, a camera (usually mounted on a tripod), a microphone and a monitor (to see and hear what you are getting on the tape).

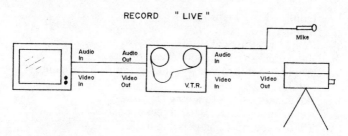

RECORD   " LIVE "

For recording an "off-air" television program (broadcast over a regular TV channel) you need a special television set, the VTR, and possibly a monitor.

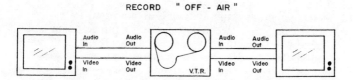

RECORD   " OFF - AIR "

For playback you need only the VTR and a suitably large monitor; if the monitor doesn't have a built-in sound system you will also need an amplifier and speaker.

PLAYBACK

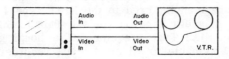

All North American television equipment uses 117-volt AC power and you must plan for sufficient extension cords and outlets to plug everything in.

While most TV cameras and microphones are compatible with helical scan recorders, it would be wise to check that you have the right cords with the correct plugs; that all the necessary adapters, etc., are present. Also check that the equipment you will be using really does work together before you head off into the television sunset. Next, read the instruction manuals again.

VTR Operator's List

1. Inspect for cleanliness.
2. Inspect tape path.
3. Keep tape in container.
4. Keep container closed when empty.
5. Handle reel properly (pick up by hub or center hole).
6. No unnecessary touching of tape.
7. Never mark tape with grease pencil.
8. Take care when rewinding tape.
9. Inspect for scatter winds.
10. Inspect tape reel for smoothness.
11. Do not let ends of tape run through heads.
12. Trim off damaged end of tape.
13. Tab down tape and return to container.
14. Always store tape in vertical position.
15. Stabilize tape (when a tape is received from outside let it return to room temperature). If possible let sit for 24 hours before using.

NOTE: It is virtually impossible to erase a tape acci-
dentally, i.e., near a telephone, television
monitor, etc.

Production Supervisor
Capital Cable TV

Care and Handling of Video Tapes

VTR machines should be clean at all times.
Even when the machine has not been used dust will
collect on the heads and cause dropouts on the
tape.

The tape path should be examined periodically
to ensure that all tape guides are guiding the tape
not pushing it and that the tension is correct. If the
tension is not right you will get "Flag Waving" at the
top of the picture and tape crunching on 3/4" cassettes.

Edge Damage

When a tape has been rewound and you can
see uneven edges of the tape on the take up reel it
is called a "Scatter Wind." A tape should never be
stored in this condition. The best way to avoid this
is when you have finished a recording or viewing a
tape, run it forward until you come to the end of the
reel then rewind the tape completely.

Inspect take up reel for smoothness (chips,
dirt, etc.). Always pick up tape by the hub or center hole. Because of excessive handling the first few
inches of tape become damaged. This should be
trimmed off.

Work areas should be kept clean, air conditioned and humidity controlled--40 to 50 percent. The
temperature should be 20 degrees C. The storage
area should be kept as clean as the working area. No
smoking should be in effect in both areas.

3M Seminar Notes

3/4" Cartridge Machines

The 3/4" cartridge or cassette recorder is the latest style of helical scan recorder. These recorders are capable of recording and playing back color as well as black and white provided you have the right auxiliary equipment (color video cameras, a pre-recorded color tape and a color monitor). Operation is essentially the same as for the 1/2" recorder except that threading is automatically accomplished with the tape cartridge. Because of the automatic threading and accompanying automatic take-up of tape slack it is extremely difficult to stop on a particular frame and/or edit to a specific point with some machines. Since the tape is enclosed it is not possible to manually find an edit point by rolling the tape backwards and forwards as can be done with a reel-to-reel machine. The 3/4" recorder seems to come with a built-in RF adaptor to enable connection to a home TV set (the special video monitors are much more expensive than a home TV set).

Since color cameras are still very expensive most television work is still done in black and white. Many national organizations supposedly provide training materials in color for local use (often business or government agencies) and some 16mm films are available on videotape.

General Operation

The manufacturers have usually done a good job of preparing instruction manuals for their equipment. Obtain the instruction booklets for all of the equipment that you are using, study the procedures, and practice using the equipment until you are confident about your ability to operate and diagnose any difficulties (lost manuals will be replaced by the selling dealer).

- all equipment must be plugged into the correct input and outputs.

- the "camera/line/TV" input selector switch must be correctly set for the input being used.

- the recorder must have the power switch turned ON and have the RECORD button depressed to get a picture on the monitor. Since the tape doesn't need to be moving to do this, you can easily get a preview picture on the monitor.

CAMERA LINE TV Selector and connected equipments

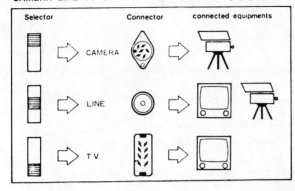

When recording with a microphone, set the selector to CAMERA or LINE.

- keep the RECORD button depressed when switching the function lever into the FORWARD position if you wish to record.

- do not depress the RECORD switch for playback since it will erase the tape.

- the recorder will automatically shut off when the tape runs out (or if a break should occur) but you must put the function lever back to the STOP position before re-threading, otherwise the tape will not be in the proper position.

- a new sound track can be added during playback if you plug in a microphone and press the AUDIO DUB button.

- any kind of "low-impedance" microphone will work with the VTR provided it has the right connector.

- the AUX IN jack can be used to connect a record player, radio or tape recorder into the system (an amplifier or public address system can also be plugged in here, particularly if you are recording in an auditorium which has a built-in P.A. system).

- use a threading diagram and manually advance a couple of inches of tape after you have threaded the machine (the mechanism can get jammed or the heads damaged if the tape is threaded incorrectly).

- always make a short test tape before beginning a recording session.

AV 3400 maintenance

HEAD CLEANING:

1. Set the Videocorder function lever to STOP and allow the rotary video heads to come to a stop.

2. Move the video head (there are two of them inside the 'drum' around which the tape passes) to the cleaning groove by gently pushing the head with the tip of the head cleaner.

3. Carefully hold the edge of the head with your fingertip to keep the head from moving.

4. Saturate the tip of the cleaner with the cleaning fluid (supplied). Press the tip lightly against the head and clean by moving the tip horizontally. *Never move the tip vertically.*

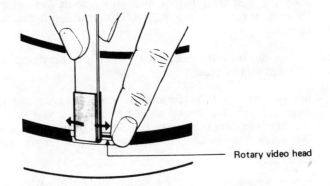

Rotary video head

5. Another head is located at the opposite side of the rotary video head. Rotate the assembly so that the other head faces to the cleaning groove. Repeat cleaning as described above.

6. Clean the stationary audio/control head and erase head in the same manner.

- follow the manufacturer's instructions carefully when cleaning the heads or other parts of the VTR (heads are expensive to replace if you damage one by careless handling). (The heads are the small protrusions which rotate inside the drum-shaped cover on top of the recorder.)

- all levels (brightness, contrast, sound, etc.) are automatically controlled during recording. SKEW and TRACKING controls are only used if the picture is distorted during playback. The monitor controls are used to change the picture brightness, etc., during playback.

- playback on a conventional home television set is possible if the VTR is equipped with an RF modulator (TV transmitter) which is then connected to the antenna terminals on the set.

Common Problems

- don't smoke around a VTR; the ashes will be attracted to the tape and clog the recording heads.

- turn the VOLUME down on the monitor to prevent annoying feedback during recording (noises picked up by the mike are amplified and picked up again and again, causing a loud howl).

- the playback on a new VTR may seem to have a radio playing in the background where none existed during the recording session (check it out because microphones are sensitive). If you are sure that there was no radio on, see your VTR supplier and he can probably fix it (your VTR thinks that it is a radio--electronics are funny sometimes).

- if the picture on playback has a wide horizontal bar running across the whole screen it may be due to the contrasting light values of the subject. A white shirt against a dark suit will cause a grey bar, as the electronics "average" the scene. On manually controlled recorders or with extremely contrasty subjects the image will "tear" (very distracting to the viewer). Wear colored shirts and tone down bright spots by using "dulling" spray or moving the lights (changing the camera aperture will sometimes work if the scene is too bright over all).

- snow is often caused by interference from fluorescent lights. Replace any fluorescent lamps which "flicker" and the snow will usually disappear. Black blips and complete loss of picture are caused by dirty recording heads. Stop the recorder and clean the heads carefully. Let the cleaning fluid evaporate before rethreading.

NOTE: The other handbook articles on television should be consulted for tips on operating cameras and auxiliary equipment.

SINGLE ROOM TELEVISION SYSTEMS

A complex set-up of equipment is not required for
many television applications. A single television camera
mounted on a tripod and connected directly to a television
monitor (TV set) can be used for image magnification or to
allow more people to see a demonstration. The same camera can be attached to several TV monitors for large group
viewing. If necessary, a P.A. system can be used to amplify the speaker's voice. This system can also be used to
provide programming simultaneously to several rooms. A
videotape recorder (VTR) can be added to record the program for later use or to play back a prerecorded tape.
(See also the other articles in this chapter.)

Hook-Up

As you can see from the following diagrams, the
physical linkage of the equipment is simple. The image is
picked up by a camera (the lens is "video in"), processed
by the camera and sent out ("video out," sometimes marked
as "VTR") to the monitor or video tape recorder ("video
in," sometimes marked as "camera"); if the video tape recorder is used (or several monitors are linked together) the
signal goes out the "video out" terminal and into the "video
in" of the next unit.

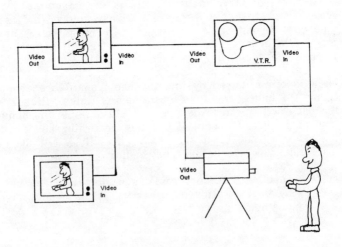

- the sound system works in a similar manner.

- connections are usually made with screw connectors or multi-pin plugs.

- make sure that the output switch on the camera is set for the correct output terminal ("VTR," "VHF," or "RF").

- make sure that the input switch on the VTR or monitor is set for the correct input terminal ("camera" or "monitor").

- input switches on monitors need to be switched for "external" when not showing off-air programs (internal).

- every piece of equipment will have to be plugged into a 117V outlet; most also have an ON-OFF switch.

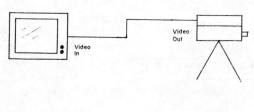

ONE   MONITOR - ONE   CAMERA

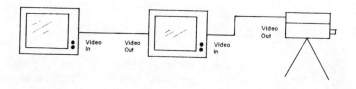

TWO   MONITORS - ONE   CAMERA

- read the instruction manual before operating the video tape recorder.

- many of the cords used are similar; check that they have the correct connectors.

- monitors which have provisions for "video out" usually require a load or resistance on the output to prevent "snow."
If there is no switch for an internal load a special ter-
minator may be made up by your equipment supplier to
be screwed onto the "video out."

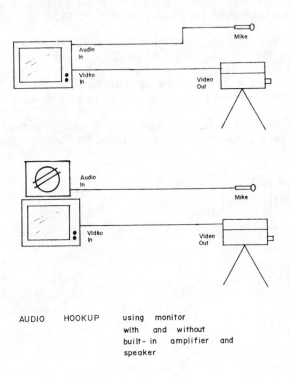

AUDIO   HOOKUP   using   monitor
                  with   and without
                  built- in   amplifier   and
                  speaker

Camera Operation

- most cameras have an OFF-STANDBY-ON switch.   Use
the STANDBY switch to keep the camera in readiness for
picture taking; turn the camera ON when you are actually
taking a picture.

- do not point the camera at bright lights or directly down.
Both actions will cause permanent black marks on the
picture.

- focusing, zooming and setting the light level are all accomplished by moving parts of the lens.   Practice until

you know how to do this.   (Work indoors will require an
aperture setting of about f4 or f5. 6; outdoors will require
about f16.)

- extra light on the subject is always useful.

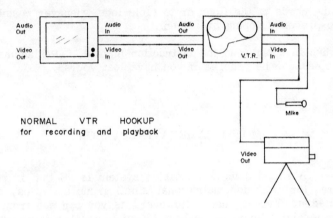

NORMAL   VTR   HOOKUP
for   recording   and   playback

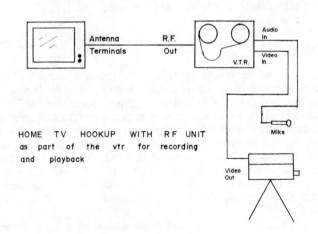

HOME   TV   HOOKUP   WITH   R F   UNIT
as   part   of   the   vtr   for   recording
and   playback

Maintenance

- keep all equipment clean and dust free (cover equipment with a dust cover when not in use).

- use photographic lens tissue and cleaner for the camera lens.

- tape cords to the floor or to table legs whenever possible to prevent tripping over them.

- when in doubt read the instruction manual. (Replacement copies can be ordered if you have lost yours.)

MULTI-CAMERA TELEVISION

A single camera television system is all that is required for most demonstrations, small group activities, or immediate feedback use. However, as you can see from commercial television, several visual inputs can improve more elaborate presentations by offering a different viewpoint, by allowing two or more images to be viewed simultaneously, or by allowing for the insertion of other types of visuals (slides, films, photographs, etc.).

Camera Switching

In the simplest form two or more cameras can be linked together with simple double-pole, double-throw switches for camera selection. This "switcher" will cost about $2.00 home-made; commercial mechanical switchers will cost about $50.00. There will almost always be a short (or sometimes long) period of picture flip (the picture is all messed up and seems to roll up or down) as the cameras are switched on a tape playback. There will not be any roll if you are using more sophisticated equipment (which may include "sync" generators).

One of the most useful functions of a more complex switcher is to allow you to fade/dissolve smoothly from one picture to another or to superimpose one image on top of the other (for adding captions, titles, etc.). Several

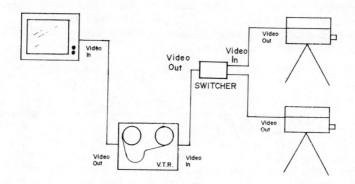

manufacturers make a reasonably inexpensive (about $750) switcher-fader which will work with matched cameras (these generally have to be the same model and manufacturer).

A problem of using several cameras is to balance their picture contrast so that they all have equal contrast. This will have to be done by changing individual camera

apertures or by carefully regulating the "video level" control on the VTR.   Pictures which do not have similar contrasts will be difficult to watch and will cause recording/playback problems (more complex systems use an oscilliscope to balance the images).

Film Chains

A television camera can be focused on a still picture (mounted on cardboard if possible) or on a slide or film image projected on a wall or rear projection screen.   This is the simplest way of adding such images.   Films may have a black bar which slowly moves across the picture since the film and TV image may be out of synchronization; this is satisfactory for in-house operation (not usable on broadcast TV).

Flat pictures will need supplemental lights (mount lamps about 18 inches away on either side of the picture so that there are no reflections) and if mounted on cardboard several pictures can be stacked on the easel and dropped forward to change pictures (a three ring binder will work as an easel with punched cardboard).

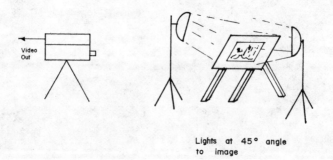

Lights at 45° angle
to image

Commercial "multi-plexers" are machines that allow several film slide images to be focused into one camera for more professional inclusion of supplementary images.   These machines often cost several thousand dollars and of course require their own separate room and a technician for operation.   Special film projectors (both **16**mm and Super 8mm) overcome the synchronization problems mentioned earlier.

Special Effects Generators

A special effects generator is a high status appeal unit which enables two pictures to be seen on the screen at one time.   It is the unit which produces split-screen effects, "wipes," etc., on commercial television (similar effects on film are usually produced in the film laboratory).

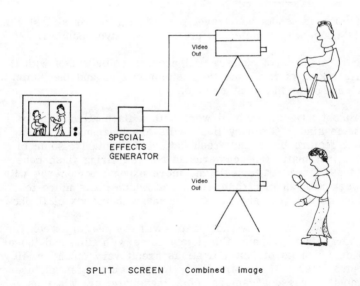

SPLIT   SCREEN   Combined   image

In my experience, non-professional television operations can survive without a special effects generator (in actual fact, so do many smaller commercial stations), although a switcher/fader is very useful (at least one manufacturer includes a special effects generator in their basic switcher/fader, since both need an internal "sync" generator unit).

CHOOSING A STILL CAMERA

There are almost as many kinds of cameras as there are people, and if one reads the manufacturer's literature or listens to a camera enthusiast, it seems as though each camera is the best in the world for your needs. In this article I have first considered the basic steps that everyone should follow in selecting a camera from among the glittering array of models, then the needs of more specialized photographers. The glossary contains some of the terms the camera buyer will find useful.

I: Identify Your Needs

One, what kind of photographs will you be taking?

- family snapshots and travel pictures (prints or slides) can be taken with simple box or instamatic type camera.

- several sizes of camera will produce color slides with the right kind of film, but the instamatic type and the 35mm camera are the most common.

- almost any camera will work with a flash attachment of some kind. Ordinary flash units are inexpensive to buy but require bulbs and fresh batteries regularly; some of the instamatic type cameras use a self-firing flash cube (doesn't need batteries); and more expensive cameras will work with an electronic flash unit which costs more to buy initially but should last for many thousands of flashes.

Two, how many photographs will you take in a week, or a month? Photographic film deteriorates with time and those wonderful shots of last Christmas aren't very much fun 10 months later. If you are likely to take only a few pictures a month, choose a camera (box, instamatic or twin lens reflex) that uses rolls with only 8 or 12 exposures. Since a 35mm camera uses rolls of 20 and 36 exposures (unless you load your own) it would probably take several months for you to finish the roll and get your photographs returned from the processor (the other alternative is to shoot only part of a roll and send it in for processing, wasting the rest of the roll).

Three, how much do you want to spend on a

camera? Cameras designed for small children cost as little
as $1.50. They actually work and are a very good invest-
ment for a beginning photography class. Snapshot cameras
run from about $20.00 to $100.00, including most of the
instamatic types and many of the instant developing (Polaroid) models. (Kids like Polaroid cameras because they can
see what they took immediately.) Basic 35mm cameras
(non-interchangeable lenses and range finder types) are included in this price range.

Single lens reflex cameras and twin lens reflex
cameras begin at about $80.00 and run upwards of $500.00.
Most single lens reflex cameras are in the popular 35mm
size and twin lens reflex cameras are usually 2-1/4" square.
View cameras begin about $200.00 and range upwards, as
do such professional types as the 2-1/4" single lens re-
flexes.

Generally speaking, you get what you pay for when
you buy a camera, although the more expensive camera may
not be better than a similar but less expensive model. Because of differences in national wage scales it is usually
cheaper to buy an imported camera than a North American
manufactured one of the same type. Most U.S. camera
companies, however, already import the camera with their
own label. Asian cameras (chiefly Japanese) will normally
be less expensive than European cameras. Quality is a
function of price nonetheless, and provided the more expensive camera has the same features (without a lot of added
frills or gadgets) it will probably be a better buy. Remember that repair costs also affect your real camera price,
so choose a camera from a reputable dealer and check the
leading camera magazines and Consumer's Reports for current tests and ease of repair data.

The fourth factor in buying a camera is your own
personality and taste. Try several cameras before buying
if possible and talk to owners of each kind.

- get the feel of the camera. Does it fit your hands? Is
  is too heavy? Too light? Does the camera look good?
  Can you carry it easily?

- try out some film. Does it load easily? Can you focus
  and frame the picture easily? Does the camera feel right
  when taking pictures?

- will the camera take the kind of pictures that you will
  primarily be shooting?

- do you really need all of the extras that add so much
  more money (self-timer, 1/1000th of a second, black
  body, fl. 4 lens, etc.)?

There is no sense getting a complicated camera if
you have only a casual interest in photography. Admittedly,
some cameras do not seem to allow much scope to expand
if you become more interested, but you can always sell or
give the camera away to another beginner, and if you are
willing to experiment you will find your simple camera very
versatile.

Regardless of your decision, you should eventually
settle on a camera which you know is ideally suited to your
needs and your pocketbook. Now comes the important part--
PRACTICE. You will never take decent pictures without
practice, no matter how good your camera is! The least
expensive camera made can take excellent photos if its
owner knows how to use it. Buy some film and experiment;
shoot pictures and evaluate the results until you feel confident in your ability to handle your camera.

Second Hand Cameras: Many good deals can be made
by purchasing a used camera. The criteria for such a camera are the same as for a new camera, plus a check to insure that the camera hasn't been abused and is in good
shape. Steer clear of cameras which have loose backs,
dents or excessively worn finish. If possible, take your
choice to a competent repair shop and get their advice or
else shoot a roll of film to test the camera before purchasing it.

II: Beyond the Basics

Special Needs:

Nature photography (animals, birds, etc.) will require a camera which will accept long focus (telephoto--like
a telescope) lenses, and will have a fairly fast speed to
stop action (1/500th of a second is quite adequate). A tripod mount will also be essential.

Close-up photography (flowers, copying still pictures,
micro-photography, etc.) will necessitate your choosing a

camera which will accept special close-up lenses and adapters. As well, you need to be able to frame your subject
accurately. While any camera can be converted to do this
kind of photography if you are willing to accept some incon-
veniences, the usual camera for this work will be a single
lens reflex type.

Sports photography will require a camera capable of
stopping fast action (maybe as high as 1/1000th of a second),
although you can "pan with the action" or catch the action
when it is stopped (a trapeze artist is stationary at the top
of his flip) with an ordinary camera.

Architectural photographers generally need a camera
with a tiltable lens board to correct for perspective problems
(uncorrected, a tall building appears to be tilting away from
the camera). This is generally a view camera.

Photographs for publications sometimes require large
negatives to produce acceptable results (generally 2-1/4"
square or larger). General purpose publications can use
35mm negatives but cover shots, fashion photos, etc. will
often require larger formats.

Anthropological, ecological, legal and other special
photography may require small, inconspicuous cameras.
Spies are not the only people who take pictures of people in
informal or candid settings. A large, noisy camera may
intrude on the physical setting even when permission has
been obtained for the picture taking.

Social action photography, where the picture taking
is part of the process of group identification or improving
communication skills can make good use of the instant developing cameras. Previously Polaroid was the only manufacturer, however today several manufacturers make both
cameras and film. Unfortunately such film is not widely
available outside of large urban centers.

Many varieties of film are only made for 35mm and
professional cameras. While most photographers will never
have a need to use infrared or other exotic films, the ex-
perimenter or photographic artist may desire this capability.

Accessories:

Often the purchase of a camera will be only the first

step towards a considerable collection of photographic apparatus. After all, you need a carrying bag and a tripod, a light meter and some filters, perhaps a second or a third lens ... the list is endless. Just remember to stop and carefully evaluate every prospective purchase.

- do you really need it? will you use it?

- is this model the best value for the money? (Much of the equipment sold through department and drugstore camera counters is not designed for heavy duty use.)

- is there something else that will do the job better, or can you do the job with existing equipment and a little ingenuity?

DON'T BUY ANY EQUIPMENT UNLESS YOU HAVE A CLEAR NEED FOR IT AND YOU HAVE EVALUATED ALL OF YOUR POSSIBLE CHOICES TO ENSURE THAT THE EQUIPMENT REPRESENTS YOUR BEST BUY.

SIMPLE TAPE-SLIDE SETS

One of the easiest and most economical ways of obtaining a visualized instruction set or demonstration is through the use of slides and tape-recorded commentary. Today we have a wide variety of means of producing slides in color or black and white: a simple Instamatic type camera will prepare quite acceptable slides (and can even do close-ups with the proper attachments), but more experienced photographers will probably choose a more expensive 35mm camera. The narration and sound effects can be prepared on either a reel-to-reel or a cassette recorder (monaural or stereo). Using a single projector and one tape recorder for playback we have a package of equipment that is simple to operate and very dependable. Unfortunately many of the demonstrations or lessons prepared to utilize this equipment lack planning, originality and organization. This shows up most crucially in the lack of continuity from beginning to end of the tape-slide set, and in that most sets are too long to maintain interest.

Before Starting

For a discussion of the planning process refer to the section on planning (Chapter 2). This process is similar regardless of the medium that you choose for presentation of your message.

To summarize the planning process you should remember that the best sets are not prepared by taking all of the slides (or even the best slides) that you have, arranging them in order, and preparing a commentary for them. You must define your topic and its audience, plan your basic script (visuals and commentary), then obtain slides that fit the script (either from your files or by original photography) and tape the narration. If your basic idea was sound and if you ironed out the bugs of continuity and conciseness before shooting, you can develop a good tape-slide set. But keep it short!

Photography

It is better to use nothing than to use poor slides or other materials. Poor or questionable photographs (out-of-focus, under-exposed, poor taste, badly composed, off-color, etc.) have no place in a slide series. (Under-exposed photos are too light; over-exposed photos are too dark.) Retake them if necessary until all of the slides are of a consistent high quality (this is doubly important if you want to get duplicate copies made of the set). Most color reversal films (the Kodachromes, the Ektachromes, GAF color film, and others) will provide good quality reproduction for screening or duplication. Your choice of film will probably depend upon personal taste or availability of film and processing in your area (most cut price films are not a bargain), and best results will come once you know enough about a particular film so that you will be able to predict its results in any circumstance (this just takes practice). All of the film manufacturers provide instruction sheets inside the film boxes and some of them have extensive reference materials to explain the creative and technical use of their products.

- Ektachrome High Speed, Kodachrome-X, GAF 200 and GAF 500 will allow you more latitude when you are shooting under low light levels (in the shade or indoors).

- Kodachrome films are balanced toward the red end

of the spectrum, and seem to favor the reds and bright colors of your subjects (Kodachrome-X works very well for circus pictures and other occasions where the colors are garish). Ektachrome is balanced toward the blue-green colors and favors them. GAF films have a more pastel effect, as do some of the European films.

- remember that outdoor films will look yellow when used indoors. Use "tungsten" film or the proper filter for interior work under artificial lighting (fluorescent lights have a variety of colors, some of which cause the photographs to appear purple).

- switching back and forth from horizontal to vertical photographs in a series can sometimes be distracting (particularly if you are using a horizontal screen and the vertical photograph will not fit).

- even a simple snapshot camera can take decent photographs if the photographer uses some common sense and takes advantage of the accessories available for special types of shots (such as close-up work).

- above all else, keep your presentation short. Some (indeed many) topics or demonstrations could be accomplished with twenty slides and five to seven minutes of narration. Between thirty and fifty slides will probably be enough to exhaust any topic (don't take more than fifteen to twenty minutes to present them). A short series will induce your audience to return a second time; a long series will merely produce boredom and groans the next time a tape-slide set is mentioned.

NOTE: If all of your slides are horizontals and the subject is such that the context will not change for a reasonable length of time, you might consider having the slides converted into a filmstrip. A filmstrip is a 35mm wide length of film containing all of the visuals in sequence and has two advantages: first, it is reasonably inexpensive to provide multiple copies; and second, it is easy to use since the images cannot get out of order, lost or jammed. Obviously its inflexibility is its biggest disadvantage. Filmstrips can be prepared locally using a "half-frame" camera and copy attachments, or by professional audio-visual laboratories.

A presentation will only be successful if the materials
are inspected, and poor or misleading slides rejected.

Titles

     Titles are most effective if they are colorful and neat (this applies to all kinds of artwork: charts, graphs, diagrams, etc.). Lettering should be as large as possible, keeping the number of words quite short (five lines of five average words is a maximum). Signs, lettering on the chalkboard, press-on lettering, and large letters laid out on the sidewalk or lawn can all be effective.

> NOTE: If you can hold the completed 2" x 2" slides up to a light and read them without a magnifying glass, people in the back row can probably read them on the screen.

Commentary

     Keep the commentary short and concise (see above). Do not repeat yourself endlessly; leave the listener free to follow the visuals as much as possible. Explaining a process or step may be necessary, but ten minutes on one slide is not.

- background music at the start and end of the tape is a good means of providing a cue to your audience that you are about to begin, and later a signal that the presentation is over. Authentic sound effects can be used to advantage to provide realism but should be used with caution.

- a harmonious bell, a waterglass "ping" or an electronic "beep" are all means of indicating the time for the projectionist to change slides; special sounds such as an automobile horn or a dog's bark should not be used as the novelty effect soon wears off. Alternatively, soundless electronic change cues can be used provided the specialized equipment needed will always be available. (See the following article on Multi-Media Presentations for a discussion of more complex presentations and electronic controls.) The important idea here is to keep the tape and slides together, since few things are more frustrating than a projectionist who is either one slide ahead or one slide behind the narration.

- obtain someone who is used to public speaking or reading out loud to do your narration on tape (a poorly read

Correlating slides and music is an important part of producing a tape-slide presentation.

narration will put everyone to sleep). A well modulated voice, free from distracting accents or slurring, will make listening more enjoyable.

- rather than using a narration, why not compose a musical or sound effect track to accompany the set--inspiration, motivational, etc.? Many visual messages require no words to explain them.

- if your audience is composed of people who speak more than one language, it would be most advisable to prepare a narration in each language.

- if the commentary is to be provided live, it is important to have a well-rehearsed script (and a reading light).

Presentation

Once the set has been completed, check it again for continuity, conciseness, clarity and good technical quality. Arrange the slides in the projection tray (check to insure that they are all in the right order and right side up) and set up your equipment. Keep a spare projection lamp and a flashlight on hand in case of trouble and you're ready. The applause will be gratifying and the instructional benefits considerable from your well prepared tape-slide set.

MULTI-MEDIA PRESENTATIONS

Multi-media is a much overused term today, and it is little understood. This article will try to sort out the possibilities and the problems of a multi-media approach.

First, what are we talking about? Many communicators and media personnel are finding that a variety of media may be necessary to best convey the intended message and to involve the viewer. Any presentation using more than one medium of communication (sight, sound, taste, smell, etc.) and/or more than one presentation medium (slides, film, audiotapes, television, etc.) can properly be termed a multi-media presentation. We also use the term to describe multiple screen presentations where several images

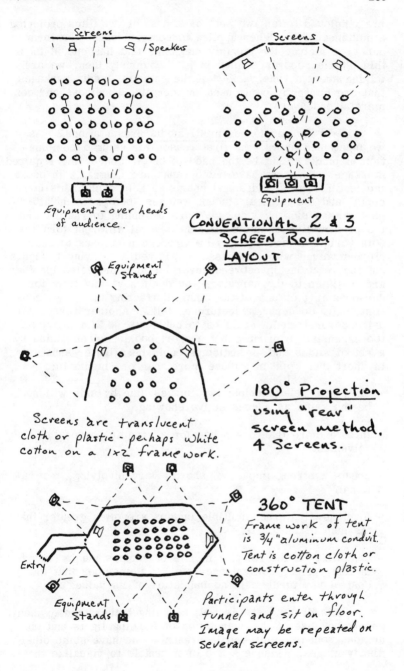

Screens / Speakers

Equipment - over heads of audience.

Screens

Equipment

CONVENTIONAL 2 & 3 SCREEN ROOM LAYOUT

Equipment Stands

Screens are translucent cloth or plastic - perhaps white cotton on a 1×2 framework.

180° Projection using "rear" screen method. 4 Screens.

360° TENT

Framework of tent is 3/4" aluminum conduit. Tent is cotton cloth or construction plastic.

Entry

Equipment Stands

Participants enter through tunnel and sit on floor. Image may be repeated on several screens.

are employed (often two sets of slides, or two films projected simultaneously).   When applied to common usage the term can even include the monthly magazine that has one of those thin plastic records stapled in it.   Obviously then, we are talking about a wide variety of the potential media packages that are currently being used in education, business and commercial endeavors.

Why do people use multi-media presentations?   As we mentioned above, the first reason for using a combination of media might be the need to better convey the required message.   Thus we have photographs and diagrams in books, the lecturer uses slides and charts to help explain his concepts, and the medical student watches "before" and "after" photographs side by side.   We are beginning to realize that the presentation of information in several different forms, with variations and changes provided, can help us to become more involved with the message.   If you are trying to figure out the relationship between several slides projected together and to listen to the narrator, you don't have any time for day-dreaming or any of the other distracting things we conventionally do during a lecture or talk.   Another reason for using several media could be to cut costs; a film might be too expensive to produce but a short booklet accompanied by a set of slides and an audiotape could be a better substitute. In short then, you might use more than one media to:

- show new relationships; two images side by side will not be the same as a consecutive showing.

- involve more than one sense for a greater personal involvement.

- create a strong impact (if short), very involving, motivational.

- form new patterns; multiple images are often greater than the sum of the parts.

- capitalize on the relative merits of various media (sound, motion, price, convenience, etc.).   Remember that the cost of any medium is no indication of its value.

Disadvantages: As well as being bothersome to many people because of the connotation of flashing lights and obnoxious sounds, multi-media presentations have some other disadvantages.   Planners are often unable to visualize the

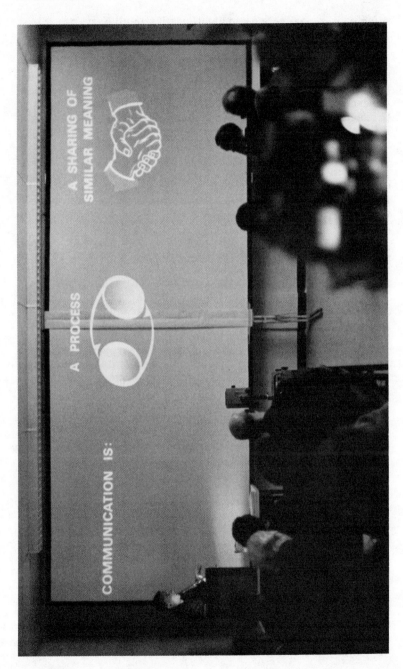

effects of a particular combination of stimuli (say two slides and some music) without actually viewing the combination. This inability to visualize the results can cause time-consuming and costly delays in production (or else an improperly tested production that will bomb). Combining several media in a public presentation requires equipment that will operate dependably and can be easily moved. Unfortunately, the presentations that I have participated in required up to eight slide projectors, two tape recorders, several electrical control devices, three film projectors, six screens and four multi-armed paperhangers to run the whole mess. If you set out to overcome this equipment problem you run into quite considerable costs (anybody who has seen the Ontario government's A Place to Stand or similar films will agree that it is sometimes worth the cost).

Simple systems: If all presentations were as complex as the ones described above you might soon have to admit defeat and go back to your home movies. A couple of simple examples should however convince you of their benefits:

1. A history class is studying the changes that have occurred along the French/German border from 1812 to the present time. A map of contemporary Europe is projected on a screen while changes are projected on a second screen beside it. The students also have copies of the maps to retain for future reference.

2. An art group is studying the technique of silk screen printing on cloth. There are several samples at various stages of completion hung on the workroom walls, and the group is looking at a series of short Super 8mm loop films demonstrating the process while they attempt the steps on their own materials.

3. Two students in a sociology class prepare a slide/16mm film/audio-tape/overhead projector presentation complete with live costumed guests to illustrate the living conditions on a nearby Indian reserve. They have taken all the film and photographs themselves and spent a total of about $100.00 for their 15-minute display.

Electronic controls: One of the biggest difficulties with operating a multi-media presentation is to keep the materials in the proper order and synchronization. In many cases several individuals are used to act as human "programmers" to change slides, turn equipment on and off, etc.;

PREPARING A VERY LARGE SCREEN

in other cases electronics have taken over.   Punched paper
tape may be used to drive a controller for several machines,
and is very similar to automatic letter-writing typewriter
systems.   In the same way computer tapes can be used (at
enormous expense).   A more common solution is to use a
stereo tape recorder, record the audio (sounds that you want
the audience to hear) on one track and record control signals
which the audience will not hear on the other track.   Kodak
makes a simple unit that will control one projector using this
principle (Carousel Sound Synchronizer) and several recorder
manufacturers make complete units (e.g., Wollensak or Sony
cassette recorders with slide control) that do not require any
additional hardware.   Also in the simple category are the
various systems that apply an inaudible tone to any tape recording that will control the projectors (careful ... sometimes musical tones will actuate the mechanism).   More complex systems are also available and can run into the hundreds
and thousands of dollars to control a wide range of equipment
or functions (two slide projectors can operate so that one
picture dissolves into the next automatically ... costing at
least $500).   General Motors may be able to afford $100,000
for a single multi-media presentation but the rest of us
should try and accomplish the same results using less expensive means.

Design Tips (especially when using human programmers):

- develop a script with times that indicate when various
  equipment goes on and off, what materials appear when.

- have at least one rehearsal, remember that you will be
  working in semi-darkness, agree on who will be in charge,
  what signals will be used between operators, and what the
  group (and the program) will do in the event of trouble (a
  projector lamp burns out, circuit breaker pops, etc.).
  Are you going to stop the show or will you go on and fly
  by the seat of your pants?

- the standard room arrangement with a screen at the front
  and all the chairs facing forward may not be the best arrangement.   Try out various arrangements.

- keep the presentation short, preferably several short segments with breaks between for a total of twenty minutes
  maximum.

- keep the narration short and relevant.

- if part of the program is going to be very loud (noise, gunfire, etc.), try also building in some quiet time for contrast and to allow the participants to recover and reflect upon the experience.

- always follow up the program with some kind of opportunity to discuss or question.

- check out the visuals ... a dark slide will be impossible to see if it is shown at the same time as a very bright slide.

- try smells, hand things around for the participants to feel.

- keep the picture sizes similar unless you are trying to create something special (a large slide on the screen at the same time as a small one will overshadow the smaller).

- visuals and sounds should work together to produce the desired effect. Soft music and pastoral slides combine to relax the viewer but the same music with a sequence of slides showing an industrial process may be confusing.

- coordinate slide changes so that they are logical, and so that you are looking at the correct visual for the narration.

Operating Tips:

- make sure that you have adequate power supplies, check out the location of fuse panels, circuit breakers, and light switches.

- plan for plenty of time to set up and test your equipment.

- rehearse.

- have a flashlight, spare power cords, spare projection lamps, three-way plugs, tape for fastening down cords, projection stands or tables, screens or sheets.

- make sure that all projectors are shooting over the heads of the audience.

- check out the sound levels with the equipment running (it is very hard to judge sound levels when you are in the midst of a pile of equipment with their distracting noises).

DISPLAYS AND EXHIBITIONS

Displays and exhibitions often use only print materials, although they certainly do not need to do so. Some of the displays that I have helped design have had a variety of purposes and content:

- a photographic exhibition to illustrate a manufacturing technique. Special emphasis was on the people involved in the craft industry. The display used large (8" x 10" to 20" x 24") photographic prints mounted on cardboard. The photographs were hung with strings from the ceiling of the display room or fastened to a cloth covered display board.

- an exhibition of a model building technique. The model railroaders involved in this display built a 4-foot long diorama which illustrated the step by step procedure for its construction. One end was bare wood, the other finished diorama with each "foot" of display progressively showing the construction. Neat hand lettered signs completed the display.

- an educational "walk around" and "sit in" display. Cardboard boxes were painted bright colors and stacked on coffee tables in a lounge to provide the support for the visuals. Visuals were photographs, photographic blow-ups of magazine articles, montages, cutouts from magazines and hand-lettered statements. The boxes were obtained from a "recycle" dealer and were painted with a roller and latex paint.

- a more permanent display was constructed of hollow core wooden doors hinged together to stand on their own. Degrade and rejected doors were used, painted and covered with exhibition materials. Enamel paint made a smooth enough surface that rubber cement could be used for mounting photographs and posters. Press-on lettering was used for verbal material. Everything was removable for re-use of the display stands. Hinge pins were removable for disassembly.

- 1x2 or 1x4 lumber can be framed into display stands and covered with pegboard, masonite, plywood, chipboard, cardboard, or cloth. As with the doors above, hinges join the units for standing. Braces are sometimes needed to provide rigidity. Display materials can be pinned, glued,

screwed, etc., to the display depending upon the type of
covering used.

- Foam core art board or corrugated cardboard can have
  photographs or other materials mounted on one or both
  faces. Use "dry-mount" tissue, available at any good
  photographic store, double-sided tape, or rubber cement
  for mounting. The completed "boards" are light enough
  to be suspended from the ceiling with heavy thread.

     The cost of a display will obviously vary depending
upon the materials selected for the framework and upon the
materials being displayed. A display should attract attention,
provide information or motivation and follow-up details (name
and phone number, etc. for further information). Displays
should be brightly colored and well-lighted. A dark dingy
display will not attract any interest. Handout materials at
a display are often a waste of money, everyone automatically
picks up a copy and then throws it away. Perhaps it would
be better to emphasize how to obtain further information.
Lettering should be large and easy to read.

- keep the display neat and uncluttered.

- keep the display in good repair, fixing any loose corners,
  etc., immediately.

- displays should be touchable, people will always touch.
  Cover fragile materials with plexiglass.

- displays for children must be set close to the floor, and
  should have more touchable or moveable components.

- set the display "eye-level" for an adult at about 4'8" to
  5'2" rather than the 6'0" eye-level of the guys assembling
  the display.

- the best displays are self-explanatory, they do not need
  an attendant.

- slides, films, music, etc., can provide a good addition to
  a display but require a constant operator.

Displays:

- Hollow core doors, hinged, removable pins.
- Paint bright colors, cheap, attractive.
- Self standing, re-usable.
- Large letters, clean & uncluttered.
- Phone number for follow-up.

- Similar unit constructed of 1×2 or 1×4 lumber (laid flat).
- Cover with pegboard, masonite, cardboard, cotton, etc.
- hinge units as above.

Displays:

- Cardboard boxes: painted, lettered, stacked.
- Glue visuals to box sides.
- Hang mobiles and mounted visuals
        from ceiling.

Triangular shelf
fastens to hinged units
to display books, artifacts,
etc. Vertical faces
are still available for
other materials.

Two pieces of card
join to form stand.

Mount visuals
on cardboard
or foam core
board & cut.

6 INTERACTION TECHNIQUES

STREET THEATRE: A TOOL FOR ACTION

One of the strongest means of involving people emotionally is through the use of street or improvised theatre. While most people do not ordinarily attend "the theatre," they do recognize and easily identify with short skits or dramatizations. Audience participation can be encouraged and since street theatre does not involve props or sets it can take place in almost any location.

Planning

As with any type of media you should start by identifying the message you wish to communicate, the audience you wish to reach and, just as important, how and when you will present the play.

- a small group of people (4-8 total) can plan and organize the theatre; ideas should be thrown into the pot for discussion and you should attempt to actually "walk-through" ideas before discarding any that seem impractical.

- get as much information about the topic as possible.

- keep the message simple.

- use actions rather than words; pantomime and "charade" techniques can be used with amateur actors to eliminate the need to talk too much.

- forget about using elaborate props and sets; instead, use simple means of identification for the actors (such as white painted faces, colored scarves, or distinctive hats) and pantomime appropriate actions to suggest the props you don't have (an actor doesn't need an axe to portray the cutting down of a tree).

- as on the silent screen you may need to exaggerate actions and facial expressions to make them meaningful.

302

- practice the play, showing it to your friends for constructive criticism and improvement (it is very easy to contra-
  dict yourself in a play and only the audience will be aware
  of it).

- remember your audience; for maximum effect, keep it
  humorous, <u>short</u> and relevant to their lives.

Scripts

The first plays you attempt and plays that are going
to be given several times probably need scripts that provide
dialogue, actions and timing. With practice, however,
troupes should be able to perform plays with only a bare outline of actions and an indication of the type of dialogue required. Each actor will then do his part to contribute to the
overall effect and will be responsible for maintaining pacing
and improvising his own lines. It is essential, however, to
have identified the actors who will perform the key roles and
in what sequence. The other actors will take their cues
from these high points. Improvisations will probably be most
effective when the members of the theatre troupe know each
other well.

The Performance

Street theatre can be performed anywhere--on the
streets; at shopping malls; in coffee houses, churches, offices or at meetings--anywhere that your particular audience
may congregate.

- ordinarily you should try to surprise your audience. Posters and other forms of advance notice lessen the shock
  value of your play and allow people to tune out your message (often by not showing up).

- interruptions to planned events are very effective; you have
  a captive audience to whom your play is both a surprise
  and a break from the routine (often you can make advance
  arrangements with the organizers to interrupt at a prearranged time or as you find it appropriate. This avoids
  completely disorienting the coordinator of an event you are
  trying to support).

- move quickly, steal everyone's attention, get the action

over with and disappear. While leaflets amplifying your
position or someone passing the hat to finance your cause
are effective follow-ups to the play, the actors should not
stay around as a focus of attention. Discussion of your
ideas will not take place while the audience is watching
you.

- use megaphones, portable PA systems, or tape recorders
  to amplify your voice or to provide sound effects if necessary, but generally theatre is more effective if it is inti-
  mate. This means using words as little as possible and
  learning how to project your voices.

- bright colors and large graphics (signs or posters) attract
  attention.

- use the language of your audience, remembering that words
  are not the only language we use.

- build in a role for the audience to help them get involved.
  The cast might ask the audience to answer a question
  (something they can answer en masse) or to perform an
  action such as clapping in time to a song. Members of
  the audience could also be given specific roles provided
  they are simple or repetitive.

- satire is an effective technique but do not ridicule or insult your audience (this turns them off to your message),
  and keep it simple.

- poetry reading or a song can be combined with actors'
  pantomiming the action.

- don't use special lighting--this isolates the audience and
  makes them viewers rather than participants. Likewise
  try to avoid formal stages. Steps or a couple of tables
  pushed together will serve to elevate you if required and
  also keep you close.

Working on the Street

     Perhaps the most difficult form of theatre occurs
when you actually work "on the street." Here you are exposed to many kinds of unplanned distractions and possible
reactions.

- theatre on the street must be short and simple; the audience doesn't wait around.

- pedestrians have a "right of passage." Do not totally block the street or sidewalk.

- some communities require permits for demonstrations on the streets. If you decide to ignore the permit you must be prepared to accept the consequences, including the possibility of fines or jail terms.

- be familiar with local laws so that you and your troupe are aware of the various activities that you can be arrested for doing.

- practice on the streets to get the feel of working outdoors.

- the troupe must be disciplined in terms of its responses, particularly when working on the street or when disrupting events (concerts, meetings, restaurants, courtrooms, etc.). Don't get emotionally involved (have a prearranged escape plan). Keep cool.

- remember you can't choose your audience on the street.

Try It

Street theatre has been found effective at transmitting messages and for arousing interest. In particular, it has been used to facilitate social action (often called guerilla theatre when performed in conjunction with sit-ins, peace marches, etc.) and to motivate people to action.

The techniques are easy and skill improves with practice provided you critically evaluate your own performance. You can't expect to be polished actors on your first attempt and audiences may be critical. However, your real task is to present a message, simply and with enthusiasm. Adapt other people's ideas and constantly look for situations to exploit through your drama.

USING ROLE PLAY IN GROUP DISCUSSIONS

It is sometimes quite difficult to initiate a good discussion with a group, especially if the group members either
do not know each other or know each other too well (as in
an office or voluntary organization with a lot of interpersonal
conflicts). Role playing is a technique to get the group discussing a particular topic.

Role Play is a learning activity where two or more
people act out prepared "roles" or "parts." The "audience"
is usually a small discussion group which uses the player's
(actor's) performance as the topic of their discussion. The
players are normally members of the discussion group who
have been selected or volunteered to act out the roles. Note
that in a skit or play the actors are given the exact dialogue
that they will use. In a role play the players are usually
given very general directions about what they should do.
They make up their own dialogue as they go along. The
players normally do not use costumes, make-up or props.

1. Prepare written directions for each player (see sample
    role play instructions, page 308).

2. Select players from the discussion group and allow them
    a few minutes to study the individual directions. Nor-
    mally players will see only their own role directions.

3. Introduce the topic of the role play to the discussion
    group. The group members should be given one or two
    questions which they will answer after the role play.
    These questions will form the topic of the discussion
    following.

4. Introduce the players to the group. For example: "This
    is Ranjit, a rich farmer."

5. Start the role play and allow it to continue until the
    players are finished, or until you feel that it is neces-
    sary to stop. For example, you might stop the role
    play after five minutes if the players had been distracted
    from the main topic of the role play.

6. Stop the role play. The players can now take their
    places as part of the discussion group.

7. The discussion leader should then help the group to answer the questions based upon the activities of the role play.

8. Sometimes the discussion leader may wish to restart the role play, either with the same or new players. During the discussion someone may make a comment that could have changed the outcome of the role play. As a discussion leader I have often said: "That is an interesting point. Why don't you take the part of Player A and Mr. XYZ can be Player B. Pick up the role play at the point where you have said 'xxxxxxxxx,' and let's see just what does happen."

    Role play exercises can also be done without prepared roles at any point during a group discussion. After the group has discussed a problem for some time, the discussion leader can select role players to act out their solution to the problem for the group.

    The purpose of a role play is to learn from seeing "what might happen if...." Often there will be no correct

answers and no one right way of doing something. The
players show one way that the problem could be solved.
The discussion group examines that solution and proposes
others.

Sample Role Play Instructions

MIDWIFE: You are a rural midwife with about
1000 families in your area. In one of the villages,
you met with the women a few months ago and talked
about family planning. You explained the importance
of family planning and the use of contraceptives.
Since the condom is the easiest contraceptive to obtain locally you explained how the condom prevents
the male sperm from reaching the female egg in the
woman's womb. The women in this village cannot
read well so you demonstrated the use of the condom
by unrolling the condom on your finger. You then
sold several packets of condoms to the village women.
Today you have returned to the village and see that
one of the women who bought condoms is pregnant
again. She sees you and is very angry. You should
talk to her and find out what is her problem.

VILLAGE WOMAN: You are the illiterate wife
of an agricultural laborer. You have seven children
and your husband's income is too low to feed them
properly. Several months ago the midwife talked to
you and some of your neighbors about stopping having
children. Even though you didn't understand much of
what she said you decided to try. You bought the
package of rubber things and wore them on your finger every night exactly as the midwife had shown
you. Now you are pregnant again and your husband
laughs at you for believing the midwife. Today you
see the midwife crossing the street and you decide
to get her banned from the village. You call out
loudly to her and run after her.

GAMING IN THE COMMUNITY

Simulation-gaming is an old learning method which is enjoying a new popularity. It presents interesting possibilities for work with community groups or students, participation of passersby at displays, training of volunteer workers, etc.

There are many kinds of simulation-games. Little girls playing house learn how to fill some of their future roles; teenagers often may learn the skills of driving on a driver-simulator; groups may learn more about effective ways of working together through some types of exercises, or interested citizens may learn about some of the problems of international diplomacy through a structured "game. "

Simulation-games may be simple or quite complex; some require a team of organizers, several dozen players, days or weeks of playing time and perhaps a computer. But many others are quite simple and are equally effective; and these will probably be of more use in working in the community. All simulations used for teaching purposes are simplified working models of the real world. Many details may be omitted, but the processes should be essentially the same as those of the real world so that the participants can transfer their experiences to the back home situation.

You might decide to use a learning game for several reasons:

- it can provide a safe and inexpensive situation for people to practice new or unfamiliar skills. In the game "Living City" participants have the opportunity to design a new community and to see how the results of their early decisions pose later constraints. They can try several different ways of coping with the future.

- it can provide practice in making decisions in situations which arise infrequently, but which require instant response. Disaster planning might be an example of this use; "Community Disaster" is a general exercise on this subject.

- it can provide an experience not otherwise readily available. An example here would be the game "Dirty Water," in which the participants have an opportunity to try to cope with various water pollutants in a hypothetical situation.

- games can provide an opportunity for people to learn directly by experience, rather than through a second-hand experience delivered by a lecturer. In the "Star Power" exercise, players live through some of the problems of inequality and its consequences in society.

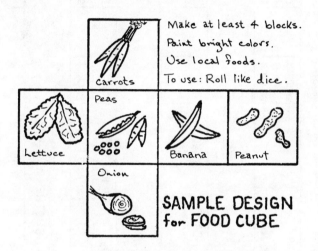

Make at least 4 blocks.
Paint bright colors.
Use local foods.
To use: Roll like dice.

Carrots

Peas

Lettuce

Banana

Peanut

Onion

SAMPLE DESIGN for FOOD CUBE

There are many commercial games available now, some of which may suit your purpose; others can be used with minor modifications. Even better in many situations is to make your own simulation game. This isn't as difficult as it sounds and has at least two major advantages:

- you have an exercise specifically tailored to your group, its needs and the constraints within which you must work.

- the experience of constructing, testing and revising the simulation can provide many insights for the group con-concerned.

Whatever the source of the material there are a few basic things to keep in mind as you use simulation or learning games:

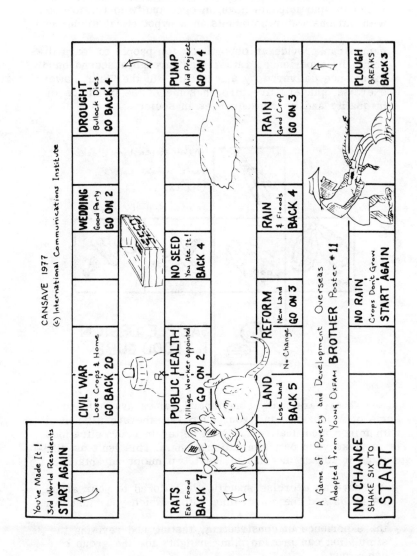

CANSAVE 1977
(c) International Communications Institute

You've Made It!
3rd World Residents
START AGAIN

CIVIL WAR
Lose Crops & Home
GO BACK 20

WEDDING
Good Party
GO ON 2

DROUGHT
Bullock Dies
GO BACK 4

PUMP
Aid Project
GO ON 4

PUBLIC HEALTH
Village Worker appointed
GO ON 2

REFORM
New Land
GO ON 3

NO SEED
You Ate It!
BACK 4

RAIN
& Floods
BACK 4

RAIN
Good Crop
GO ON 3

LAND
Lose Land
BACK 5

No Change

RATS
Eat Food
BACK 7

A Game of Poverty and Development Overseas
Adopted from Young Oxfam BROTHER Poster #11

NO RAIN
Crops Don't Grow
START AGAIN

PLOUGH
BREAKS
BACK 3

NO CHANCE
SHAKE SIX TO
START

- become <u>very</u> familiar yourself with the rules and operating procedure before you use the game. A "dry run" with a few friends can help immeasurably to keep the experience running smoothly and effectively.

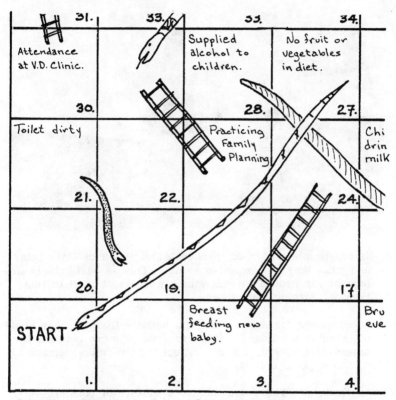

SAMPLE SECTION from **Public Health adaptation** of **SNAKES** and **LADDERS** Game.

- make sure you have all of the game pieces, sets of instructions or whatever else is required. Last minute changes or substitutions only confuse the players and detract from the learning experience.

- introduce the exercise carefully. While you may want to keep the ultimate purpose of the exercise hidden until

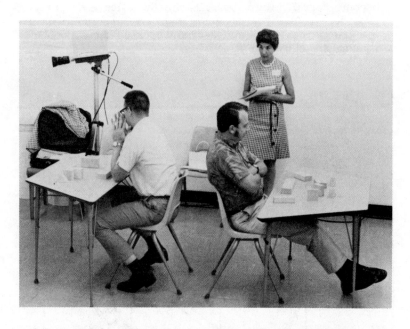

later, people will need to have a clear idea of their roles
and what they are expected to do. This is particularly important for groups or individuals who aren't used to this
type of learning experience.

- be prepared for more noise and activity than in other kinds
  of learning situations. (This may be of more concern to
  others around you, but may affect the overall acceptability
  of this type of activity.)

- be flexible. There are usually a variety of possible out-
  comes to any simulation; trying to manipulate happenings
  towards a particular end may only frustrate the players
  and cause them to question the validity of the whole experience. In general, any outcome (positive, negative or totally unexpected) can provide experience and insight for the
  players which can be the basis for later fruitful discussion.

- leave enough time to complete the exercise and for discussion afterwards. The correct amount of time is difficult
  to judge since some groups will take much longer than
  others to work through the same exercise.

Time for discussion or debriefing following a simulation is of crucial importance. While some people will learn
a good deal simply from participating in the experience, most
will find it much more fruitful if they spend some time ex-
changing experiences with other players (seeing how the same
actions looked from other perspectives), getting an overview
of the action and making applications to their real-world situation. Of course, not all this discussion needs to take place
in a formal situation; it can start there with the gamesmaster
or observers contributing their insights but can often continue
quite fruitfully in small groups over coffee or in the bar once
it has been initiated.

Using simulation games requires pre-planning and
preparation on your part, but can provide effective participation in the learning process.

Live-in Simulations

Most simulations are designed to require no more than
a few hours. Some, however, can be designed to continue
over several days and are much more complex. In this situation the participants don't play the simulation, they virtually
live it by temporarily adopting the simulated world as the
"real world"--food, accommodations, and social activity all
becoming part of the learning experience.

The cost in time, effort and resources of such an experience must be balanced against the potential learning.
Usually an extended simulation incorporates two activities and
learning experiences simultaneously:

- a camp or residential activity which brings relative
  strangers into close contact and provides an intensive
  small group experience.

- a simulated society--usually designed to focus the participants' attention on economic, social or political organization factors.

Organizing the residential aspect is fairly straightforward. A great deal of expertise is readily available from
youth groups, churches and recreation departments.

However, the goals and design of the simulation must
always be kept in mind while organizing the camping logistics.

To be realistic the simulation must incorporate some of the
frustrations and situations of the real world, but there
should not be more tensions than the participants or directors
can cope with.

The game needs to be designed to meet the established
objectives. Collecting rules and scenarios of relevant games
(both short term and extended) and then modifying them to
fit local requirements is probably the most efficient way of
working out a game design.

Most games divide participants into three to five
groups with conspicuously varying standards of living and
with appropriate surpluses or shortages of goods, equipment,
and luxury goods. Usually, groups are kept separate for
the first few days to develop both a group feeling and their
own political, economic and social structures. If the political and economical organization has been imposed upon the
group, the initial period provides an opportunity for the
group members to determine if the structure is satisfactory
or if it needs changing.

Factors to be considered in designing a live-in game:

- surpluses and shortages--trade
- distribution of food and luxuries--labor
- accepted techniques for change and conflict--war
- currency
- language barriers
- outside traders
- aid-welfare programs
- individuals expelled from groups--jail, labor camps
- individuals or groups who fail to provide for them-
  selves--involvement
- resources of the site--natural resources.

If possible, a shortened run-through of the game design with a small group can be helpful in working out the
bugs.

The simulation should be finished several days before
the end of the camp to provide enough time to debrief and
analyze what has happened.

NOTE: Sources of the simulations mentioned can be found
       in the bibliography.

SIMULATIONS AND GAMES: DESIGNING AND ADAPTING

There are many excellent simulations and games available commercially, however you may wish to design or mod-
ify your own if existing materials are not perfect for your
needs.   Circumstances vary from country to country as well
as province to province (or state to state).   Modifications
might be required to adjust to local terminology, legislative
or cultural differences.   When working with specific cultural
groups the illustrations must also be changed to represent
the local people rather than "strangers with problems which
do not affect us."

The level of content may not be suitable for your
group.   Materials may be made more complicated or simplified by changing the terminology, by selecting more appropriate situations to explore or by modifying the basic format (such as by using teams rather than individuals to solve
complicated problems).   Thus adult games may be modified
for use with children or children's games disguised for use
with adult groups.

Procedure

It is far easier to make relatively minor revisions to
an existing exercise than it is to begin completely from
scratch.   Once you have successfully revised a number of
simulations and made them more useful to your needs you
can begin to explore making materials for situations where
nothing seems to currently exist.   When this happens, stop
and look again for something that is currently available to
suit your needs.

If in fact nothing is available to suit your needs, you
must start by defining your instructional objectives and then
looking at the subject that you want to simulate.   In any
real world situation we have a wide selection of component
items, some of which are crucial to the operation of the
system.   The first task in designing a simulation will be to
look at the situation in question and extract its essential
characteristics.

Having obtained a list of the essential components of
the system it is now necessary to design a simulation or
gaming model which will allow us to manipulate these elements

Revision/Design Process

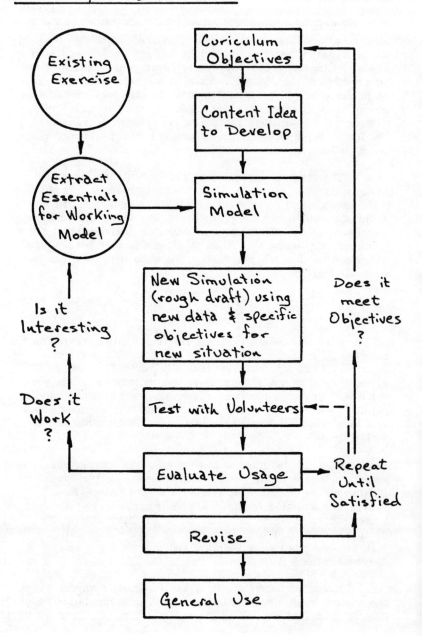

in a way that will be useful. In designing, as well as revising, we must fit the content into a system or pattern from which we can learn. In training nurses to recognize abnormal lung sounds we might build stethoscope ear pieces onto a small tape recorder; the actual chest, etc., of the patient would not be necessary since we are wanting her to recognize sounds through the stethoscope. If, however, we wanted to train her where to place the stethoscope diaphragm most effectively and the different sounds to be heard at each place, then we would need a much more elaborate model.

- Start simple. If you have used a crossword puzzle with your group successfully, let them make their own. It will not be as easy as they think; there will be solutions they had not intended or definitions for which no one can find a solution. The format is straightforward and the only mistakes they should make will be in the manipulation of the content.

- Another simple entry point is a simple "in-basket." Let the group scrounge enough copies of the various forms required, search out the changes necessary for their own institution to make it realistic, and prepare new documents. (Keep the names of individuals fictitious to help retain their credibility, and prudence may dictate that forms borrowed from local sources should have the names of the specific institution obliterated.)

Do not be discouraged with failures. Your first attempts may not yield perfect results but you can build on these to produce better materials as time goes on.

Producing successful materials is seldom an individual task. A "team" might consist of a subject matter specialist, a person familiar with simulation techniques, and one or more persons as the users. It may sometimes be possible to combine the first two individuals but we have found that showing the developing materials to colleagues and friends for their comments and suggestions has invariably improved the results. The actual testing of the new materials cannot be done without a user population. We often use disinterested volunteers who do not know us personally. These individuals are recruited to test out new materials which may or may not be successful. They generally enter fully into the spirit of the activity and can give more constructive comments than will come from someone who knows the objectives of the exercise more fully. Next the materials should be

given to another colleague to use independently; this will test
the reliability of the exercise and its instructions. Revisions
must be made and the materials tested again.

Reproduction

Many of the simulation materials that you produce
yourself can be reproduced in small quantity on your office
copier. Any good photographic laboratory can provide duplicates of charts, X-rays, or photos for inclusion. Verbal
material can be duplicated one copy at a time by hooking
two tape recorders together.

For larger quantities we have found that offset printing from typewritten originals is the most economical. Any
large town or city has a number of "quick" printing firms
who do this type of work if your institution cannot. Line
drawings and sketches can be included without added charge
provided they are prepared with black ink. Likewise newspaper clippings, etc., can be included with the typewritten
copy. Simply paste illustrations in place on the same sheet
as the typing. Photographs can be reproduced at slightly
higher cost. Proper set type, as in a book, is very expensive.

Game boards, posters, and other large materials, as
well as color illustrations can be economically prepared by
the silk-screen process. Art work can often be prepared by
art students at your local college or high school. Tape recordings, etc., can be duplicated in bulk by commercial
firms. Check your telephone yellow pages for suppliers for
these and other services.

It has been our experience that some of the best
simulations have been inexpensive and very simple. Fancy
packaging, expensive game boards and glossy components do
not guarantee the quality or utility of the exercise. Many
users will want to revise the materials before using them,
thus when designing your simulation you might save others
the problem of discarding a large part of the exercise by
keeping your materials simple. Most teaching units will
have access to some kind of duplicator and a typewriter.
Components that need multiple copies may be given a sample
form in the operator's guide for the user to reproduce.
Other items could be listed for local purchase by the user.

THE TELEPHONE: A COMMUNITY
INFORMATION SERVICE

Everyone knows how to use a telephone but how many
of us know about some of the other services of a telephone
company? While your telephone company may not advertise
them, most of the following equipment and services are available. Try the marketing division of your telephone company
for prices and installation details.

Speaker Phones

Some telephone companies call them "Speaker Phones,"
others call them "Conference Phones," but they are basically
a telephone with a loud-speaker system and one or more
microphones. Newer sets weigh about 20 pounds while older
units may weigh several times that; all plug into a standard
telephone jack and a 110-volt electrical outlet. In many
areas they may be rented for $10 to $15 per month and are
also available for single use occasions.

With such a unit several people can converse with
another quite easily, regardless of the distance. A common
use is in schools where a whole class will telephone someone long distance to address the class. Obviously, for best
results you should make arrangements ahead of time before
placing an important call, to ensure that the person you are
calling will be available and prepared. For a long distance
call the operator will usually connect your call at a predetermined time if you require--this saves taking time to
place the call during a class or meeting.

Smaller models of the conference phone are also available to amplify your normal telephone. The telephone receiver sits in a special cradle and you must talk towards a
sound collecting cone. These are generally not very acceptable and should be avoided.

Conference Calls

Strictly speaking, a conference call is a telephone
call where several people can participate at the same time.
Thus the "speaker phone" system is used to allow several
people at one location to talk to another point. Another

type of conference call involves several groups or individuals at a number of points. Such a call might be useful if several community groups in different cities wished to discuss a common problem without having to get together in one location. Today it is possible to arrange to use television equipment to provide a video signal (picture) as well. Speakers can then both see and hear the other participants. This type of conference call must be arranged with the telephone company well in advance of the required date.

Again, since long distance rates usually apply, it is necessary to plan ahead.

- make sure that all participants will be available at a predetermined location and time.

- organize your thoughts to avoid costly delays in speaking and try to have all necessary notes and materials on hand to avoid having to leave the phone to get supporting letters, etc.

24-Hour Telephone Answering Services

Community groups, as well as business organizations, sometimes find it important to have 24-hour telephone services. In most cities there are answering service organizations which will provide a human operator to answer your phone as needed. Sometimes this is part of the telephone company but often it is a private organization. The telephone company hooks your phone line up in such a way that it can be intercepted by a central switchboard when you wish the service to be in operation. At this central office one operator can handle several lines, resulting in a low monthly rate. Your phone operates normally when it is disconnected from the switchboard, and calls can be made out on the phone at all times.

A second way of handling such calls is to buy or rent a machine to provide a recorded announcement requesting the caller to leave his name, phone number, etc., after the "beep." The same device then records a short message from the caller. When you return you can replay the messages to find out who called. This system is very useful but has the disadvantage of not being able to handle extraordinary calls to which the human operator may be able to respond more adequately.

Comfort Lines

Recently we have seen a large number of phone numbers that may be dialed by a person wanting special information or assistance. Thus we have Dial-a-Prayer, Time, Weather and similar numbers (usually complete with advertising) as well as Suicide and Drug Treatment "hot lines." The former type of calls can be handled by automatic equipment and might be a useful means of providing updated information about the community. At least one city has had such a service, revised hourly, which provided factual information about current police-community relations in an attempt to prevent harmful rumors. Most of the distress center "hot lines" are manned by trained personnel (not necessarily professionals) who will talk to callers, calm down the suicide, or give information to help bring the drug "tripper" back to reality. Home phones can be connected into such a system but a central office is more economical and convenient.

In some areas the telephone company will list the telephone numbers of these services in the front pages of the directory where they can be quickly located.

Telephone and the Media

Phone-in radio shows are very popular but have definite time limitations. "Phone-in after the program" seems a viable alternative. By arranging to have several knowledgeable persons available to answer the phones it is possible to respond to questions or collect information from a large number of listeners. Incidentally, collecting information by phone is often quicker and easier than in person--people generally respond quite well to phone requests.

Newspapers and other print media can also be correlated to telephone campaigns to elicit verbal rather than written responses.

Groups should also consider organizing campaigns to be heard on local radio programs if they wish to contribute to discussions of current issues. Well-informed callers can be organized to "plug" a particular stand on an issue, and having a number of callers taking the same stand will lend an aura of public support. Individuals or organizations could also be organized to relay "news" to the various media so that coverage of fast-breaking events will be possible (some

radio stations offer money prizes to the first person who
phones in with a news item that is used).

Mobile Telephones and Ham Radio

Battery-operated telephones are available for use in
locations where a regular phone is not possible. Thus isolated camps, for example, can be in contact with medical
and similar services. These phones are not always available
for short term use, however, so the services of a local ham
radio club might be checked out as an alternative. A "ham"
with a mobile license can locate almost anywhere and, by
calling another ham who then telephones for assistance, an
emergency communications link is possible. CB radio, so
popular these days is simply a low-cost but short distance
communication system using principles similar to ham radio--
it is a shared public communication facility.

Other Services

- it is usually illegal to affix a recording device to a telephone unless it has been supplied by the telephone company.
  These recorders provide the distinctive "beep" which in-
  forms the caller that the conversation is being recorded.

- WATS (Wide Area Telephone Service) lines are toll-free
  long distance lines. A fixed monthly rental is paid regardless of the number of long distance calls (WATS lines are
  usually obtained for incoming or outgoing calls, depending
  upon the needs of the organization).

- computer data, typed messages and visual materials may
  also be transmitted over telephone lines, as may burglar
  alarms and similar signals.

- the telephone companies now offer a service whereby computer users in one city may access information in another
  without having to pay long-distance rates.

FIELDTRIPS AND DEMONSTRATIONS

Demonstrations and fieldtrips are a common element

in our schools where students are "treated" to an opportunity
to see some event that is not normally part of the school
atmosphere. Less recognized but still present are the many
uses of these techniques with adult and community groups.
For example in the last several months I have seen a local
photography club demonstrate the use of a simple camera
for taking portraits (using a polaroid type camera), a community group demonstrating flower arranging with local weeds,
and participated in a trip to see a government resettlement
scheme. Listening to the radio I hear that the Department
of Agriculture is arranging weed spraying demonstrations and
the local pollution pressure group is offering to conduct city
aldermen and other interested citizens around local polluting
industries.

        As with more conventional mediums it is necessary
to have a clear objective for the use of fieldtrips or demonstrations. Demonstrations usually bring the event to the
viewer, fieldtrips take the viewer to the event.

- arrange alternative programs in case of last minute
  changes of plans.

- ensure sufficient transportation for fieldtrips, renting
  buses where necessary, have maps available for drivers.

- collect fees in advance and purchase tickets, etc., in bulk in advance.

- prepare a program of activities, and attempt to stick to the program.

- arrange for a "briefing" to explain what is being seen.

- self-guided demonstrations or fieldtrips can be organized with large groups to allow individuals to proceed at their own speed. Printed notes or tape recorded commentaries can provide the necessary description of the event being observed.

- ensure that everyone can see and hear, using visual materials, P.A. systems, closed-circuit television, megaphones, C.B. radio, etc., as required.

- always arrange for a trial run to determine timing, etc. before settling on final arrangements.

- toilet facilities are as essential as transportation for a field-trip. Large groups can be delayed considerably by the necessity for a bus load of visitors to wait for the use of a single toilet.

- food and refreshment stops need to be planned at logical

Fieldtrips require planning and supervision.

times in the program.   It is very frustrating to have to
gulp down a cup of coffee because the coffee break is too
short.   Alternatively it is annoying to have to leave an
interesting site because "we can't keep the coffee shop
waiting."

- provide time and knowledgeable persons for answering questions that arise.

- check for special restrictions before the activity begins.
  Many institutions will not allow cameras or tape-recorders
  on their premises, and I have even known occasions when
  a guest invited in to demonstrate a technique refused to
  allow the taking of photographs.   The necessity for hard
  hats is a similar restriction that causes considerable disruption if not planned for in advance.

- a photo set, tape-slide presentation, video-tape or film of
  the process being viewed can be used as an introduction,
  follow-up or even to replace the demonstration or fieldtrip.

     Fieldtrips and demonstrations require considerable ad-
vance planning to be successful.   A poorly planned activity
is probably worse than no activity at all.

7 COMMERCIAL MEDIA

OBTAINING ACCESS TO THE MEDIA

One of the major problems in obtaining access to the commercial media results from their needs to satisfy very broad public interests and make a profit. Thus "broadcasters", the radio and television stations, have periodic "rating" checks and less popular programs are dropped. Newspapers and magazines conduct surveys of their readers and "audit" their circulation changes to determine the need for content changes. Even the supposedly expandable newspaper has limits to the amount it can print (unless you pay for an advertising supplement) and, more particularly, all of the media have limited staff. It is impossible to respond to every group or to send a reporter to every event.

Businessmen overcome these problems by either purchasing advertising or publishing their own "trade" or "in-house" journals. The community group often publishes a newsletter (see Newsletters: Their Design and Function) and distributes promotional "flyers" for special events. Both of these groups can purchase advertising space in the commercial media if the usual press release or solicited media coverage fails to meet their total needs. The big problem of course is the expense.

Historically, newspapers were one of the first signs of a new thriving community and from hand-set type the letterpress newspaper has evolved through time as the weekly community newspaper. Today the thriving community paper uses the offset process with its inexpensive use of visuals (see "Print Media: Reproduction Processes"). Many community groups have taken advantage of the availability of low-cost secondhand offset presses and "quick" printers to produce their own newspaper or newsletter. If labor is free and distribution is arranged this can be a reasonable way of getting access to commercial style media: produce your own. (See references in the bibliography for details of these ideas.)

Similarly residents of a number of communities have

become dissatisfied enough with the commercial radio and
television services to establish their own stations. In
the Canadian Arctic several communities have very low-power
FM facilities to reach the several hundred residents of their
town or village. Local community events and recorded music are the usual fare. Stations seldom operate more than
a few hours per day. In the cities and large towns something more powerful is required. For some it means acquir-
ing the ownership of an existing radio station or applying for
and operating an FM station; for others it means seeking access to the local origination channel on a cable TV system.
Operating your own radio or television station is a lot of
work and is expensive. However this is sometimes the only
means that a segment of the community, feeling disenfran-
chised by the regular media, can take to "broadcast" to their
audience. In media jargon they are usually "narrow-casting"
because of the smallness of their audience. (See "Citizen's
Media: Some Cases," which follows.)

Establish Contacts

        No matter how small the circulation, every commer-
cial broadcast station or newspaper must keep involved in
the community if it is to survive (your problem is that the
broadcaster may have a different idea of "community" than
you do). Thus you can almost always find a public affairs
department (or reporter) who has a regular column or program dealing with local events. In the case of the local
origination channel on cable TV the whole channel may be
devoted to community events and community designed programs. These people are often short of new program ideas
and will welcome your suggestion of a topic or a guest.
Get to know whom to contact at the various media and become familiar with their program needs.

        Personal contacts are crucial. It is possible to mail
a notice to "the editor" and get a small note in the weekly
happenings column. Regular coverage and special features
cannot be obtained this way. You must get to know the media, its audience and its needs. Learn who the reporters
are that must cover your type of event and suit your materials to their personal style and needs.

        I once organized a press conference on less than
twenty-four hours notice. We sent telegrams to every media
outlet and followed them up with phone calls. We managed to

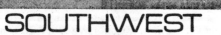

SOUTHWEST

Maureen Utley is your neighborhod reporter. Contact her at The Journal, 425-9120 with news of your area. Deadline 5 p.m. Friday for publication Wednesday.

CPR TRACKS

CITY BOUNDARY

Daily Paper with regular reporters & format.

People

The 64th Cub and Scout Group of Edmonton held its award night recently. Winners of the outstanding cub award were Roy Sharplin and Jackie Allbon, ~ also won the cub's choice award. M~ Londry and Michael Barton won ~ ership skills award while Troy ~ Craig Negrey won the most ~

Donnie Willoughby r~ for the scout who pro~ ance to a cub pa~ ~ers

re~   ~ard in cubs, the five ~ar represents an area of ~t, such as nature, citizen~ ~sical fitness.

~gan Community League has a new ~utive. President is Al Evenson; first ~ce-president, Bob Gilson; second vice-president, Roger Soderstrom; secretary, Marianne Benning; and treasurer, Campbell Graham.

Coming events

N~ ~eavers, youngest memb~ ~ scout organization, are exp~ ~ 28 for the fifth South West Bea~ ~, the annual beavers sports day in the ~outhwest district, to be held from 10 a.m. to 3 p.m. on the Riverbend Public School grounds, 14820 53rd Ave.

GREENFIELD Elementary School, 3735 114th St. is holding registration for kindergarten at 7:30 p.m. today. The child must be five years of age on or before March 1, 1978. Bring birth certificate and health records. The election of members to the local advisory committee will also take place at this meeting.

STRATHCONA Composite High School, 10450 72nd Ave. is producing the musical *You're a Good Man, Charlie Brown* today through until April 30. Curtain time is 8 p.m.

A RUG HOOKING and handicraft display by Pleasantview Happy Hookers will be held today in the community hall, 57th Avenue and 109th Street at 7:30 p.m.

GREENFIELD Elementary School, 3735 114th St. is showing the movie *Napoleon and Samantha* Thursday at 3:45 p.m.

Fire calls

Firemen on the south side were busy during the week answering a total of 35 calls, of which 24 were fire calls.

None of the fires was serious, but firemen remind residents that no burning permits are issued within city limits. Rubbish and grass must be hauled away, not burnt. Grass fires were the major causes of the fires.

Firemen also answered seven service calls and four medical aid calls.

Till Talk

by Ursula Tillmann

Spruce Grove's teen centre at McLeod Rink is getting there. You might not have noticed anything different from the outside, but wait until you see what's behind the scene.

I had the first taste of what the teen centre will be like last Tuesday. Kids of all age groups were cleaning-out corners, but most of all painting walls and doors.

Luckily I didn't sit down on one of the benches. But, instead my camera got stuck on some fresh paint, which didn't match the color though.

However, what I should point out is the enthusiasm for youngsters, some getting paid.

Using all colors 'groovy'.

Thanks to mai including McLeod Magic, and Parkla on a centre whicl

I asked teenage start on their cent and watch televi bored."

Having a plac providing that na facility. Stony Plc doesn't happe

But.

News from

Rochfort Bridge

By Mrs. W. Russ
Phone 785-2400

Joan Caithness spent a few days in Edmonton relatives.

from Powell River are spending a few days visiting Bruce and Millie Shuck and family and renewing old acquaintances.

Mr. and Mrs. Gordon ck, son of Shell Shuck, and v visited Bruce and Shuck.

and Annette Wat- children were

DA COLUMN

Locating county fires a problem

By Wilfred L. Cody
and William Bayda
District Agriculturists
Box 510, Stony Plain
T0E 2G0

The agricultural advisory ...mittee recently heard a ... Rev Saunders,

property. A system is being worked out to identify home sites in the subdivisions. The main difficulty in all this, of course, is in remembering this pertinent information in a time of crisis.

Mr. Saunders suggests posting this information on the telephone dial. Later this ...priate stickers for ...ailed

WEEKLIES have special audiences.

get coverage by almost all of the local media. We were
however dealing with a national news story involving several
millions of dollars. As well, the story related to a topical
government agency which had been the subject of a recent
scandal. It would be impossible to accomplish this again
unless you have a very important story. Normally you
should schedule a press conference at least a week in advance, hand deliver invitations to your contacts and follow-
up with a phone call. If the media aren't too busy they will
try to fit you in, PROVIDED THAT YOUR STORY IS NEWS
WORTHY.

Do disasters, murders, scandals and sex seem to
receive undue attention in the media compared to the "good"
work that your agency is doing? Perhaps you aren't familiar
enough with the needs of your local media.

- just prior to Christmas is an impossible time to get coverage of any community events. Even national public service
  spots (commercials for non-profit agencies which are carried free) are eliminated or scheduled at 4:00 a.m.

- Sunday night and weekends in general are low staff times
  for the media. If you have a good story that can be recorded for later use it might get national TV news coverage on a slow weekend. You won't know when it will appear however until after the event.

- are your stories new? and original? The media can only
  use so many stories each year of donations of money or
  ho-hum program activities.

- tie your stories to topical events. If you had 1000 members of your group fasting on Christmas day as a fund
  raising activity you could likely get excellent coverage if
  you contacted the media in advance. The same 1000 people fasting during the summer would likely not receive any
  attention.

- provide interesting people with interesting ideas. Controversy does sell, and if you have someone able to speak
  well about a controversial topic you can often get coverage.

Media planning is sometimes done months in advance.
The regular columnist may be depending on a last minute
idea for today's article but the public affairs department will
also be working on next year's "specials." Contact the
media early.

Be Creative

Don't rely solely on press releases mailed to a city editor or his equivalent. As mentioned above the releases, ideas, etc., should be delivered in person whenever possible. Remember that most media are visually oriented. They need photographs or other visual ideas to effectively handle your story.

- novel ideas are always useful, although they can easily become mere gimmicks.

- visualize every message with creative and imaginative photographs, maps, charts, graphs, etc. We are all familiar with the dull photograph of someone presenting a check or trophy--such a photo is meaningless to the general viewer. A much more useful photograph would illustrate the activity for which the presentation was being made.

- phone or write the editor to request information on a topic: "Why isn't there anything on this topic in your newspaper today?"

Look to the Future

The media are planning to be in business for a long time--their needs are continuous. While they may be busier at some times than at others, they will welcome the group that has a well thought out public relations or educational program which will continue for several months or even years. They get to know your goals and activities. Even more importantly they get to know your regular public information officer.

Long term activities create some problems for your group. You must plan long term campaigns instead of single shot press releases. You must build an audience who will be interested in your activities. You must have a responsible public information officer with enough money to work effectively.

- provide continuity through a consistent theme or a particular style of writing.

- be very self-critical and constantly seek means of improving your program.

- general interest information will often attract an audience which will become interested in more specific activities.

- strive to create a positive public image, however some
  controversy is helpful in getting viewer or reader attention.

- use a variety of media in a coordinated effort. If no one
  listens to your weekly radio show perhaps you need to get
  a parallel column in the local newspaper to promote the
  radio.

- always provide names and addresses or phone numbers for
  obtaining further information.

- respond positively to requests for information from the
  media, even on controversial issues. You can then usually expect a more favorable response from the reporter
  at a later date when you need a favor. Small organizations cannot afford to brush off the media with a "no comment. "

    There is obviously a limit to the number of regular
columns and programs available in the media. One of the
reasons that the District Home Economist has a regular
space in the weekly newspaper is that she regularly provides
topical information. Tailor your public information program
to fit the needs of the media and the particular audience
of that media. Whether you are trying for a one shot
press release or a long running "show, " you must get to
know the media reporter, his particular needs, and his
audience.

THE PUBLICITY CHAIRMAN

    One of the advance harbingers of spring each year is
the outburst of renewed activity among organizations and
groups emerging from the mid-winter hiatus of December
and January. And one of the essential ingredients for the

success of many enterprises, from the spring tea to the appearance of a renowned speaker, is publicity.

It's been my experience over the years spent in radio, television and newspaper work that all too often the person given the position of publicity chairman has it thrust on him against his will and can unwittingly do his group harm while in the process of learning the job.

What are some of the qualities in the person handling publicity that make either the material she sends in or her own presence welcome to those in the media? And what are those that cause negative reactions--the "tell her I'm out" sort of response?

It seems to me that those in charge of publicity must be sincerely enthusiastic about the cause they are working for, while at the same time maintaining a sense of proportion about the fact that there are other causes. Time and space have to be shared.

Some publicity chairmen approach their work with a sort of missionary zeal and are offended if everyone they meet isn't immediately converted.

Take Time to Find Out

Doing the publicity for any organization can be a most interesting responsibility for the right person. Part of being the right person, in my view, is to take the time and make the effort to find out what sort of information the various media can use to best advantage--in what form they prefer to have it--and who is the best person to contact.

It's important to know whom not to send material to and what a particular branch of the media can't do.

I've had publicity chairmen arrange with me to conduct an interview with one person and then show up at the appointed time with two or three, all of whom came prepared to contribute. It couldn't be done.

Perhaps a rule to cover this might be: when tempted to substitute one knowledgeable person with a delegation--don't!

I advise publicity conveners who ask for suggestions
to find out a little about the timetable or schedule on which
the newspaper or radio or TV show works.   A visit or telephone call 15 minutes before deadline time may bring a reaction that sounds very much like a brush-off.

Something else that often results in disappointment,
both for the person wanting something drawn to public attention and the one in the media who is approached, is lack of
awareness on the part of a publicity chairman about the
amount of advance notice required to get something printed
or aired.

Get Facts Straight

A good publicity chairman gets the facts straight and
complete.   Times, places, dates, prices, speaker's topic
and details of his biography should all be double-checked.

Nothing is more frustrating than to discover at the
last moment that an important piece of information is missing, when the publicity convener is not within reach and no
one around can think of the name of anyone else in the organization.

Striking a happy balance between too little and too
much publicity material is important too.   "Snowing under"
every person in the media from whom there is the remotest
possibility of getting coverage doesn't mean being an efficient
publicizer.

The classic example of this approach was the publiciz-
ing of Canada's centennial year.   The tons of material with
which the media across the country were inundated and the
amount that must have been tossed in waste baskets from
sea to sea still haunt me.

A poor relationship between organization and press
can result when the publicity convener goes to several people under the same roof with the same material and the
same requests without letting one know that the other has
also been contacted.

Many groups and associations have internal struggles.
They're often a sign of good health rather than sickness.
However, when the result is conflicting opinions expressed

to the media or an overlapping of approaches, it can be highly detrimental to that organization as far as understanding and cooperation by the media is concerned.

I had a call not long ago from a woman who began the conversation with the words, "I've been stuck with the publicity job." I was reminded of how many times I've heard it put that way. And yet, with a little pre-planning that may even include asking someone in the communications field for some advice, this can turn out to be a stimulating and educational role.

THE PRESS RELEASE

It used to be that a press release was only sent to "the press"--the newspapers. A press release is one of the means of disseminating information that you think is worthy of public notice (another way might be through a regular newspaper column or in an article printed in your organizational newsletter). Today, therefore, press releases are used to provide information to all of the mass media, and in addition may be distributed to such small audience media as trade and in-house publications. Remember, though, that the editor of a media service, be it radio, television, a newspaper or a magazine, is interested in "news" that will interest his audience; he is almost always working against both a deadline and a tight budget and will not be interested in receiving a press release that is poorly written or out of date. While almost anyone can write press releases with practice, you can do even better by following some basic guidelines.

Writing the Release

The first paragraph of a press release must contain all of the essential information you wish to communicate. Check any newspaper article and you are sure to find that it is written in an inverted form: the reader's attention is captured in the first paragraph and the following paragraphs provide additional details in declining order of importance. An editor faced with a space problem may then delete the bottom paragraphs to fit the space or time he has available

PRESS RELEASE

(cap) ~~Unfortunately only~~ *T*en farmers attended the conference
at the Hayburn Co-op last weekend ~~to hear the stumulating~~
~~lecture~~ on the use of *e* ~~new~~ improved *vaccines* ~~immunizing agents~~
˅ for the treatment of Mutlar's disease. The lecture was
~~generously~~ *e* sponsored by the ~~diligent management of the~~
C ~~Hayburn~~ *e* Co-op and th *e* ~~perceptive and forward thinking~~
County Agriculture Committee. Dr. R. J. Baker, ~~D.Vm.,~~ *e*
veterinarian, was the guest speaker and *e*
~~employed as Veterinary Specialist very ably lectured for~~
~~forty-five minutes. One of Dr. R. J. Baker's remarks was~~ *e*
remarked
˄ that "many farmers are too slow to see the beneficial
˅ ⊙ effects of the new drugs.~~on today's market."~~ "Teddy" *Mr. E.*
of the Co-op showed *e* *e*
Johnson ~~professionally assisted with a~~ slide ~~s presentation~~
of ˄ *e* *vaccines.*
~~showing~~ local ~~results of the~~ use of the ~~immunizing agents.~~

RETYPED RELEASE

Farmers Slow to Adopt Vaccines

Ten Farmers attended the conference at the Mayburn
Co-Op last weekend on the use of improved vaccines
for the treatment of Mutlar's disease. The lecture
was sponsored by the Co-Op and the County Agriculture Committee. Dr. R. J. Baker, veterinarian,
was the guest speaker and remarked that "many
farmers are too slow to see the beneficial effects
of the new drugs." Mr. E. Johnson of the Co-Op
showed slides of local use of the vaccines.

without rewriting the article.   Since your release is providing the media with the information as you want it to appear, make sure that it is kept as short and succinct as possible but is written so that it can be trimmed without losing its meaning.

Keep the writing simple, avoid flowery phrases, jargon and long sentences.   The example (page 340) illustrates the kind of corrections necessary for a poorly written release.

Clearly label the article as a "press release" and, if timing is important, give the time at which the information may be made public.   Provide the name and telephone number of a person to contact for further information.

Check your facts.   Accuracy in writing a press release is absolutely important.   Incorrect names or figures indicate sloppy work on the part of the writer and will be an embarrassment to everyone concerned.   Direct or indirect quotations should always be checked with the source for authenticity.   Send out a correction if necessary when you have goofed rather than allowing a mistake to continue.   As well, you should always be totally open and honest about your purposes; do not confuse your own opinions or desires with the facts.

When announcing a meeting or similar activity, check to ensure that you have included the purpose, date, time, price and location of the meeting as well as special points of interest such as information about the guest speaker.

Make the release interesting as well as merely informative.   Trivialities do not belong in a press release; minute details may be very important to you but many readers are more interested in an overall picture of how your activities affect them.   While some subjects do not lend themselves to humor, it does not hurt occasionally to poke fun at yourself.

Illustrations

Tables, charts, and graphs can sometimes be used to accompany press releases but the average editor is more interested in photographs which will grab the reader's attention and illustrate the article.   An attractive series of photos may even result in a major feature.

Faculty of Extension · The University of Alberta · Edmonton

university
extension

news release

YUKON SUMMER SCHOOL

The Yukon Territory is a distinctive area of the North. In order to provide
an opportunity to see and to learn about this area, The University of Alberta
Faculty of Extension in cooperation with the Boreal Institute for Northern
Studies and the Government of the Yukon Territory has set up the Yukon Summer
School.

This first Yukon Summer School has been designed for administrators, managers,
professional specialists, and others who are involved in planning or carrying
out activities in the Yukon. It is particularly aimed at those who are from
outside the Territory or who are very recent arrivals and are interested in
familiarizing themselves as rapidly as possible with the special conditions
affecting northern and Yukon operations. There may also be some people who
have a personal interest in the Yukon and want to use the School as a way of
expanding their knowledge.

The general objective of the School is to provide participants with an opportunity to learn more about the Yukon Territory: its government, history,
native people, ecology, geology, and industrial development. The program
is a combination of lectures and field trips. The lecturers will be experts
in their fields who are also residents of the Yukon.

The Summer School group will leave Edmonton for Whitehorse on Sunday, August
21, and return to Edmonton on August 27. The registration deadline is
July 15. The course fee is $850 which includes all transportation, meals
(except for those in Dawson City), lodging, materials, and instruction. Complete details or brochures may be obtained by calling (403) 432-3022 or
(403) 432-5061.

Ann Prideaux
Administrative Assistant
Phone (403) 432-5061
April 26, 1977

Professional photographers appear at first to be rather expensive but their results will often be more effective than those of the amateur. You must provide the setting, models and ideas for the photographer and he will produce photographs which will be guaranteed to be acceptable technically. Neither a professional nor an amateur can guarantee the acceptance of any photo but poorly focused or washed-out snapshots will not be used by any editor. Once you have found a good photographer you would be well advised to retain him for subsequent material, since he will soon be familiar enough with your organization's needs that he can make suggestions that will improve the results.

Do not use photographs of your membership or staff just because they hold some position in the organization; make sure that each and every photo tells a story for your organization and provides a reason why the reader should want to learn more. Provide 4" x 5" or larger prints. If of sufficient interest they can be used by both the print media and television (always send them in a cardboard mailer to prevent bending).

Distributing the Release

If you are in the regular business of sending out press releases you will gradually find out who are the specific individuals that your release should be sent to. Certainly, in a small town everyone knows the editor of the weekly newspaper and the local events announcer for the radio station. Otherwise, direct your release to "the editor" or "city editor" or "farm editor" appropriate to your news. A complete address will ensure that your letter is delivered (include street address, etc.). Urgent releases may be hand delivered to the appropriate office of the media (don't leave it at the front desk).

Press releases must always be typed, double or triple spaced on one side of the paper. Number all pages and indicate "more" at the bottom of all pages except the last. When multiple copies are required, the release should be clearly duplicated. Carbon copies should not be used (type original copies for every recipient if necessary) and smeared or hard to read copies should not be sent. Double-check the release before mailing; remember to have someone else read it over; and also check that every envelope has the correct postage.

Further Contacts

      Every press release should clearly indicate the source, i.e., the name of the person and/or organization issuing the release. In addition the release should contain the name, address and phone number of someone to contact for further information. You may feel that the press release contains all of the essential information for your intended audience but the editor may not agree. If you want publicity give him someone to contact who really knows about the event you are trying to promote. (A public information officer friend of mine has stopped putting her name on the bottom of press releases. She doesn't really know much about the programs being promoted so it just wastes time to phone her. The contact name and/or phone number appears in the body of the release--see example.)

RADIO FOR PUBLIC INFORMATION

      In this world of instant mass communication it is still difficult, and often expensive, to reach specific segments of the general public. I am sure, also, that one of Parkinson's Laws must be that "a group or organization which has information which should be disseminated widely will have neither the resources (money and contacts) nor the ability (public speakers, artists) to do so." One of the reasons for this is that we tend to ignore radio, that often forgotten sister of glamorous new television.

- radio is relatively inexpensive.

- people still listen to radio.

- radio makes extensive use of public affairs and public service information.

- radio provides a forum; listeners can call in and question a speaker or engage in a dialogue.

- large cities have several radio stations, each of which has a specific (and very loyal) audience. Smaller centers may have only one station but most of the populace will listen to it for at least part of the day.

- radio is a reasonably safe medium for the speaker; no lights or stages, no cameras, only a microphone and an interviewer. It's just like talking on the telephone. Often you can just talk on the phone in your own home and have the interview aired later on the radio.

Public Service

A radio station maintains its audience by offering its listeners the type of information and entertainment that is wanted by those listeners. In one setting this might dictate high quality symphonic and similar "cultured music," along with political comment, university level public affairs and continuing education programs. At another level this might mean "pop" music and news about the happenings and coming events of the teen crowd. In any case the station will welcome material directed at its audience; if you look in your local newspaper or listen to your local station(s) for a day or two you are likely to hear:

- a public health nurse being interviewed on an open line program about preventing food poisoning at community and church suppers.

- a psychologist talking about kids and the kinds of toys to buy at Christmas.

- an ex-drug addict explaining his experiences and soliciting funds for a self-help group.

- a home economist reporting on a survey of the best food buys this week.

- coming events (the bulletin board), meetings, fund raising drives, picnics, etc.

- discussion of local events (generally open line programs), commentary on the news.

In some centers the radio stations may also be willing to help serve specific ethnic and minority groups by providing time for foreign language or special interest programming.

How to Be Effective and Get Invited Back

Having a radio station in your community isn't of much value if you can't engineer an invitation to speak on the air, but equally important you want to be invited back (particularly if you want to make a regular contribution).

1.   Check out the radio station.   What is its audience?   What kind of programming does it have?   Then try to select the station that serves the audience that you want to reach and gear your presentation to complement its programming.

2.   Capitalize on news events.   The best time to get an opportunity to present a case for better sanitation and cooking procedures at public events might be just after several cases of food poisoning from a church supper.   A discussion of the value of day-care centers might be appropriate at city budget time, and public relations about the crippled children's camp during the United Fund campaign drive.

3.   Remember that most radio stations today are using very short interviews rather than the long involved ones of the past.   For topics which fit a discussion format the most common style is the open line or "forum" where the listener can call in and comment.   Here the guest has a chance to explain the topic more fully, and hopefully the listeners' questions get answered.   The short interview will usually be taped (and edited if necessary) and may be replayed several times as commentary or "news."   The open line program will be live and usually aired only once.

4.   Be well prepared.   Make sure that you have all of your facts straight; make notes of such things as individuals' names and titles so that you get them correct when you are talking about them.   Have a capsule description of what you want to say written down to help the interviewer or moderator.   Have a name and address or telephone number for follow-up information and bring a couple of copies of it written down (few things are more embarrassing than to forget your own phone number).

5.   Cooperate with the station staff; no one will appreciate the nervous guest who engages every employee in conversation in an attempt to calm his or her own nerves.

6.   Don't be evasive; answer questions honestly or say that you don't know.

7. Talk to the <u>interviewer</u>, not the great audience
out there in radio land.

8. Try to talk over the subject ahead of time with
the host.   You will both be more familiar with the topic and
it will help you to relax.

Cardinal rule: only one person talking at a time.
Also keep from making extra noises such as rustling
paper or drumming fingers on the table.

In conclusion, <u>reading</u> a prepared talk can be very
dull (both for the audience and the speaker).   If the subject
you will be discussing is controversial and the station
wants to preview it ahead of time, you might suggest pre-
taping your discussion rather than submitting a prepared
typewritten script.   Be informal, be yourself and be informative.

BROADCAST COMMUNITY TELEVISION

<u>Switzer Theorem*</u>

If a program service is worthy of unrestricted
distribution on a cable system, it is worthy of
unrestricted "on-air" distribution in the same
community.

Not only cable companies, but other local groups
should broadcast and should have the right to low-power
broadcast licenses.   There should be a television equivalent
of the "citizen's band" which was provided for public use of
the two-way radio spectrum.   More stringent control should
be applied, but there is no reason why low-power $15,000

---

*Mr. I. Switzer is a cable television engineer who believes
that communities shouldn't be trying to gain control of a
cable company but, instead, should be forming broadcast
television (or radio) "mini-stations" for local programming.

TV transmitters could not be on the air giving expression to the wide range of views and opinions prevalent in the area.

I feel very strongly that public service television (and radio) must be by broadcast means. AM radio is probably a greater potential communications medium for isolated, underprivileged communities than is television, because of its low operating costs and the very low cost of AM radio receivers. Transistor radios can now be bought for as little as $3.95. They can be given to every man, woman and child in a community. They don't need to be plugged into power lines (often a problem in remote communities) and can often communicate as effectively as television. AM radio is the favorite medium in developing countries abroad.

Cable and Community Television

Basically, cable is a communications system, not a broadcasting system. It will be many decades before the "wired city" is a reality, while the "wired nation" may be fifty to one hundred years away. In the meantime--for the next thirty, fifty or even one hundred years--mass communication will be by "wireless."

- cable is terribly expensive except in urban areas with very high population densities.

- cable has very few channels available compared to "air broadcasting," at least for the next five years.

- cable does not reach everyone in the communities it now serves.

- cable is capable of providing a large variety of supplementary communications services. Community television could be one of those services.

However, community television cannot wait for the "wired city." The social and political needs and purposes for television exist now and must be fulfilled now. The "wired city" will come only when all electronic communications functions, such as picture-phone, information retrieval, shopping from the home, banking by wire, etc., become services of mass appeal.

I am skeptical of the rate at which demand for such

services will develop. I look back to 1960, back at my own
home and my own life style. My life in 1971 has not changed
significantly. I have automatic laundry equipment, air conditioning, telephone, television, radio--all things that I had in
1960. I don't have color television in my home. Many millions of people just have never considered color television to
be a necessity. I spend my money on other things. After
a decade in which the integrated circuit revolutionized electronic technology there is not a single integrated circuit in
my home. Sophisticated technology is at work in my office,
in my government, in some of my schools--but not in my
private home. The wired city will not have arrived until
individual householders, in tens of millions, are ready to
accept, and can afford, these communications marvels. Perhaps now you can understand some of my skepticism. Cable
television will not be a practical "mass-communications"
medium for many, many years.

I have used the term "mass-communications" to mean
communications with a potential of reaching all the people
within a community. Really, what good is a system that
reaches those fat cats who can afford cable TV subscription
rates? And even then, does anybody really watch the local
cablecast service? People mistakenly assume that all they
have to do to get their message across is to get on television, but other people have to be watching.

The only television services that people do watch in
significant numbers are the high power VHF television stations. These are the television equivalents of AM radio stations and everyone is equipped to receive them. These channels are now virtually all used to sell soap flakes or cars,
and to titillate the masses. Don't come to me, your local
cable company, asking me to provide community service by
television--go to your local television station. If you have
anything to say to the people of your community it has to be
said by broadcast and over the most effective communications
medium you have: the AM radio and the VHF television
channels assigned to your area.

What is the role of cable? Cable is a communications system, like the telephone. For the next few years
cable will act as a supplement to broadcast television, helping it over the rough spots of propagation and interference
that sometimes plague some channels. When broadcast television finally reaches its ultimate state of service as a medium of public information and education, cable TV will be
serving a variety of other purposes.

Broadcasting

The obvious thing is to have the cablecaster broadcast his signal. UHF channels are available anywhere. Don't let anyone tell you that there is a shortage of spectrum-- anywhere! Bullshit! The UHF allocations plan (and the VHF plan) are based on completely obsolete principles and are perpetuated more for the economic protection of the present broadcast industry than for any other reason. Certainly, low power "drop ins" would be available in every community. Let the local cable company broadcast its signal from the roof of its cable studio or from its "head end" tower using a 100-watt "translator" type of transmitter and a small antenna, giving an ERP of about 1,000 watts. This would provide broadcast coverage over most cable communities for less than $15,000 and with negligible annual operating costs.

Consider the benefits:
- receivable by everyone in the community.
- relieves cable company of responsibility for providing subsidized service to low income groups or to people at some distance from the main cable lines.

Disadvantages:
- hardly any.
- an imaginary, mistaken belief that energetic local cablecasting will draw subscribers. (I will debate this with any individual or group of cable operators you care to bring to me.)

If a program service is worthy of unrestricted distribution on a cable system, it is worthy of unrestricted "on-air" distribution in the same community.

8 CITIZEN'S MEDIA: Some Cases

INTRODUCTION

During the last ten years an increasing number of communities have rediscovered the potential of radio, and organized to own their own radio stations.

Here in Canada the federal government and the publicly owned Canadian Broadcasting System have been working on the equipment and program needs of the small isolated community. With this help many of the small Indian and Inuit communities of the far north operate stations. In several cases they have received assistance in organizing and operating from the CBC, in others they became interested and worked on their own. The newspapers of Southern Canada regularly carry short features on these stations, often coupled with a request for used records. Typically the station runs a few hours per day, is very low powered, relies on volunteer staffing, and offers a mixed diet of recorded music and local gossip cum news.

In the United States the larger centers have had community owned stations develop to meet the needs of specific audience groups. Most commercial stations are fairly conservative and usually operate to make money. The alternate stations often offer more radical treatment of political issues, support and report truly local happenings and generally cater to minority groups missed by the commercial operators. In the last three or four years this trend has come to Canada as well and most larger centers either have a community station, or are in the application process to receive one. Most such stations seem to be set up as cooperatives (one member-one vote) and membership carries with it the responsibility of operating and/or financing the station (cooperative stations are normally non-profit as well).

It can be argued that the big-city cooperative stations do not cater to real community needs any more than do the large commercial stations. Indeed in at least a few centers a large chunk of the middle-class majority would actually be discouraged from participating. It is important to recognize however that significant segments of the community do feel ignored by the mass media. Most radio stations ignore controversial local events (city council debates, human rights, housing problems, etc.) because their audience doesn't want to listen to programs about such events. Big stations are big and profitable because they do cater to the wishes of their audience. Likewise the big station may not want to cover a controversial issue because of the fear, real or perceived, that they might offend a sponsor. Operating your own radio station may be the only means you have of disseminating your ideas, be they political or religious, radical or ultra-conservative.

There aren't very many community owned television broadcast stations yet, however their time may come. In the meantime we have PBS and cable stations. The Public Broadcasting System, an American educational service, now reaches into most large centers in Canada too, and provides good coverage of US National issues. The local cable service provides better reception of television signals and usually is required to provide one or more channels of locally originated programming. This may mean a simple display of community messages, time and weather, national and international news (usually taken right off a teletype wire-service line), blue movies, "movie of the week," cable company local productions, or community produced programming. Your local operator may provide some, all, or none of these types of service. It is likely however that in order to obtain his license he promised to deliver at least one channel of community service programming. Making use of this channel may mean a lot of work (if you produce your own programs) but that is likely easier than organizing and operating your own station, radio or television.

When I was writing the first edition of this Handbook the community channels on cable had a lot of potential. Everyone, layman or expert, seemed to be predicting that the communities would take over the control of the local cable community channel. It seemed to be the answer to our dreams. To discover and report on what has really happened in the intervening years I have visited a number of cable systems in Canada. For comparison I looked at two community radio services. In the cases which follow I have tried to report on some of these activities and to explain the advantages or disadvantages of working within each system. It should be remembered that these are case studies, and your local situation might be very different.

CASE NUMBER ONE:
QCFM, EDMONTON

QCFM is a non-commercial five channel radio sta-
tion(s) using the FM capability of the local cable-TV system.
Four of the channels operate 24 hours per day, seven days
per week.   The fifth channel programs about 16 hours per
day.   The service costs $24.00 per year for hook-up by the
cable company.   At present it serves about 500 legally
hooked-up subscribers plus approximately 15,000 others who
either listen to one of the channels running as "background"
to the various cable-TV services or are illegally hooked up.

The station's basic philosophy is that no one listens
for more than three hours at any one time.   They therefore
use tapes of about 3-1/2 hours duration which reverse and
rerun continuously.   At the end of every three day period
tapes will be removed and new programming begins.   As
well the tapes are interrupted by live or taped special programs at scheduled times (early evening hours).   Tapes will
be stored after use and may be replayed after a 6-12 month
delay.

The station has five full time employees plus "as
many volunteers as can be handled by the staff."   With a
$75,000 investment in the control room and related equip-
ment the station has facilities to equal many commercial
stations.   Most programming is music (see channel descriptions which follow), thus studio oriented.   However one channel is recorded in the community and uses the station's three
remote units.   Remote recordings may be on SONY cassette
machines with the microphone attached around the speaker's
neck for better audio or on 1/4" tape machines.   The cassette recordings are only used where the spoken presentation
will be fairly complete in itself without requiring much editing.   Volunteer workers also prepare music programs on
cassette in their homes for transfer to the 3-1/2 hour
"broadcast" tapes.

Channel 1: Children's Audio.   Beginning as an electronic baby sitter for children ages 4-7 the format has now
expanded to include 12-15 year olds.   As well as the FM
channel this programming serves as background audio for
the community announcements channel on TV.   From 4-5 p.m.
a "live" music dedication hour is inserted and 75-90 calls
will be received on a good day.   Once a week the dedication

program will be simultaneously broadcast on the regular
community television (cable) channel.   For the older kids it
is mostly music, for the younger set it is songs and stories.
Some of the content is recorded locally (local writers airing
their children's stories, etc.) but the station really depends
upon the output of the record companies.

Of particular interest is the summer crew--kids 9-14
years old have been coming in to record their own shows.
During the summer they pretty well run the channel.

Channel 2: Music from Home.   The second most
popular channel caters to the ethnic groups of Edmonton with
mostly music, some information and talk.   An ex-music
store owner works as a free-lance consultant to produce the
regular tapes for this channel from his personal collection
of 100,000 ethnic records.   Every Friday nite the cable TV
station's four telephone lines come alive with requests for
the simulcast of his live request program.   Other nights of
the week generate as many as 20 requests on the daily cable-
radio only show.

Also on Friday nights is a varying series of 1/2 hour
programs prepared by various ethnic groups.   Work is currently going on with six such programs with two already on
the air.   A particular difficulty of this channel is the government regulation that requires an English translation of all
program material.   With volunteer workers this is an extra
chore which sometimes leads to the cancellation of a series.
Likewise community groups or interested individuals do not
realize the time involved to prepare a regular program--
what seems like fun the first week becomes heavy work after
a month or so and deadlines get missed--another cancellation.
Ethnic groups as a whole, however, are very loyal and if
anything they are usually almost impossible for the station
to get rid of if the occasion ever arises.

Channel 3: Spoken Word.   QCFM attends teacher's
association workshops, university conferences, seminars,
rotary club meetings and school debates.   It's all in a day's
work when you are trying to find good spoken word to replay
on radio.   First make the contact for a possible program
then record the speech or talk, edit the tapes adding intro-
ductions and musical interludes, transfer to 3-1/2 hour tapes,
and finally contact the group again to tell them when the program will be aired.   The main problem always is "what can
we record this week?"

In terms of costs this channel is more expensive than the other four combined (two staff required full time).

Channel 4: Easy Listening. This channel also does double duty as the audio background for the cable TV news printer. It programs at least 33 percent Canadian music (recordings), uses few vocals and almost no announcements.

Channel 5: Community Station. This channel is really misnamed since most of the year it is shared between the student radio stations at the Technical Institute and the University. The former, CHNR, features teen music and the latter, CKSR, a more sophisticated mix. Summer scheduling (when CHNR goes off the air since the institution has no summer students) is mainly music. Programs are often prepared by volunteers in the winter months and stockpiled for summer use.

Citizen Participation. Volunteer programmers from the community are required to submit a detailed written brief of their ideas for station evaluation. If the idea is accepted a staff member is assigned to train and otherwise assist the programmer as required. Volunteers are encouraged to do their own technical operations and production as well as organizing resources (records, guests, etc.). Training is done on the job using the station's regular facilities. Assembled programs prepared out of the studio (at home often) are accepted for broadcast from experienced volunteers.

For the Future. QCFM will soon add five additional FM channels, all rebroadcasting signals brought in from the United States (rock, easy listening, religious, etc.). As soon as reception equipment can be obtained the station also expects to offer nine short wave channels. These stations, mainly European, will provide better reception of news and music from home for Edmonton's ethnic communities.

CASE NUMBER TWO:
CFRO CO-OP RADIO, VANCOUVER

Several years ago a group of residents in Vancouver decided that the media outlets in the city weren't being objective. As a result they organized their own radio station

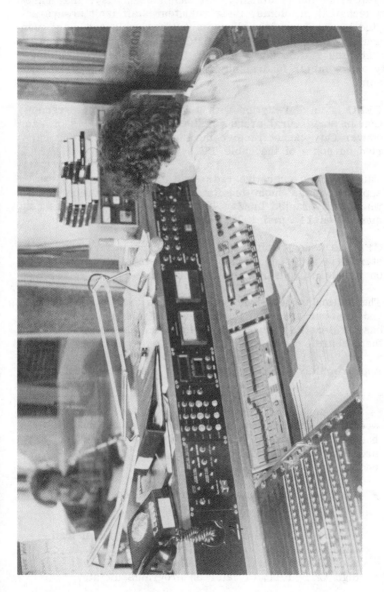

Volunteers at work on the "Morning Show."

to represent the community. It hasn't been easy, they have had technical problems, their volunteer staff isn't always accepted by the conventional media professionals and many Vancouverites have never heard of "Co-op Radio." On balance though, the station now seems to be accepted in the community and a major fundraising drive looks as if it will be successful.

- CFRO is an FM station with a 3.7 kilowatt signal, reception in some rural areas is often clear while parts of Vancouver City cannot receive the signal. The signal is carried on some of the cable TV systems.

- Vancouver Co-operative radio was organized in 1973, an application was submitted for an independent station license which was granted in May 1974. The first broadcasts commenced on 14 April 1975. Quality keeps improving.

- CFRO is a non-profit venture with no commercials. It started in a "grant economy," now it must stand or fall on its ability to serve the community.

- The station is debt-free, memberships ($2.00 per share) and member assessments provide a strengthening financial base. Benefits, grants, contests, etc., all contribute their share.

- Approximately 150 people work at the station as volunteers.

A large portion of the musicians heard on the station are local, providing a forum for city groups and bands. The station operates seven days a week, but broadcasts are scheduled to reach their major audiences:

- weekdays the morning show catches people as they get up and travel to work. Sign On: 6:30 a.m.

- weekdays the evening programs reach special audiences with music and culture, public affairs and special events. Sign On: 4:30 to 5:00 p.m.
  Sign Off: 10:45 or later as programs dictate.

- weekends Sign On varies from 10:00 to noon, Sign Off 11:00 p.m. to midnight, programs are educational and informative as well as entertaining. Lots of local music and culture.

THE MORNING SHOW

The sun isn't quite up yet, but the alarm clock is ringing. The morning air is fresh and damp as it comes through the window that you left partly open last night. As the last trace of that final dream recedes from your thoughts you reach across the table beside your bed and turn the alarm off. Between now and the time you have to be at work there's much to do. So, you want something to help you get moving. The radio is there next to the bed, so you turn it on. Classical music - nice, but you've got to get going and it will just hold you back. You twist the dial - rock music and the announcer is selling you an instant solution to your financial problems. You don't want to dance and your finances can wait until tonight. Then twisting the dial once more you happen across a voice that's almost familiar; it could be someone you know, but you're not sure. The news is being read. It doesn't sound like any newscast you've ever heard. The stories are unusual. The information is different from what you're used to. So, you leave the dial.

Following the news, someone is interviewing people on the street. Regular people like yourself; people on their way to work, shopping, sitting in a park, or going to school. Then there is some funky, old jazz music that you've never heard and before long you're humming the tune.

By now you're dressed and drinking a second cup of coffee - the radio host is talking to someone in the studio about how to do home repairs. But, you're going to be late if you don't hustle.

The sunlight is bright now and the room has warmed up. It's been an invigorating morning. The music was just right, you've learned something and even had a good laugh. The radio host is talking now - '...and this is the Morning Show, here on Co-op Radio.' You turn the radio off on your way out the door, but you take note of the dial as you go.

THE MORNING SHOW :
102.7 FM — 6:30 to 9:00 a.m. weekdays

Public affairs programs are committed to city politics but provincial and regional concerns also get aired as they affect Vancouver residents. Background commentaries and interviews provide a context to local events. As far as possible live and taped remotes are used rather than studio productions since the studios are small and the station is dedicated to representing its constituency.

Many of the staff of the station are socially conscious individuals. Staff are sometimes "paid" from special grants or other operating budgets but CFRO depends upon its volunteers. Training includes everything from techniques of operating equipment to interviewing to production. New volunteers join a programming group in an area they're interested in. From the group they will learn the skills needed to make programs. Some volunteers eventually move on to become freelancers with public and commercial AM stations, "not necessarily a step up."

The "Streeters": Radio on the street. Most mornings the views of individual citizens are heard as CFRO conducts its "streeters," on the street interviews. Station volunteers use portable tape recorders (cassette mainly) to record comments of individuals stopped on the street as they hurry through downtown Vancouver. Longer interviews are also conducted in the streets and the parks. Street interviews provide a good way for new volunteers to understand Co-op radio's policy towards representing its listeners and a training ground for interviewing skills. Interviewees are encouraged to "listen to yourself tomorrow on Co-op radio."

Music: CFRO has permanent microphone lines to two of Vancouver's live music clubs.

"There's only one place in town where local musicians who write and play their own brand of rock--be it country, blues, folk, jazz, r and b, or the rock 'n' roll variations-- are encouraged to perform; which is why we go to where the REAL music is happening and bring you a LIVE set every week...."

Local musicians are taped and form a major part of the recorded music heard on the station as well. While the musicians do have outlets in local clubs for their music they would likely not receive any opportunity to broadcast without Co-op radio. Exposure on the station thus helps local artists to gain national recognition through their performers' union.

Obviously such music does not appeal to everyone, CFRO does have other musical programs.   Individual programs are generally geared to specific audiences with local talent and local performances getting the priority.

Children's Programming: Tired of Walt Disney and the usual commercial children's records?   Try CFRO's weekly children's programs: Jingle Pot Road and Flannel Caboose.   Once a month Jingle Pot Road is put together and hosted by the kids themselves--ages 6-12 or so.   Jingle Pot Road features music, stories, jokes and information, much of it specially written for local children by local artists and authors.   The Flannel Caboose on the other hand is a specially prepared series of adventure stories written and recorded for CFRO.   Sound effects abound as "Bolsom Brown" and his friends take to the air in these liberated children's stories.

As part of the station's policy of integrating special audiences into regular programs the children's staff are working to find regular times and formats for inclusion of materials of interest to children in such programs as the Morning Show.

Worker's Council: CFRO is listener owned and operated.   Memberships in the Co-op and annual member assessments help finance the station.   Even more importantly, any listener can join in the operation and management of the station--everything from sweeping the floors to producing programs to deciding station priorities.   Such participatory democracy requires mechanisms for planning and operation: the Worker's Council is one such mechanism.   Every production group (Morning Show, Children's programming, independent producers, etc.) is eligible for elected representation; the Council meets weekly with the co-ordinator to carry on between meetings.   All operational decisions are made by the Council and ratified, if necessary, by the periodic Board Meetings and Annual membership meeting.   Most importantly for CFRO, the Council manages the station, sets policy, and coordinates both committees and volunteers.   Those volunteers who work hardest for the station likely have most influence in operation, but even the rawest newcomer has representation.

Use of Volunteers: CFRO has had paid staff, working in a "Grant economy."   They have often had money for people rather than capital improvements.   At the time of the

EDITING (CONT.)

[EDITING TOOLS]   WHITE LEADER   SPLICING TAPE
        EDITING BLOCK   RED   RAZOR   GREASE PENCIL
                                   LEADER

the tape is held away from the record head if you switch the control lever to "STOP" and then you won't hear anything if you move the tape.

STEP BY   The Actual process of editing involves the following steps: 1) Locating
STEP   the beginning of what you want to take out; 2) Locating the end of what
you want out; 3) Making diagonal cuts and removing unwanted material, 4) Rejoining
remaining tape; 5) "Packaging" finished tape.
    As an example, suppose you have the following segment on tape: "I want to say-is
that thing running?- this about that." You want "is that thing running?" out.

FINDING THE BEGINNING

1. The first step is to play the tape until you reach the beginning of the phrase, then hit the pause button (not the
"STOP" lever!). "Rock" the reels back & forth, listening for
the pause between the "AY" of say & "is". It's the spaces
you'll be hunting for usually-words sound much different
in slow motion!
    Narrow down the point you want 'til you've got it ex-
actly centered on the recording head. (Think the spot is
hard to find? Imagine finding it at 3¾ or 15/8 IPS-see p.11,TOP)
Then mark that very spot with the grease pencil, careful
of marking up the head. Release the INSTANT STOP and listen to make sure you're at the precise spot you want.
    If your next mark will be far away, you will find it use-
ful to return the grease mark to the center of the head
and set the tape counter at '000'. This will save hunting
through miles of tape for your little mark later.

• ROCKING THE REELS

• MARKING THE SPOT

FINDING THE OTHER END

2. To locate the space between "running" & "this", you follow the same procedure as above: locate the general
area, hit the pause button, rock the reels, mark the spot
(note counter number). Remember to leave enough si-
lences on the tape so the final product will be conver-
sational, not jumpy.

USING TAPE COUNTER
SAVES YOU HAVING TO
HUNT FOR THOSE
LITTLE GREASE MARKS

MAKING THE CUTS

3. Now back the tape up to the 1ST mark (counter no.'000')
and turn the control lever to "STOP". Gently pull the tape
away from the head and lay it down in the groove of the
editing block. The backside-with the mark-should be

• PUTTING TAPE IN THE BLOCK

17

Sample page from **CFRO** training handbook.

author's visit however (Spring 1977) the use of paid staff
was being totally discontinued due to the lack of money for
salaries. Even the station engineer, a statutory require-
ment, was to be a volunteer. Judging from the enthusiasm
of the volunteer staff so far, they are likely to be successful.

CASE NUMBER THREE:
CABLE TELEVISION IN EDMONTON

The City of Edmonton, with a population of approximately 500,000, is divided geographically between two cable
companies: Capital Cable TV and QCTV. The two companies jointly program the "community" channel (Cable 10)
on a turnabout basis:

Capital: Mon, Tue, Wed.
QC: Thur, Fri, Sat.
QC reruns programs from the week on Sunday.

Capital has the license to service most of the satellite towns,
thus the city and surrounding area is covered by a single
locally originated channel. Subscribers pay about 50 cents
per month toward the cable programming (QC's 1976 budget
for the community service was approximately $230,000.)
The community service competes for audience with a total
of 11 other channels:

CBXT - English language Canadian Broadcasting Corpora-
        tion
CBXFT - French language Canadian Broadcasting Cor-
        poration
CFRN - Privately owned network affiliate
CITV - Privately owned local station
CKRO - (on one channel only), regional city station
News - Electronically generated news, weather, etc.
ABC, CBS, NBC, PBS - all from Spokane, Washington
Education - Local educational consortium

Because of the small audiences and the interconnec-
tion of Channel 10, many subscribers are unaware of the
dual nature of the programming of the two stations, and in
point of fact the differences are meaningless to the average
viewer. Community programming is mainly programming

VIGNETTES OF COMMUNITY CABLE TV
(Photos by Capital and QCTV)

FOR the community rather than BY the community. The
cable channel serves as training ground for the local commercial stations and good program ideas (and sometimes
personnel) are copied for larger audiences on the commercial stations. Both cable stations have rather small but
adequate studio facilities that lack the technical class of the
better financed broadcasters, however they can in fact do
almost any kind of production that they might desire. Regardless of this, technical quality remains perhaps the cable-
casters biggest headache. They see themselves in competi-
tion with every other available signal, therefore quality must
be competitive. As a result both stations discourage (almost
prohibit) the use of 1/2" video equipment and remote operations require extensive advance planning and equipment support. QC in fact uses its studio type cameras for remote
operations (two cameras, switcher, camera control unit, and
video recorder all in a special mobile van unit). In comparison to CFRO Co-op radio and their on-the-street interviews with a simple cassette recorder the use of television
in the community becomes complex. Most productions are
done "in-studio" and sparse budgets limit the use of film or
photographs.

Typical Programs: The Pentecostal Church has been
running a church initiated magazine type program weekly for
about a year. The program is done live from the QC studio
for a full half hour. Any rehearsals are done earlier at the
church. QC sets up the studio and operates the Camera
Control Unit as well as the control room (video tape recorders, etc.). The church provides the Host, Video Switcher,
Director, Floor Director, Audio Operator and three Camera Operators. Use of three separate "sets" (set-up areas
in the studio) allows the program to flow without interruption.
The "magazine" format includes singing and music, interviews, small discussions, and guests as on a talk show.
The church provided its own sets for the show.

Another QC program is a 1/2 hour live colloquium
crewed and operated by students at one of the local high
schools. Technical support comes from the station.

Every other week QC broadcasts the city council
meetings live with a one-camera set-up. The sessions are
re-broadcast on the Sunday following.

Once a week QC broadcasts one-half hour live of its
QCFM music request show--a televised disc jockey!

On Capital, another program is pre-taped on Sunday mornings without any station assistance. A group of Chinese youths prepare an ethnic magazine, completely crewing their own show, using the studio at a time when it is vacant and normal staff not available.

Capital started with one-half hour per week of programming plus a character generator (electronic typewriter which creates word messages on the screen and repeats them endlessly or with updates). Today they work on a 13-week cycle, at the end of 13 weeks a program is normally finished. The tapes are saved and may be rerun later if appropriate. The 13-week format is easier for obtaining commitments from performers/volunteers and gives a nice neatly defined time schedule for both station and performer. Most programs are pre-taped before the 13-week session begins. As well, Quality turns off its portion of the channel for the month of August for staff holidays except for a community message board provided by the character generator.

Use of Volunteers: "The day of the volunteer is slowly disappearing," even the students taking communications at the local technical institutes have their own school studios and want to earn money if they work for the community channel.

QC Thanks You for being part of
Community Programming

10538 - 114 STREET
EDMONTON, ALBERTA **QCTV LTD** Bus. 425-8410

QCTV notifies
groups about
the "air" time
of their programs
And sends studio
photos of the participants.

PROGRAM ....

TO BE SEEN

DATE ....

TIME ....

CABLE CHANNEL ....

Program: _____ Date: _____

Volunteers are mainly trained on an internship basis:
come, watch, learn, and try it out.   First, help setting up
the studio, move mikes, etc.   Next, graduation to "floor
director," and eventually work as a camera operator on a
simple production.

"We can't afford for them to foul-up, so they (the
volunteers) had better be pretty serious about being a volunteer, or don't waste our time."

Since it is becoming more difficult to obtain volunteers for crew positions the stations have increased their
staff of full and part-time employees.   The stations feel
that if they spent time training volunteers (whether in technical or program skills) there wouldn't really be any end
result on the community channel--just training.

PLEASE BEAR WITH US FOREVER,

TECHNICAL PROBLEMS ARE PERMANENT.

For all these problems however, Capital has a list
of about 70 people available on a volunteer basis to crew
their programs--and it takes much of one permanent staffers
time to compile the crew rosters and fill out the needs with
part-time employees.   Problems between paid and volunteer
staffs seemed minimal.

New Program Ideas: Both stations have program
directors to screen new program ideas regardless of whether
they originate from staff or community.   In some cases a
controversial idea will be discussed with management before
acceptance.   Both stations require an extensive program
proposal--format, content, style, proposed guests, etc.; and
they are very cautious about new programs or unknown people.

"Our staff are not traffic cops to let somebody in and
keep others out, but we are trying to integrate this channel
into the regular TV spectrum.   We must have regularity to
our programs, and we must know in advance what is going
to happen.   Even the TV listing in the newspaper guide requires advance information.   Quality is also important."

"Originally cable TV was to be the BAREFOOT

capital cable 10

SCRIPT SHEET

PROGRAMME TITLE	IT'S A SMALL WORLD	DURATION	28 MINUTES	
COMMUNITY PRODUCER	NANCY GIBSON	REC. DATE	Apr. 22 2 pm.	TELECAST DATE ? June 1
DIRECTOR		NO. OF GUESTS	2	John Jones, Exec. Div Robert Foster, Cdn Hunger Fdn Alta Rep. Cdn Hunger Fdn

STUDIO REQUIREMENTS: (USE OTHER SIDE OF SHEET IF NECESSARY)

3 chairs, coffee table, globe

VIDEO	SEG. TIME	RUNNING TIME	AUDIO
Intro - slides/photos	90 sec.		Tape: It's a small world - to be inserted later.
* Regular intro to be prepared & inserted later.			
Intro of show, guests		1½ min	Studio.
(question & answer) discussion period			
Slides (20)	10 min	15 min	✓ (discussion)
Closing remarks		25 min ↓ 28 min	✓ ✓

SUMMARY: What are the Agencies doing?
A look at the Canadian Hunger Foundation.

PLEASE FILL OUT AND BRING WITH YOU TO THE STUDIO   7024 - 101 AVE.   465-6571

MEDIUM--the open door for the community. However, it is still television, especially on cable where the community channel is merely one of many channels."

Available Services: OK, assume that we have managed to have a program idea accepted for use on the cable channel, we have our staff and performers all lined up. What can we expect in the way of services from the cable station?

- technical advice, program advice and assistance in producing and directing the show.

- press-on lettering for graphics, you make your own; or the limited services of a free-lance graphic artist; or the use of the character generator for superimposed titles, etc.

- extremely limited budget, perhaps, for film, slides, etc. (no filming is done by the station).

PLEASE BE CLEAR
AND ACCURATE!

capital cable tv ltd.

TAPE # _____   VTR CUE SHEET & PROMOTIONAL INFORMATION

	PRODUCTION AND NUMBER		TIME	PLAYDATE	REC.MACHINE
A					
B					

	COMMUNITY PRODUCER	DIRECTOR	# OF PARTICIPANTS	DATE RECORDED
A				
B				

	TECHNICAL DETAILS (opening, closing cues, tape faults - specify)
A	
B	

	Special instructions and promotional information - eg. guests, topic etc.
A	
B	

- mobile television studio for major events which would be of wide interest. Excerpts can be used for individual programs.

- 16mm and 8mm movie projectors as well as 35mm slide projectors for including visuals.

- studio time, including technical crew if necessary, and video-tape facilities (3/4" cassette or 1" reel to reel).

- limited promotional facilities: TV Guide, and newspaper listing.

For the Future: Edmonton seems to be a very conservative community which is busy making money. Only a small minority cares about "community" issues. Community groups often have only 1-2 members who really carry the momentum for their organization. The seemingly "urgent" issues get diffused and public affairs programs generated by the community groups become almost impossible. In the reality of this situation at least one station--Capital--is considering initiating its own public affairs programs. The problem is one of budget, the broadcast stations have a much larger budget and while they seem to have abdicated the area of community issue programming it is hard to compete. Capital doesn't want to be the same as the broadcast stations, but to be an accepted part of the television scene means competing in terms of program quality.

GLOSSARY

This glossary contains some of the commonly confused terminology in five areas: Photographic, Motion Picture Production, Screen Language, Television, Print Materials. In practice many of the terms are used in other areas; however, they are separated here for clarity in understanding.

Photographic

ASA: abbreviation for American Standards Association, refers to the relative speed of photographic film. A film with a low ASA number, such as ASA25, requires more light than an ASA400 film to take a picture under the same circumstances (light can be added through increasing the size of the aperture opening, slowing the shutter speed, or by using flash or flood lights).

Automatic Lens: a lens containing a mechanism to close the lens down automatically to the required aperture for picture taking and open it again for focusing for the next shot.

Bellows Unit: an adjustable tunnel which fits between the camera and the lens to facilitate taking close-up pictures (or for focusing a view camera).

Between-the-Lens Shutter: a camera shutter manufactured as an integral part of the lens.

Black and White Prints: a black and white photographic image printed on paper. Any size possible. Almost always made from a b & w negative. Prints the same size as the negative are called contact prints; they are useful for selection of shots to be enlarged. Good b & w enlargements are easily made with a minimum of equipment providing care is exercised.

Black and White Slides: A projectable b & w image. Not
   very common. Can be made using a b & w reversal
   film or duplicated from a negative. Special purpose
   high contrast slides can be made on "litho" or high
   contrast ortho films such as printers use. These
   can then be colored with felt pens for title slides,
   etc.

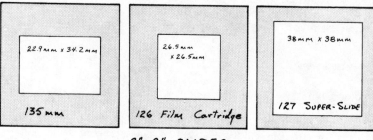

135mm — 22.9mm x 34.2mm
126 Film Cartridge — 26.5mm x 26.5mm
127 Super-Slide — 38mm x 38mm

2" x 2" SLIDES

Black Body: a camera which has all the metal parts painted
   black to decrease reflections when doing copy work
   or photographing shiny objects.

Close-up Lens: any lens that permits the subject to be
   closer than normal to the camera (useful for flower
   and insect pictures, etc.).

Color Prints: A color photographic image printed on paper.
   Any size possible. Most are made from a negative
   film. Color dyes used tend to fade in sunlight.
   Drugstore prints tend to be pretty poor; for high
   quality prints use professional materials and a custom printer (a person who specialized in high quality
   special orders). The extra cost of "custom" services provides much better quality.

Color Slides: a projectable image in color. Several sizes
   from 16mm to 8" x 10" or larger. Most common
   ones fit a 2" x 2" mount. Usually made on a color
   reversal film.

Coupled Light Meter: a light meter, either inside or on the
   camera, which is mechanically or electronically connected to the shutter to save time and make the camera operation less complex.

Daylight Film: a film ordinarily used for shooting outdoors. Will look very yellow or red if shot under incandescent lighting without a filter.

Diazo Film: a light-sensitive material for making transparencies. Available in many different colors. Exposed by ultraviolet light and processed in ammonia gas.

Electronic Shutter: any shutter controlled by an electronic mechanism; supposedly makes for better and more accurate operation.

Extension Tubes: metal tubes which are placed between the lens and the camera body to facilitate taking close-up pictures.

Eye Level Viewfinder: a device for focusing and/or framing the photographic image, must be raised to your eye level for use. (See also Waist Level Viewfinder.)

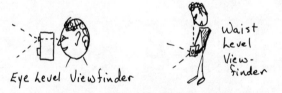

Eye Level Viewfinder   Waist Level View-finder

f stop: the stops or positions corresponding to the size of opening of the aperture (the adjustable hole in the lens) indicating the relative amount of light striking the film. A small f/rating indicates a "fast" lens. In other words, it can take pictures in a darker setting.

Fish Eye Lens: an extremely short wide-angle novelty lens with very broad coverage.

Fixed Focus Camera: a camera with a lens which is effectively "in focus" from about 4 feet to infinity; i.e., does not require focusing.

Focal Length: in layman's terms, a measure of the effective angle of coverage of the lens. A short focal length lens is a wide angle lens, a long focal length lens is a telephoto lens. (See also Normal Lens.)

Wide Angle

Normal

Telephoto

LENS COVERAGE

Establishing
or Long Shot
(LS)

Medium Shot
(MS)

Close Shot
(CS)

Close-Up
(CU)

Extreme
Close-Up (ECU)

All terminology is relative, ie: the ECU
above might be the establishing shot
for a look at the man's tonsils.

Focal Plane Shutter: the piece of metal or rubberized cloth
that sits just in front of the film plane which opens
and closes to take the picture. Mainly used on removable lens cameras.

Graphic Arts: the printing industry, which uses large quantities of special purpose films and papers. Most
graphic arts cameras are large view cameras (sometimes called process cameras) with vacuum backs to
hold the film smooth. Most graphic arts films record
only the high contrasts of black and white (no grey).

Hand-held Meter: a light meter which is not attached to the
     camera and is held in the hand for use. A reflected
     light meter measures the amount of light reflected
     back towards the camera from the subject. A spot
     meter is a very accurate reflected light meter which
     measures the light from a very small area of the
     subject. An incident meter measures the amount of
     light falling upon the subject and requires the photog-
     rapher to walk up to the subject.

Instamatic Type: a camera using a plastic "pop-in" cartridge
     containing the film. First developed by Kodak, the
     camera is very easy to load and unload.

Lens Converters: optical accessories which go between the
     lens and the camera to increase its effective focal
     length. A 2x converter added to a 50mm lens makes
     it equivalent to a 100mm telephoto.

Macro Lens: a lens that will operate normally and focus
     close enough to take close-up pictures. Normally
     macro lenses will permit 1:1 or 1:2 image reductions.

Manual Lens: a lens which requires the photographer to
     change the aperture setting manually for focusing and
     picture taking.

Microfilm: a special high contrast duplicating film available
     for copying records and other documents for safekeep-
     ing. While the home photographer doesn't have the
     facilities to do large volume microfilming, small runs
     are possible when perfect quality is not essential.

Microphotography: photography through the microscope.

Motion Picture Films: projectable photographic films for
     use in a camera capable of recording motion. A
     wide variety of both color and black and white, nega-
     tive-positive and reversal materials are available for
     use under almost any light conditions.

Negative Material: a film or other photographic product
     which reproduces an image with tonal (and/or color)
     values reversed. Black and white negatives repro-
     duce a white original as black and vice versa. Color
     negatives have both color and density reversed.

Normal Lens: a lens which will give a picture approximating

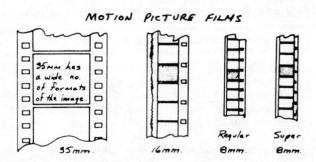

MOTION PICTURE FILMS

35mm has a wide no. of formats of the image.

35mm.   16mm.   Regular 8mm.   Super 8mm.

Super 8mm and Reg. 8mm film is the same width. The difference is in the image area and sprocket hole locations.

Regular 8mm is made by splitting special 16mm film in half, after processing. Super 8mm and Single 8 use the same format.

what the eye could see.   To find the normal lens for a camera, measure the diagonal distance across the negative area in millimeters, that distance will be roughly the focal length of the normal lens in milli-meters.

Plastic Lens: cheaper cameras may be made of plastic, in-cluding the lens.   While a plastic lens is extremely inexpensive in comparison to a properly polished glass lens, the plastic lens can give quite acceptable results (except that they scratch easily).

Polaroid Materials: photographic films and papers which use "in-camera" development to give an instant (ten sec-onds to two minutes) print.   Available in both color and black and white for special cameras.   Multiple or duplicate copies are usually difficult to obtain and quality of the duplicates is poor (unless you use the special material which produces a black and white print and a negative for future use).

Positive Image: film or other photographic image which represents the original image with the same tone and colors as the original; i.e., black is black, red is red, etc.

Preset Lens: a lens which has a mechanism for presetting the required aperture so that it may be opened (to

allow more light to enter) for focusing, then closed
for picture taking at the proper aperture.

Range Finder: a system of focusing through a form of tri-
angulation, using a special set of lenses above or beside the taking lens.

Reversal Materials: film or other photographic material
which produces a positive image without requiring a
negative step.

Single Lens Reflex: a camera which uses the picture taking
lens for the viewing lens. It has the advantage that
you see exactly what the film will record.

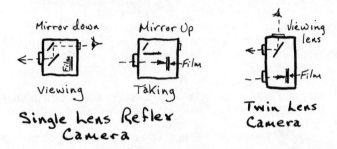

Stabilization Paper: a black and white photographic paper
which is used when a large volume of temporary
prints is required. (Very effective for press releases and TV work.)

Telephoto Lens: any lens that has a focal length longer than
the normal lens. A 135mm telephoto is very popular
for a 35mm camera. It has a narrower angle of
coverage than the normal lens.

Through-the-Lens Meter: a reflected light meter which
evaluates the amount of light passing through the
lens of the camera. The meter is inside the camera and may record the light over part or all of the
image using a variety of measuring systems. Properly used, it should give a more accurate reading
than a normal hand-held meter.

Twin Lens Reflex: a camera which uses two lenses, one
above the other. The top lens is for viewing and

has no shutter. The bottom lens is used for taking
the picture. The top lens does not see exactly the
same image as the bottom lens for close-ups.

Type A Film: a film balanced to use with photoflood bulbs
(3400° K).

Type B Film: a film balanced to use with 3200° K light.

View Camera: a camera which has a removable back to
allow the photographer to focus directly at the film
plane (image is upside down and reversed). Camera
is mounted on a tripod and focusing is done underneath a black cloth. (Remember the frontier photographers!) Used for 4" x 5" and larger formats.

Waist Level Viewfinder: a device for focusing and/or framing the photographic image which can be used with
the camera at waist level. (See also Eye Level
Viewfinder.)

Wide Angle Lens: any lens that has a focal length shorter
than the normal lens. It has a broader coverage than
the normal lens. A wide angle lens is useful for
taking pictures of large objects when you cannot get
very far away.

Motion Picture Production

Camera Film: the film used in the camera. Many camera
films cannot be projected because the emulsion is too
soft.

Composite or Answer Print: a duplicate copy of the edited
film containing both picture and sound in their (hopefully) correct relationships. This is the last stage
where changes can still be made.

Conforming the Original: editing the original film so that
it "conforms" to the finished work print. Since we
have edited the work print, we must now make the
same cuts and splices in the original to be able to
print our final production.

Dolly: a movable platform for use under a camera tripod.

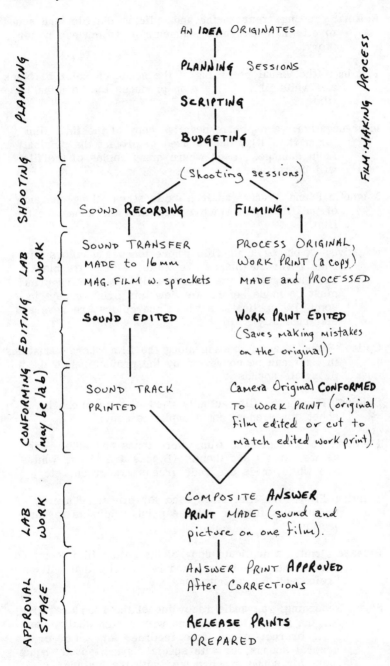

FILM-MAKING PROCESS

PLANNING

AN **IDEA** ORIGINATES

PLANNING SESSIONS

SCRIPTING

BUDGETING

SHOOTING

(Shooting sessions)

SOUND **RECORDING**   **FILMING.**

LAB WORK

SOUND TRANSFER
MADE to 16mm
MAG. FILM w. sprockets

PROCESS ORIGINAL,
WORK PRINT (a copy)
MADE and PROCESSED

EDITING

SOUND EDITED

WORK PRINT EDITED
(Saves making mistakes
on the original).

CONFORMING
(may be lab)

SOUND TRACK
PRINTED

Camera Original **CONFORMED**
TO WORK PRINT (original
film edited or cut to
match edited work print).

LAB WORK

COMPOSITE **ANSWER
PRINT MADE** (sound and
picture on one film).

APPROVAL STAGE

ANSWER PRINT **APPROVED**
After CORRECTIONS

RELEASE PRINTS
PREPARED

Editing: cutting, rearranging and splicing the film and sound
     to eliminate unwanted segments or to make a better
     story.

Filming: the visual recording of the scene on color or black
     and white film. This step produces the "original"
     film.

Inter-negative: a duplicate negative copy of the final film
     (or part of it) which is used to protect the original
     from damage. Used where many copies of the film
     will be produced.

Magnetic Sound Track: an iron oxide stripe along one side
     of the film upon which is recorded the sound for the
     film.

Negative: a photographic film where tones and colors have
     been reversed (blacks are white, whites are black,
     reds are green, greens are red). A positive print
     must be made before we view this print (except in
     some TV applications where the colors are reversed
     electronically).

Optical Sound Track: a strip along the film where variations
     in light can be converted by the projector into the ap-
     propriate sounds.

Original Film: the film actually used in the camera to
     shoot our scenes; not a duplicate copy.

Positive: a photographic film where tones and colors are
     as we usually see them. (Blacks are black, whites
     are white, reds are red, greens are green, etc.)

Printing Film: the film stock used for preparing a copy of
     the camera film or release print. Suitable for pro-
     jection.

Release Print: a duplicate copy of the edited film; contains
     both sound and picture, and is the film that will be
     "released" for distribution.

Sound Recording: an audio recording of the sound required
     for the film. May be done with a high quality cas-
     sette or reel-to-reel tape recorder for "wild" or
     general sounds, or with special "synch-sound" equip-
     ment for sound synchronized with the picture.

Sound Transfer: a duplicate copy of the original sound re-
    cording, usually on 16mm wide, iron oxide coated
    film stock. This aids in editing.

Wild Sound: sounds that have been recorded at the same
    general time that the picture was shot, but not
    synchronized with the picture. Wild sound can be
    added to the film during editing and can even be
    synchronized. For example, if we were shooting a
    house being built we might record the sound of a
    man hammering, move the tape recorder away so
    that it wasn't in the picture, shoot the scene of the
    carpenter hammering in another nail, and then, if
    lucky, combine the sound and action during editing.

Work Print: a duplicate copy of the original film which can
    be projected, viewed and edited. Using a work print
    saves the original from scratches and from being ac-
    cidentally cut up.

Screen Language

Shot: one single run of the camera.

Sequence: series of shots, usually on the same topic.

Scene: long sequence with a beginning and an end.

Straightcut: use within a scene to move between shots of
    the same subject. No time transition, as shots shift
    instantaneously.

Fade-out, Fade-in: scene brightness decreases to black and
    vice-versa. Used in moving from one idea to an-
    other with a long time or space gap implied.

Dissolve: fade-out and fade-in overlapped to show passage
    of time or distance. Long dissolve (up to 5 seconds)
    provides a slow transition, shortest is usually about
    1/3 second and provides a very quick change. Nor-
    mal dissolve is about 2 seconds. It is usually best
    to dissolve on action shots, although very well
    framed static shots will not "jump."

Matched Action: shows one continuous action through sev-
    eral different viewpoints. Each shot (viewpoint)
    requires a separate camera (or a repeat of the

action for each shot). The point at which the action
was "cut" in the first shot is picked up in the next
with no addition or subtraction of action or time.
Hands or other noticeable objects must be in exactly
the same place in every shot of the sequence to avoid
"jump cuts" where an object appears to jump from
one point to another without apparent reason. Fast
action may not require exact matching.

Cut Away: a shot of reaction or some other related activity
that builds emotion, relieves screen boredom or fills
in for a missing point in the action. For example:
1) shot of man digging hole (long shot); 2) shot of
dirt being piled up (close-up); 3) shot of man completing hole (long shot). The shot of the dirt pile
eliminated the need for 30 minutes of the man digging.

Super: two scenes run simultaneously so the images are
superimposed. Often used for titles.

Television

Audio Tape: an iron oxide-coated tape which will record
and store audible sounds (such as voices) for later
playback. Often called magnetic tape, it is used on
a tape recorder.

Broadcast Television: a television system where the program or signal is "broadcast" into the air from a
large antenna. The program can be received on a
home television set.

Cable: the wire which hooks television sets together in a
cable television system.

Cable License: the license which is allocated to a cable
operator to provide cable television. The license
sets out the requirements and responsibilities of a
cable operator. Often called "a license to print
money" since it is generally believed that cable operators can make generous profits on their investment.

Cable Operator: an individual or company with a franchise
(license) to operate a cable television station. Also
the manager of such a system where the owner lives
elsewhere.

Cable Television: a system of "wiring" homes together with
a television cable (like a telephone cable) to provide
a better picture or an increased number of TV channels available for selection. Again, as with the telephone system, the subscriber pays a hook-up charge
and a monthly rental fee. The "cable" hooks up to
the ordinary television set in exactly the same manner as the antenna normally does.

Charter Board, Media Co-op, Board of Directors, Community
Board: terms which refer to organizations which
would be established to work with (not for) the cable
operator to provide community television programming.
Some proponents would prefer them to be the holder
of a license to produce the programs for a community
television channel, leaving the cable operator with the
task of distributing the programs over his cable system.

Closed Circuit Television (CCTV): a television system where
the TV camera and microphone are connected directly
(usually by wires) to the television set (monitor).
The television signal is not broadcast through the air
as is the normal commercial television program, and
cannot be received on any television set that is not
physically connected. Often used in schools and in
security surveillance systems.

Community Access: a term used to indicate the ability of
a member of the community to participate in the production of a television program. Usually a commercial television crew will make a program "about" a
community. "Access" implies that the community
will use the media tools to make a program about
itself.

Community Antenna Television System (CATV): a cable system where the cable operator or owner has erected
a large antenna which is hooked up to several television sets (maybe several thousand sets in a large
community) to improve television reception. Often
used in apartment houses so that each tenant does
not need his own antenna.

Community Channel: the term used to describe one or more
channels on a cable television system reserved for
local community programming. (See also Community
Access.)

Community Feedback: the process of obtaining responses
   from a community regarding an issue under discussion. Phone-in radio shows solicit listener "feedback."

Community Involvement: a term which refers to the working of individuals and/or groups on a community
   project or problem.

Community Television (or Community Programming): variety of definitions; usually meaning television programs
   which originate from the local community where they
   are shown. These could include anything from local
   newscasts and sport events, to local drama productions and talk shows. Used also to mean locally produced programs which members of the community itself have prepared rather than being prepared by
   professional broadcasters.

Copyright: the protection that an artist or writer receives
   to restrict copying of any creative material. Copyrighted materials should not be reproduced without
   permission from the artist or author (and often the
   payment of a fee).

Director: the creative person who controls the artistic and
   technical quality of a program.

Edit, Editing, Editing Capability: terms referring to the
   ability to take scenes from film or videotape that
   were shot at different times and to combine them
   into a single smooth presentation, or to remove
   material from a film or videotape to make a shorter
   production.

Educational Television (ETV): a term which, when adapted
   to Canada, means television programming of "courses
   of study" to an audience of "students." Includes
   such programs as "How to Play Bridge" and "Sesame
   Street."

EVR, Instavision, Videocassette: commercial trade names
   for machines or systems for playing back a prerecorded program, and in some cases for recording
   programs.

Film: the photographic material used to make a motion

picture or a still photograph. (See also Videotape and Kinescope.)

Film Chain: the machine which allows a motion picture to be shown on television (can be 16mm or Super 8mm).

Graphics: lettering or drawings which are used on television to help explain concepts where words are not adequate. May also include segments of film for the same purpose.

Hardware: equipment, machines, black boxes and related wires necessary to record or play-back any media program (software).

Instructional Television (ITV): an American term referring to television programs which provide direct instruction in a specific course of study, such as "Social Studies 30" or "university credit courses by television."

Kinescope: a film record of a television program made by photographing a special television set with motion picture film. Can be viewed on a normal film projector.

Media: communications tools or processes including television, radio, newspapers, posters, books, films, slides, artistic works, photographs. A badly misused term. (Medium is the singular form.)

Microwave: a system to transmit television signals from one point to another point over long distances without using cables. A microwave system is used to bring CBC and CTV network programs to Alberta from the production centers in eastern Canada and is used to import U.S. television programs for cable television systems.

Monitor: a special television set which does not have any sound system. Used indiscriminantly to refer to any television set (e.g., home receiver).

Producer: the person who organized a film or television production. Often combined with the director as a producer/director in low budget productions.

Public Television (PTV): an American term which refers to

"public affairs" television, and the type of station which carries public affairs television. Now also refers to most U.S. educational television stations.

Software: the program, production or presentation for use on any media system (hardware). May be a book, play, speech, film, television program, etc.

Studio (Television Studio): a room or series of rooms with special lighting and other facilities to enable television programs to be produced. Usually contains several television cameras, video tape recorder and mysterious black boxes that only technicians (experts) are allowed to touch.

Talent Release: the legal document which gives a photographer or producer permission to use a photograph, audio recording or video recording of a person for inclusion in a television program, film, etc.

Video Tape: the 1/4", 1/2", 3/4", 1" or 2"-wide coated plastic tape which is used on a VTR to record television programs.

Video Tape Recorder (VTR): a machine which records television picture and sound on a magnetic tape for later replay. Commercial television stations have used large VTRs for years but now there are portable battery-operated machines.

Print Materials

Binding: stapling, gluing or otherwise fastening printed sheets into a pad, booklet or book. Common fasteners include plastic or wire coils and the common cardboard covers with bending metal posts.

Bond Paper: a good quality paper originally used for government bonds and legal documents. An excellent writing and typing paper, the best of which is made from rag pulp. Most bond papers will have a "watermark" which can be seen by holding the paper up to the light.

Bristol Board: a heavy art board available in varying thicknesses. Individual sheets of quality paper are glued together to make a stiff art medium.

Card Stock: also called "board." Any heavy paper material which resists bending. Used for covers, posters, boxes, etc.

Coated Paper: a paper that has been coated with a layer of ink-absorbent china clay. Such papers are usually very white and quite smooth. Often called art paper. Essential for highest quality printing.

Collating: arranging individual pages of a publication into proper order.

Color Separations: the special negatives prepared from a color photograph or illustration to enable the printer to print in color.

Continuous Tone Photograph: the common black and white or color photographic print prepared by a photographic laboratory from a negative. In a good photo there will be a continuous range of tones from pure white to solid black, and the gray tones will provide detail.

Copy Editing: marking the draft to give the printer exact directions for setting each line. Directions will include type size, italics, column and page sizes, etc.

Direct Image Master: a paper plate for offset duplicating. A typewriter with a special carbon acetate ribbon, special reproducing ink, reproducing pencil or grease pencil can all be used to make an image directly on the plate. Good for perhaps 500 copies if carefully made.

Draft: one of several versions of an uncompleted project. The FINAL DRAFT should be the exact text that will go to the printers, cameramen or announcers.

Dummy: a mock-up showing the size, style, and layout of a finished publication.

Halftone Photograph: a photographic illustration prepared from a special "screened" negative. The photo will contain only black and white tones, with the apparently gray areas formed by small dots of varying sizes. (Look at a newspaper photo under a magnifying glass to see the dot structure.)

High Contrast Print: a photographic print which contains
   only full black and white without any gray tones.

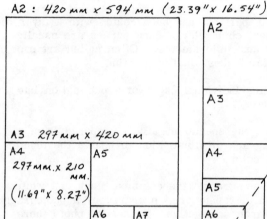

A2 : 420 mm × 594 mm (23.39"× 16.54")

A3   297 mm × 420 mm

A4
297 mm × 210
        mm.

(11.69"× 8.27")

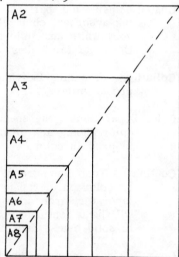

International Paper Sizes : Each ½ of larger size.

International Paper Sizes: a system of standard paper sizes.
   Each size is produced by
   halving the long side of the
   preceding sheet. A0 size is
   one square meter and A4 is
   the size of a normal piece of
   typing paper. The system is
   designed to eliminate wastage
   from cutting odd sizes from
   a large sheet of paper.

Letterpress Type

& letterpress Stamp

Justified Copy: a block of typeset
   textual material that has even
   margins on both sides. The
   individual lines of type are
   adjusted to an equal length by
   varying the spacing between
   letters and words.

Letterpress: Ink is rolled onto the

raised surfaces of type (hand or machine set) and special blocks for illustrations. Areas which are not to
be printed are recessed below the inked surface.
Most printing of this type is done by professional
printshops with a "flat-bed press."

Line Illustration: an illustration composed of solid lines
and black areas on a white background. A pen and
ink sketch is a good example.

Offset lithography:
Printing plate is wet by water
roller (A), inked by ink roller
(B), plate is wrapped around
roller (C), image is transferred
to rubber blanket (D) in reverse.

The image is again "offset" onto
the paper.

Lithography: the various lithography printing processes
work because ink and water do not mix. A master
plate is prepared with a "greasy" image, is mois-
tened with water and inked. The ink adheres to the
greasy image and can be transferred to the printing
material (usually paper). "Offset" printing uses the
lithographic process; the ink is first transferred to
a rubber roller and then to the paper.

Newsprint: a common term to refer to the inexpensive wood
pulp paper used by newspapers. Can be obtained in
sheets and rolls. For making quick drawings and
work where permanence is not required.

Offset Duplication: see Lithography.

Offset Paper: strong wood-pulp bonds and cartridge papers which range from rough to semi-smooth. They are specially designed for offset lithography.

Proof: a supposedly correct copy of a photograph or printed material. The proof is checked for accuracy, color, size, etc. In film-making the proof stage is the ANSWER PRINT.

Saddle Stitching: the staples or thread run along the line of the center crease of a booklet. The booklet can open out flat.

Saddle Stitched
(will open flat)

Side Stitching: staples are placed about 1/4" in from the edge of the bound sheets. Staples run completely through each page.

Sign Press: a simple flat bed letterpress machine with large type for making posters and display signs.

Silk Screen Duplication: a printing process for posters, etc., using an organdy, silk or wire screen stencil.

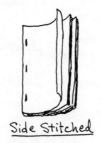

Side Stitched

Spirit Duplication: an inexpensive printing process which uses an image prepared with a special carbon "ink" soluble in methyl hydrate. The most usual ink color is purple. A "spirit duplicator" uses a master prepared on paper (in reverse) and the "hectograph" uses a master prepared on gelatin (again in reverse). The paper is dampened with methyl hydrate and is placed in contact with the master to transfer the image. High quality duplicator paper must be used.

Stencil Duplication: a printing process which uses ink or paint forced through a cut-out design in an otherwise impermeable stencil. "Cyclostyle" and "mimeo" machines as well as the "silk screen" poster ma-

Hand crank "spirit" Duplicator

Wooden Silk Screen Frame
can be made almost any size.

chines use perforated stencils. Open cut-out stencils
are used for poster making (and for shipping labels,
etc.) Newsprint or uncoated papers must be used.

Uncoated Paper: any paper which has not been coated with a
    clay finish. Some uncoated papers can be quite
    smooth if they are polished with machine rollers.

Xerography: a copying process where carbon particles are
    deposited on the page electrostatically and fused with
    heat. Inexpensive paper masters for offset duplica-
    tion and copies on clear acetate for overhead projec-
    tion can be produced as well as paper copies.

BIBLIOGRAPHY

This bibliography contains those books and periodicals which would most likely answer questions raised by this Handbook. Obviously it would be impossible to cover all of these diverse topics in any one book. A good library of reference materials is the best back-up to your own experience. Don't be put off by technical descriptions; get out and try the techniques yourself.

BOOKS

Albertson, D. R. and C. J. Hannan, eds. Twenty Exercises for the Classroom. Fairfax, Va.: NTL/Learning Resources Corporation, 1972.
A beginner's set of simple training exercises for use in a classroom situation. Can be adapted easily.

American Association of Agricultural College Editors. Communications Handbook. Danville, Ill.: AAACE, 1970.
Covers a wide range of topics: speaking, writing, radio, TV, photography, exhibits.

Biegeleisen, J. I. and M. A. Cohn. Silk Screen Techniques. New York: Dover, 1958.
Equipment, technique and design for silk screen printing.

Bigbee, Lynn, ed. Table Talk. Memphis, Tenn.: Motion Picture Laboratories, Inc.
A periodic series of leaflets on film production. (Free).

Brady, John. The Craft of Interviewing. New York: Vintage, 1977.
Well written tips, anecdotes on interviews for publication.

DeWitt, Jack. Producing Industrial Films. New York:

Barnes, 1968.
 Simple and straightforward.

Eastman Kodak Company. Index to Kodak Technical Information. Rochester, N.Y.: Annual.
 Lists all of the current Kodak publications. Also
 available from Kodak Canada Ltd., Toronto.

Eboch, Sidney C. Operating Audio-Visual Equipment. San
 Francisco: Chandler.
 My issue is 1968; probably a newer one is available.
 It is a useful training manual.

Flesch, Rudolf. The Art of Readable Writing. New York:
 Harper & Bros., 1949.
 Currently out of print but should be available in most
 libraries. Contains a method of determining readability
 of written materials. Other techniques are perhaps
 more useful but the Flesch formula can be worked by
 anyone who can count and perform basic arithmetic.

Forbes, Dorothy and Sanderson Layng. The New Communicators. Ottawa: Canadian Cable Television Assoc.,
 1977.
 Cable operator's guide to community programming.

Garland, Ken. Graphics Handbook. New York: Reinhold,
 1966.
 Very useful for the beginner and a good reminder for
 the professional. Techniques, style and equipment.

Hamm, Jack. Cartooning the Head and Figure. New York:
 Grosset and Dunlap, 1967.
 Often reprinted, this is a collection of procedures
 for cartooning people.

Hicks, Warren B. and Alma M. Tillin. Developing Multi-
 Media Libraries. New York: Bowker, 1970.
 Selection, organization, cataloguing, processing and
 storage.

Horn, Robert E. The Guide to Simulations/Games for Edu-
 cation and Training. (4th ed.) Information Resources,
 P.O. Box 417, Lexington, Mass. To be published in
 1979.
 Previous editions were edited by Zuckerman and
 Horn. Lists many of the commercially and noncommer-

cially produced simulations and games available. Cate-
gorized by subjects; includes evaluations.

Hutchins, M.   Typographics: A Designer's Handbook of
   Printing Techniques. London: Studio Vista, 1969.
      Typography and printing.

Kemp, Jerrod E.   Planning and Producing A-V Materials.
   (2nd ed.) San Francisco: Chandler Publishers.
      Professional and semi-professional techniques. The
   same planning sequence is required for high-budget commercial media and low-budget locally produced materials.

Latimer, H. C.   Advertising Production Planning and Copy
   Preparation for Offset Printing. (3rd ed.) New York:
   Art Direction Book Co. , 1974.
      Oriented toward the advertising trade but covers all
   the fundamentals of planning and copy preparation. A
   good companion to Smith's books.

Laughlin, T.   Education and Extension Communication.
   Rome: FAO of the UN, 1974.
      A prototype package of materials for "extension"
   education.

Milam, Lorenzo W.   Sex and Broadcasting: A Handbook on
   Starting a Radio Station for the Community. Saratoga,
   Calif. : Dildo Press, 1971.
      Practical information on how to start a community-
   based radio station in the U. S. A.

Miller, A. C. and Walter Strenge.   American Cinematog-
   rapher Manual. Hollywood: American Society of
   Cinematographers.
      The motion picture cameraman's bible.

Minor, Edward and Harvey R. Frye.   Techniques for Producing Visual Instructional Media. New York: McGraw
   Hill.
      Written for teachers but contains many basic tech-
   niques with universal application.

National Audio-Visual Assoc.   A-V Equipment Directory.
   Fairfax, Va. : National Audio-Visual Assoc. , annual.
      Lists most of the audio-visual equipment available
   with basic specifications. No evaluation of quality.

National Development Service. Communicating with Pictures
    in Nepal. Kathmandu: NDS and UNICEF, 1976.
    A well done study of community visual literacy. Use-
    ful guide for surveying your community.

Nelms, H. Thinking with a Pencil. New York: Barnes
    and Noble, 1964.
    Can be used to teach oneself how to sketch and draw.
    Shows many simple techniques for tracing, modifying
    sketches, stick figures, etc.

Pett, Dennis W., ed. Audio-Visual Communication Hand-
    book. Bloomington, Ind.: Audio-Visual Center, Indiana
    University.
    Originally prepared for Peace Corps use, the booklet
    emphasizes planning and basic production techniques.

Pfeiffer, J. W. and J. E. Jones, eds. Annual Handbook
    for Group Facilitators. La Jolla, Calif.: University
    Associates. Annually since 1972.
    A series of practical exercises, lecturettes, and
    evaluation tools for the human relations trainer. They
    are easily adapted for the communications trainer in a
    cross-cultural setting.

_____, eds. Handbook of Structured Experiences for
    Human Relations Training. La Jolla, Calif.: Univer-
    sity Associates. Annual volumes since 1969.
    Structured activities for group problem-solving, inter-
    group communications, etc. Correlated with the Annual
    Handbooks above and indexed in The Reference Guide to
    Handbooks and Annuals.

Smith, Keith. Community Newspapers; Print, How You Can
    Do It Yourself; Basic Video in Community Work. Lon-
    don: Inter-Action in Print (14 Talacre Road, London,
    NWJ 3PE).
    These booklets are part of a series of community
    oriented manuals to de-professionalize the media ser-
    vices.

Srinivasan, Lyra. Workshop Ideas for Family Planning
    Education. New York: World Education, 1975.
    An interesting collection of materials for workshop
    use. Useful for communications training as well as a
    model package.

Turabian, Kate L. A Manual for Writers of Term Papers, Theses and Dissertations. Chicago: University of Chicago Press, 1967.
    Layout and presentation of typed reports.

                        PERIODICALS
    Note: Use your library to inspect at least one year's issues before you subscribe to any journal.

Alternatives in Print. Chicago: American Library Assoc., Social Responsibilities Round Table.

Audio-Visual Instruction. Washington, D.C.: Association for Educational Communications and Technology.

Business Screen. New York: Harcourt Brace Jovanovich.

EPIE Gram and EPIE Reports. New York: Educational Products Information Exchange Institute.

ERIC Publications. Educational Resources Information Centers across the United States publish newsletters on such topics as adult education, mass media, educational technology, etc. Consult your library for details.

Film Makers Newsletter. Ward Hill, Ma.

Film News. New York: Film News Company.

ICIT Report. Washington, D.C.: Information Center on Instructional Technology.

Industrial Photography. New York: United Business.

Kilobaud Microcomputing. Peterborough, N.H.: 1001001, Inc.

Media and Methods. Philadelphia: North American Publishing.

Modern Photography. New York: ABC Leisure Magazines.

Movie Maker. U.K.: Model & Allied Publications.

Popular Photography. New York: Ziff-Davis.

Professional Photographer. Chicago: Professional Photographer's of America.

Rain: Journal of Appropriate Technology.   Portland, Ore.:
     Umbrella, Inc., 2270 N.W. Irving, 97210.

                    SIMULATIONS
     (Described in the section "Gaming in the Community")

Dirty Water.   Urban Systems, Inc., 1033 Massachusetts
     Ave., Cambridge, Mass.   02138.

Community Disaster.   Western Publishing Co. Ltd., 850
     Third Avenue, New York, N.Y., 10022.

Living City.   Designed by Amy and Lynn Zelmer but no
     longer available.   The simulation made extensive
     use of citizen feedback via cable television and dis-
     cussion groups.

Starpower.   Western Behavioral Sciences Institute, 1150
     Silverado, La Jolla, Calif., 92037.

INDEX

This index has been prepared in two parts. The first is a quick reference guide to processes. It directs you to the first occurrence of the topic in any particular section. Thus a reference might be to a single mention of the topic, or to a major section on that topic. The second part, beginning on page 402, is a more conventional subject word index.

INDEX TO PROCESSES

GENERAL INDEX

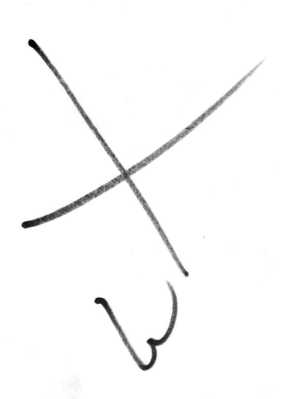